This volume brings together essays on J. S. Bach and members of his family by a distinguished group of scholars. The essays address Bach's compositions, his knowledge of the musical past, his study of contemporaries, and the cultivation of his own music by later generations. The studies draw on source criticism, musical analysis, religious and social context, performance practice, and reception history – a broad range of techniques and issues in modern Bach scholarship. The international contributors include both established scholars and newer voices in Bach studies.

This volume will be indispensable for any future work on the *Musical Offering, St. Matthew Passion, Italian Concerto*, on Bach's musical connections with his sons Carl Philipp Emanuel and Wilhelm Friedemann, and on many other topics in Bach research.

Bach Studies 2

Bach Studies 2

Edited by

DANIEL R. MELAMED

CAMBRIDGE
UNIVERSITY PRESS

Published by the Press Syndicate of the University of Cambridge
The Pitt Building, Trumpington Street, Cambridge CB2 1RP
40 West 20th Street, New York, NY 10011–4211, USA
10 Stamford Road, Oakleigh, Melbourne 3166, Australia

© Cambridge University Press 1995

First published 1995

Printed in Great Britain at the University Press, Cambridge

A catalogue record for this book is available from the British Library

Library of Congress cataloguing in publication data applied for

ISBN 0 521 470676 hardback

Contents

Figures

Preface

We are often told that this is the age of "the new musicology," but old musicology, with its focus on long-standing questions and methods, still has a lot to offer. The essays on J. S. Bach and members of his family collected here demonstrate the continuing contribution that traditional approaches can offer to the state of knowledge and to the appreciation of music from the increasingly distant past.

Many different kinds of research are represented, and the essays here show the value of combining them in the investigation of a particular problem. For example, Joshua Rifkin's essay on the *Trauerode* starts with issues of performance practice, but to understand the performance problems of the work, one must ask not only the obvious organological questions (what instruments?) but also about the organization of musical life in Leipzig in Bach's time (who played and sang?). Jeanne Swack's investigation of a familiar and vexing problem, the mutilated autograph score of one of Bach's chamber compositions, leads from immediate source-critical matters to questions of genre (the sonata in the manner of a concerto), of analysis (Bach's musical strategy), of organology (for what or whose instrument?), and of the context of the work's original performance. Throughout the collection, authors turn to a variety of sources in answering interesting musical questions – the essence of scholarship as an intellectual act.

Those dreading facts presented for their own sake – surely a pitfall of certain kinds of research – will be pleasantly surprised, because so many of the studies here focus ultimately on context and significance. The essays by Gregory Butler and John Butt consider Bach's works in light of the music of earlier and contemporary composers who influenced him. Paul Walker and Christoph Wolff address, in different ways, Bach's relation to music and musical thought of earlier centuries. Michael Marissen and Ulrich Leisinger look within and outside the musical text of two major works for clues to why Bach assembled these pieces as he did and what meanings they might have carried.

Finally, some of the essays here present things about Bach and his music that we simply did not know before: the existence of an early version of an important composition, analytical insights into another, a composition of interest to the Bach family. If these discoveries are there to be made, then certainly others are as well. I hope that scholars will continue to consider such things worth knowing and to ask the questions that will lead us to them.

The following institutions graciously gave their permission for the reproduction of sources from their collections:

Biblioteka Jagiellońska, Cracow (Fig. 12.1)

Houghton Library, Harvard University, Cambridge, Mass. (Fig. 12.3)

Johann-Sebastian-Bach-Institut, Göttingen (Fig. 1.1)

Staatsbibliothek zu Berlin–Preußischer Kulturbesitz, Musikabteilung mit Mendelssohn-Archiv (Figs. 7.1, 7.2, 12.2 and 12.4)

Hamden, Connecticut
September, 1994

Abbreviations

BC	Hans-Joachim Schulze and Christoph Wolff, *Bach-Compendium. Analytisch-bibliographisches Repertorium der Werke Johann Sebastian Bachs* (Leipzig and Frankfurt, 1985–)
BG	*Johann Sebastian Bachs Werke. Gesamtausgabe der Bachgesellschaft* (Leipzig, 1851–99)
BJ	*Bach-Jahrbuch*
BR	*The Bach Reader. A life of Johann Sebastian Bach in letters and documents*, ed. Hans T. David and Arthur Mendel, rev. edn. (New York, 1966)
BuxWV	Georg Karstädt, *Thematisch-systematisches Verzeichnis der musikalischen Werke von Dietrich Buxtehude* (Wiesbaden, 1974; 2nd edn. 1985)
BWV	Wolfgang Schmieder, *Thematisch-systematisches Verzeichnis der musikalischen Werke von Johann Sebastian Bach* (Leipzig, 1950; rev. edn. Wiesbaden, 1990)
Dok I–III	*Bach-Dokumente*, ed. Bach-Archiv Leipzig, 3 vols. (Leipzig and Cassel, 1963–72)
Fk	"Thematisches Verzeichnis der Kompositionen Wilhelm Friedemann Bachs," in Martin Falck, *Wilhelm Friedemann Bach. Sein Leben und seine Werke* (Leipzig, 1913)
H	E. Eugene Helm, *Thematic catalogue of the works of Carl Philipp Emanuel Bach* (New Haven, 1989)
MGG	*Die Musik in Geschichte und Gegenwart*, ed. Friedrich Blume, 17 vols. (Cassel and Basel, 1948–79)
NBA . . . KB	Johann Sebastian Bach, *Neue Ausgabe sämtlicher Werke . . . Kritischer Bericht*, ed. Johann-Sebastian-Bach-Institut Göttingen and Bach-Archiv Leipzig (Leipzig and Cassel, 1954–)
New Grove	*The New Grove dictionary of music and musicians*, ed. Stanley Sadie, 20 vols. (London, 1980)

QV   Horst Augsbach, *Johann Joachim Quantz. Thematisches Verzeichnis der musikalischen Werke* (Dresden, 1984)

SBB . . . P/St   Staatsbibliothek zu Berlin/Preußischer Kulturbesitz, Musikabteilung . . . Mus. ms. Bach P [score]/St [parts]

SWV   Werner Bittinger, *Schütz-Werke-Verzeichnis (SWV). Kleine Ausgabe* (Cassel, 1960)

TVWV   Werner Menke, *Thematisches Verzeichnis der Vokalwerke von Georg Philipp Telemann*, 2 vols. (Frankfurt/Main, 1982–3)

Wq   Alfred Wotquenne, *Thematisches Verzeichnis der Werke von Carl Philipp Emanuel Bach* (Leipzig, 1905)

Chapter one

An early version of the first movement of the *Italian Concerto* BWV 971 from the Scholz collection?

KIRSTEN BEIßWENGER

In 1969, the Johann-Sebastian-Bach-Institut in Göttingen acquired a collection containing approximately ninety manuscripts from the music dealer Hans Schneider in Tutzing. This group of manuscripts, originally in private hands in the vicinity of Nuremberg, contains exclusively instrumental works, mostly by Johann Sebastian and Carl Philipp Emanuel Bach. The manuscripts are mostly from the second half of the eighteenth century, a few from the middle of the century. Their principal copyist is the Nuremberg native Leonhard Scholz, who was baptized on May 28, 1720 at the St. Sebald church in that city, son of Georg Scholz, a craftsman. At the time of his marriage on May 30, 1747 to Barbara Popp, Leonhard Scholz was listed as a spice dealer, an occupation he pursued until his death. In 1769–70, Scholz was an adjunct organist at the St. Ägidius church under Lorenz Sichart, and in 1771 – perhaps even by the end of 1770 – became Sichart's successor there. From 1772 to 1781, Scholz was organist at the St. Lorenz church, and from 1781 until his death (he was buried on October 23, 1798) organist at the church in which he was baptized.[1]

As one might expect from his biography, most of the compositions in Scholz's collection are for organ and clavier, notated on single bifolia or individual leaves in various formats.[2] There are only a few title pages with designations of titles and composers; most of the copies simply have a title at their heads, in a few cases with the name of the composer added.

---

1 On Scholz's biography, see NBA IV/5 and 6 KB, Teilband 1, 159 (Dietrich Kilian).
2 A few of the manuscripts bear original dates: BWV 684 (1768), the *Well-Tempered Clavier* I BWV 846–69 (1771), and the *Two- and Three-Part Inventions* BWV 772–801 (1782).

Figure 1.1   J. S. Bach, *Italian Concerto* BWV 971, 1st mvt. in the hand of Leonhard Scholz. Göttingen, Johann-Sebastian-Bach-Institut

The *Italian Concerto* BWV 971, which first appeared in print in 1735 in the second part of Bach's *Clavier-Übung*,[3] shows up twice in incomplete form in the collection. One copy consists of a bifolium containing the first and third movements, the first on the outer pages with the heading "Concerto," the third on the inner pages, headed "Presto." In this copy, both movements are transmitted in the version generally known today.[4] The inner pages of another

3   The print was so full of errors that a corrected edition soon appeared, probably in 1736.
4   Neither print served as Scholz's model, as can be seen particularly from m. 142 in the first movement. In the print, there is a series of sixteenth notes, whereas Scholz's copy has 32nd notes.

bifolium contain a second copy of the opening movement, without an attribution but with the heading "All⁰ moderato."[5] (See Figure 1.1.) As is usual for Scholz, this is a fair copy; the few corrections stem from simple copying errors immediately caught and repaired. This second copy transmits the first movement of the *Italian Concerto* with variants that deserve investigation.

The variants in Scholz's version compared to the printed text involve both thematic and accompanimental material. The theme itself is different, as are many of the sequences. In the sequences, the melodic right hand often dominates, whereas the left hand is relegated to a simple, often chordal accompanimental role. Motivic details such as 32nd-note passing tones are absent in many places. In two places, the cadential and connecting passages are

5 The outer pages, both ruled, were originally blank. The first page later acquired the entry "N. 64" in ink and later, in pencil, "Clavierübung II: Concerto I B. W. 3, 139 = BWV 971/1."

one measure longer. (The variants are summarized in Appendix 1; those in mm. 1–30 are discussed in detail below.)

Most of the variants are in mm. 1–103; those in mm. 104–61 are mostly in small details, for example, the accompanimental motive in mm. 135 and 137. Particularly noteworthy are the registral shifts that avoid all notes above a". In general, the affected passages are placed an octave lower, for example, in the right hand in mm. 110–11, 152–3, and 156–7. In two places the top note above a" is lowered: in the theme, m. 5 (c'" lowered to g") and in m. 103 (b" lowered to f').

The differences between the two versions are significant. But where did the variants in Scholz's version come from? Two answers are conceivable: first, that the variants stem from Bach's own early version of the work; second, that the variants represent a corrupt version. The second possibility is particularly plausible because several works by Bach are transmitted in the Scholz collection in arranged versions, as will be investigated below.

The possibility that this could be an early version of the first movement is supported by the existence of a copy of the *Italian Concerto* now in the Boston Public Library, dating from before 1762, in the hand of the Bernburg organist Johann Christoph Oley (1738–1789).[6] Although Oley was not Bach's student, he had close connections to the middle-German Bach tradition.[7] Unlike Scholz's, Oley's version is close to the printed one; the theme, sequences, and accompanimental motives are mostly the familiar readings. Nonetheless, his copy of the concerto contains numerous corrections, many of whose readings *ante correcturam* differ from those in the 1735 print and the second edition that appeared shortly thereafter. For example, in several places characteristic 32nd-note passages are absent (e.g., mm. 37–9), and in several places Oley's original beaming diverges from that in the prints. There are also several measures in this version whose melody is slightly different from that in the prints.[8]

In the opinion of Walter Emery, editor of the *Italian Concerto* for the NBA, this kind of variant did not arise from simple copying errors. It also seemed unlikely to him that Oley, copying from a source transmitting the printed version, would have incorporated readings not found in his model, only to go back and systematically replace them with the readings from the print. It seems more likely to Emery that the corrected readings represent an early version of the work.[9]

---

6 Shelf number M 200.12. The manuscript passed from Franz Hauser and Ignaz Moscheles; see Yoshitake Kobayashi, "Franz Hauser und seine Bach-Handschriftensammlung" (Ph.D. diss., Göttingen, 1973), 143. For details on this source and its dating, see NBA V/2 KB, 39–47 (Walter Emery).

7 See NBA VIII/8 KB (Christoph Wolff), 111.

8 A detailed list of all variants is found in NBA V/2 KB, 40–7.

9 NBA V/2 KB, 39f.

A number of readings *ante correcturam* in Oley's version agree with Scholz's copy; these are listed in Appendix 2. Some of these shared readings are found in no other copies of the *Italian Concerto*, suggesting that the two sources may stem from the same parent source. The readings they share link them. Provisionally, this suggests the following hypothesis: that Scholz's copy represents an early version of the work, and that Oley's copy, closer to the print, represents an intermediate stage between Scholz's version and the printed edition. Despite the variants in Oley's copy, the middle stage it represents comes close to the work's final form; Scholz's copy, though, presents the concerto movement "under construction."

The transmission of the variant version in Leonhard Scholz's copy makes it essential to examine the possibility that it represents a later reworking of the piece, because several of Bach's works are indeed transmitted in the Scholz collection in doubtful variant forms. It is characteristic of the collection that many works are represented in two or more copies. Many of the duplicated works are transmitted in multiple versions: in the well-known readings and in an otherwise unknown reworking, often shortened or simplified. As mentioned above, the *Italian Concerto*, too, is represented twice in the Scholz collection, once essentially in the printed version and once in a reworking. To evaluate the variants in the first movement of this work against the background of the variant versions of other works in the collection, we must turn to an overview of techniques of reworking represented in the collection as a whole. This seems particularly necessary because scholars have tended to neglect the copies in the Scholz collection.

The reworkings fall into two categories: abbreviations and simplifications. Typical examples of the group of shortened works include the *Pièce d'Orgue* in G major BWV 572 (only the first section, *Très vitement*, mm. 1–28; see Example 1.1) and the Trio super "Herr Jesu Christ, dich zu uns wend" BWV 655. In the *Pièce d'Orgue*, several measures are missing (mm. 4, 8–9, 12, 14–15); these represent the suppression of identical or similar measures.[10] The Trio BWV 655, in contrast, is greatly abridged (see Example 1.2). The piece jumps from m. 8 to m. 52, with a newly inserted one-measure transition connecting them. The pedal part in mm. 5–8 is also transposed down an octave to accommodate this change.[11]

---

10   Scholz's model for this abbreviated version was another copy in his hand transmitting the first section in full, New Haven, Yale University LM4842h; see NBA IV/7 KB, 202 (Dietrich Kilian).
11   Scholz began m. 8 in the proper octave. It is thus conceivable that he copied the work from the original version and made the change as he copied.

Example 1.1 J. S. Bach, *Pièce d'Orgue* BWV 572, mm. 1–16. The canceled measures are missing in Leonhard Scholz's copy

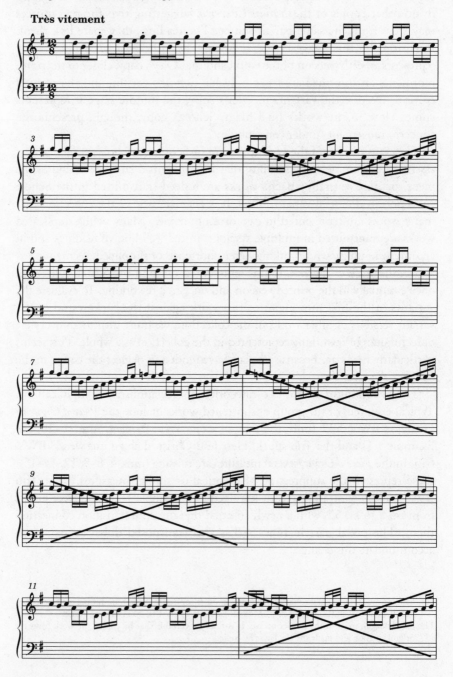

The simplified versions often result from the combination of voices or the absorption of the pedal part into the left hand. A typical example of such simplification of instrumental technique appears in the chorale setting "Christ unser Herr zum Jordan kam" BWV 684 (in D minor in the Scholz collection; see Example 1.3).[12] The soprano and alto voices in the upper staff are combined into a continuous series of eighth and sixteenth notes. In the first and third movements of Bach's organ arrangement of Antonio Vivaldi's Concerto for Two Violins in A minor BWV 593, the left hand and pedal part are combined in one system (see Example 1.4).[13] This meant that one of the two middle voices – sometimes even the pedal part – had to be eliminated. The pedal part and the left hand in the third movement, m. 85ff. were combined in a different way: all the chord tones, originally divided among three voices, were integrated into a line that moves in sixteenth notes (see Example 1.5).

Both kinds of reworkings – abbreviation and simplification – are to be found in the Passacaglia in C minor BWV 582, another work transmitted in the Scholz collection in two copies.[14] In the simplified version, all the variations

12 In addition to these technical simplifications, the passages between the chorale phrases are sharply reduced to one measure each. BWV 684 appears in a partial copy in the collection as well, containing only the first section of the work. The simplified version was the model for yet another reworking of the chorale setting, this one using the cantus firmus "Jesu, meine Freude." The non-cantus firmus sections (the opening passage and pedal point concluding passage) are identical with those in Scholz's simplified version of BWV 684; the cantus firmus sections are newly composed in Scholz's style. The passages between chorale phrases are also reduced to one measure each here.

13 Scholz's copy is in unknown private hands; photocopy in the Johann-Sebastian-Bach-Institut, Göttingen.

14 See NBA IV/7 KB, 137f.

Example 1.2 J. S. Bach, Trio super "Herr Jesu Christ, dich zu uns wend" BWV 655 in the version copied by Leonhard Scholz, mm. 1–10 (m. 10 = m. 52 of the original)

Example 1.3   J. S. Bach, "Christ unser Herr zum Jordan kam" BWV 684 in the version copied by Leonhard Scholz, mm. 1–6

in more than four voices were omitted. Among the other variations, those that were not originally conceived for manuals only were rescored so that they generally could be played without pedals. A typical example of this reduction in the number of voices is mm. 129–32 (see Example 1.6), in which the right hand proceeds monophonically without the acciaccatura-like figure and the following chord, and the left hand presents the pedal part.

In Scholz's versions the variants represent technical simplifications, through which Bach's characteristic thick polyphony is reduced in favor of a fewer-voiced texture (two or three parts). Often the voices are so combined that the piece may be performed *manualiter*. Despite adjustments in partwriting, the thematic material of the works remains substantially untouched. Variants that have no connection to their model are found only when new connecting passages are necessitated by the elimination of measures. Additionally, some works are accommodated to the musical style of the period after Bach (for example, by the use of Alberti bass figuration).

The arranger of these works is probably the principal copyist of the collection, Leonhard Scholz himself, about whose abilities as an organist we

Example 1.4   Antonio Vivaldi, Concerto for Two Violins in A minor, arr. J. S. Bach (BWV 593), 1st mvt., mm. 1–8 in the original version and the version copied by Leonhard Scholz

know nothing. Nonetheless, the extent of his arrangement of organ works (illustrated in the examples above) suggest that he took great interest in simplified versions of Bach's organ works. Clavier works are also transmitted in the Scholz collection in variant versions, but in contrast, the changes in them are much less drastic; for example, in the first movement of the Partita BWV 830, the septuplets in m. 3ff. are simplified to a sixteenth-note figure. There are no reductions in the number of voices as there are in the organ music. The only clavier work showing extensive changes is the first movement of the *Italian Concerto*.

In the absence of a source-critical chronology of the manuscripts in the collection, it is not possible to say when Scholz made the arrangements of the organ works.[15] It is also unknown whether they were intended for *manualiter* performance on the organ or for clavier. It can be ruled out that Scholz made these arrangements for the Renaissance-era organ at the St. Lorenz church, because the *Principal* on that instrument extended only to a" (as was usual for instruments from this period),[16] the *Rückpositiv* only to f".[17] Because none of Scholz's copies – with the exception of the variant version of the first movement

---

15   It has yet to be determined what models were used in copying the manuscripts of the Scholz collection. Only in the case of a few works, for example, the first book of the *Well-Tempered Clavier*, has supposition been possible. Scholz's copy of *WTC* I is related to C. G. Meißner's, suggesting a relatively close connection between Scholz and the immediate Bach circle (see NBA V/6.1 KB, 93 [Alfred Dürr]). Whether this result can be extended to other works remains to be investigated individually.

16   See Michael Praetorius, *Syntagma Musicum* II (Wolfenbüttel, 1619), 110f.

17   Johann Ulrich Sponsel, *Orgelhistorie* (Nuremberg, 1771), 150.

Example 1.5   Antonio Vivaldi, Concerto for Two Violins in A minor, arr. J. S. Bach (BWV 593), 3rd mvt., mm. 85–9 in the original version and the version copied by Leonhard Scholz

of the *Italian Concerto* – limits its range to below a", it is certain that the Scholz collection was not assembled for the St. Lorenz organ. In any event, the organ was apparently in an extremely poor state of repair. Johann Ulrich Sponsel reported in 1771 that only nine of the fourteen ranks were usable; four years later, the condition had so deteriorated that the organ was deemed essentially

Example 1.6 J. S. Bach, Passacaglia in C minor BWV 582, mm. 129–32 in the original version and the version copied by Leonhard Scholz

unusable by its examiners.[18] This state of affairs also speaks against Scholz's arrangements having been made for this organ. Little is known about the organs at the St. Sebald church, where Scholz played from 1782 until his death.

Did Leonhard Scholz arrange the first movement of the *Italian Concerto*? Because the nature of the variants in this movement is so clearly different from those in the organ works discussed above, it is difficult to assign this version of the concerto to him. The variants in the concerto are more substantial, touching the work's thematic material, the working out of its sequences, and its accompanimental figures. That passages are rewritten to avoid the highest notes (b" and c''') could point to an organist who wished to accommodate the composition to a Renaissance-era organ, and that might suggest Scholz as the arranger. But the nature of the variants speak against his role.[20] Further, there are no other transpositions of high notes in any other copies in his hand, making it unlikely that he was the arranger of this work.[21]

18 Sponsel, *Orgelhistorie*, 150; Hermann Harrasowitz, *Geschichte der Kirchenmusik an St. Lorenz in Nürnberg*, Mitteilungen des Vereins für Geschichte der Stadt Nürnberg 60 (Nuremberg, 1973), 31.

19 The first organ had a short octave in the *Principal* and pedal; we have no report on the compass of the second instrument, dating from 1657. See Sponsel, *Orgelhistorie*, 152.

20 That only the first movement exists in a variant version – and not the third movement, which Scholz also copied – could also be interpreted as evidence against Scholz's role as arranger.

21 If the elimination of the highest pitches indeed indicates an arrangement for organ performance, their elimination could also be explained by a transposition. If we assume that the highest note on the intended instrument was c''', that would mean that the piece originally stood in A♭ major, which is highly unlikely.

If Scholz was not responsible for the variant version, who was? An analytical examination can help clarify whether Scholz's version might be an early compositional stage of the printed version. On this point we can turn to the many variants in the first thirty measures and several later passages. (See Example 1.7.)

Example 1.7   J. S. Bach, *Italian Concerto* BWV 971, 1st mvt., mm. 1–30 in the printed version

The theme itself differs decidedly from that in the familiar version. Instead of the climactic syncopations in the third measure that bring the phrases of the theme to a close, the cadence is introduced by an upbeat figure of three ascending sixteenth notes. This three-sixteenth-note upbeat figure is taken up again in descending form in the following sequence[22] (upbeat to m. 9). It thus also provides a motivic connection between the opening theme and the following passage. The sequence at mm. 9–14 (and the following five measures, m. 15–20) lacks or weakens the tension-building features of the printed version. Missing is the repetition of the syncopation on c''', which, in the printed version, mm. 13–14, culminates in a syncopated 32nd-note figure. Instead, from m. 10, there is a regular series of sixteenth notes. The accompaniment, too, is completely chordal and simpler than that in the printed version.

The expansive sequence-like passage in mm. 15–20 is based in the Scholz version on a two-measure motive, and ends in m. 19 with a two-measure toccata-like figure. Harmonically, the passage in Scholz's version simply moves between dominant 7th and tonic. The two versions differ, too, in their accompaniment in this passage, the Scholz version consisting of simple octaves leading to C major and F major chords.

The right hand in mm. 21–30 is identical in the two versions, but with different accompaniment. Here, Scholz's version has a continuo-like line. In contrast, the final cadence, harmonically identical in the two versions, is melodically different. In place of the contrary motion between the two hands in the printed version, Scholz's version presents parallel motion in tenths leading to the deceptive cadence in m. 28.

A characteristic feature of the printed version is its tension-building, long-breathed melodic writing, achieved through syncopations (mm. 3, 7, 11 and 13) or insistent motivic repetition (mm. 15–20). In Scholz's version, the theme consists of two short melodic arches; these are unified in the printed version with the help of syncopations. The three-sixteenth-note upbeat of Scholz's version is gone, and its connecting role is taken over by the syncopations that dominate the sequential passage in the printed version. Connecting elements that result in larger structural units are particularly prominent in passages connecting sequential phrases. In Scholz's version, passages marking the end of one sequence and the beginning of the next are brought to a strong close; in the printed version, they are smoothly connected. Thus the first sequential unit in Scholz's version leads to a concluding eighth note (m. 14), though this is disguised by the grace note. In the printed version the first sequence (mm. 9–12)

22   The term sequence refers strictly to a series of identical motives transposed as a whole; I use it here in an extended sense to refer to a somewhat less schematic series of motives.

leads to the syncopated sixteenth- and 32nd-note figure (mm. 13–14) that slides into the figuration of the following sequence.

The passage in mm. 15–20 is decidedly stronger as well. In the printed version it is characterized by the insistent repetition of four sixteenth notes grouped as 1+3 and by its varied harmonic progression. The effect produced by the motivic repetition is supported by the left-hand accompaniment in a high register. This accompaniment joins two measures into units, the end of each marked by the pitch c. This passage, too, is more focused in the printed version than in Scholz's, with its two-measure sequential motive and unimaginative chordal accompaniment.

Even more striking is the joining of individual units into a continuous whole in mm. 15–24. In Scholz's version this unit falls into three sections: a sequence with chordal accompaniment (mm. 15–18), a toccata-like descent (mm. 19–20), and a threefold sequential passage with continuo-like accompaniment (mm. 21–3). In the printed version, mm. 15–23 are unified by the elimination of the toccata-like passage and by the accompanimental figure: the two-sixteenth-and-eighth-note motive of mm. 15–16 is split off, retained, and slightly varied through m. 24. Finally, the cadential measures (m. 25ff.), characterized by parallel motion in Scholz's version, contain contrary motion in the printed version. In both versions, the chain of sixteenth notes ends in a deceptive cadence (m. 28). In Scholz's version, this cadence continues directly into the ending measures of the opening section without a strong sense of closure because of the continuous sixteenth notes in the right hand; in the printed version, longer note values contribute to the stronger effect of the deceptive cadence.

The differences in the accompanimental figures in other sections of the movement, too, are striking (for example, mm. 43–5, 61–4, 96–9). In Scholz's version the accompaniment is chordal throughout, emphasizing the concerto character of the work. In all three passages, this accompanimental figure is replaced in the printed version by idiomatic keyboard figuration. The differences are particularly striking in the sequence in mm. 61–4, which is substantially recast by a reworking of the uppermost voice. In Scholz's version, the right hand dominates with continuous sixteenth-note motion, the left hand moving in a simple falling quarter-note figure. In the printed version, the voices are in dialogue. Overall, the character of a keyboard composition is more strongly in the foreground in the printed version.[23]

23 This kind of compositional procedure is also found in Bach's arrangement of concertos of Antonio Vivaldi; see Klaus Hofmann, "Zum Bearbeitungsverfahren in Bachs Weimarer Concerti nach Vivaldis 'Estro Armonico' Op. 3," in *Das Frühwerk Johann Sebastian Bachs. Kolloquium veranstaltet vom Institut für Musikwissenschaft der Universität Rostock*, ed. Karl Heller and Hans-Joachim Schulze (in press).

From an analytical comparison of the two versions, the hypothesis of an early version of the *Italian Concerto* is plausible. Many variants speak against their representing a later revision of the printed version. If we consider this version of the concerto in comparison to the reworkings of organ compositions in the Scholz collection, a different kind of revision in the concerto emerges. In the organ works, Scholz combined voices, omitted voices, and composed new connecting passages.[24] Doubtless he knew something of counterpoint. But in none of the examples can we find manipulation of thematic material of the kind displayed in the *Italian Concerto*. (Recall that the two versions of the concerto use two different recurring musical ideas to move the work forward: a three-sixteenth-note upbeat figure on the one hand, and a syncopated motive on the other.)

Philologically speaking, the hypothesis is supported by the readings that also appear in Oley's copy, discussed above. We cannot neglect these common readings; nonetheless, we must remain cautious. It is striking that Scholz's version is of unremarkable quality, so that one could not easily attribute it to Bach. Some of the passages, in fact, are quite weak. Perhaps we have the movement in a first, discarded draft. This would explain some of the unsatisfactory parts of the movement. In that case, details and points of refinement that distinguish the printed version would be the product of Bach's several-fold process of reworking.

Finally, it is also conceivable that Scholz's version represents an early version that was later reworked by someone other than Bach. In light of what we have seen of Scholz's arrangements, though, this is unlikely to have been Scholz himself. This hypothetical reviser might at least be responsible for the revisions that eliminate the uppermost notes.

It remains to consider when the *Italian Concerto* was composed. Walter Emery has suggested that it could date from Bach's Cöthen years, but it is difficult to say what led him to propose this.[25] He did know Oley's copy, which transmits an earlier version of the work. If Emery's dating is correct, then the version from the Scholz collection would also date from the Cöthen period (but before Oley's version), or even earlier.

It is an entirely different question whether the *Italian Concerto*, in particular the movement under consideration here, might itself be an arrangement of a work originally scored for different forces. That it might conceivably be an arrangement of another composer's work is rather unlikely, given the characteristic handling of thematic material. In particular, Bach tended to deal

24 Perhaps in one case he even composed his own chorale setting based on Bach's material; see n. 12.
25 Cf. Werner Breig, "Johann Sebastian Bach und die Entstehung des Klavierkonzerts," *Archiv für Musikwissenschaft* 36 (1979), 26 n. 12.

more respectfully with others' thematic material; in his transcriptions of concertos by Vivaldi and others, for example (BWV 592–6, 972–87), the original thematic material remained essentially untouched. In the *Italian Concerto*, though, as discussed above, the theme was distinctly altered.

One might ask whether the original form of the *Italian Concerto* might have been an instrumental concerto. Werner Breig has opined that this is certainly not the case. In his view, the structure of the outer movements of this work is substantially different from that of Bach's other keyboard concertos: it is not the solo/ripieno structure that determines the disposition of the material, but rather the characteristics of the performing medium, the two-manual harpsichord.[26] In light of the printed version of the concerto, Breig is certainly correct; in this version, typical *tutti* passages are avoided in favor of idiomatic keyboard figuration. In the Scholz version, though, *tutti* elements are unmistakable, for example, the chordal accompaniment cited above. The more conspicuous *tutti*/solo contrast in the Scholz version could lend credibility to the possibility that Bach reworked a solo concerto, if it were not that other passages decidedly contradict this hypothesis (for example, mm. 105–21, with their sixteenth-note figuration in the bass).

From all the considerations discussed here, one can reasonably conclude that the Scholz collection transmits the first movement of the *Italian Concerto* in an early version. The question of to what extent this version was later reworked by someone else remains without a definitive answer. In all probability we can rule out Scholz's hand here. Despite the possibility of a few outside revisions, the Scholz collection copy of this work most likely gives us a glimpse into Bach's workshop, illustrating his striving for perfection in his compositions.

Appendix 1   Variants in Scholz's copy of the *Italian Concerto* compared to the printed version

mm. 1–4 (5–8): Theme consists of two short melodic arches, the second beginning with a three-16th upbeat figure.

mm. 9–14: Sequence in even 16ths in r. h.; simple chordal accompaniment in l. h.

mm. 15–20: Sequence built on a two-m. motive in r. h., followed by two toccata-like measures; accompaniment simple octaves leading to dominant seventh and tonic.

26 Breig, "Entstehung des Klavierkonzerts," 26.

mm. 21–5: Accompaniment continuo-like.

mm. 26–30: Concluding cadence in parallel tenths.

mm. 37–8: No 32nd passing tones; literal repetition of mm. 35–6. Cf. mm. 97–100, 155–7.

mm. 43–5: Simple upbeat chord in l. h.

m. 48: Leading-tone figure in l. h. from C upwards; no connection to previous accompaniment figure.

m. 49: Root only of f♯ diminished seventh chord.

mm. 61–4: One-m. sequence motive in continuous 16ths in r. h.; simple quarter accompaniment in l. h. cadence in m. 64a.

mm. 76–91: Cf. mm. 15–30, in the parallel minor.

mm. 91, 93, 95: Accompaniment in quarters.

mm. 96–100: First half of each m. chordal in l. h.; no 32nds in r. h. (see above).

mm. 124–8: 8th rest at the beginning of each m.

mm. 135, 137: 16th motion in falling step figure in l. h.

m. 142: Two-m. descending 16th passage in bass range (= mm. 142–142a) ending on G in m. 143; g' in m. 143 reached by two-octave leap. R. h. rests during entire passage.

Appendix 2 Variants shared by Scholz's copy and Oley's copy *ante correcturam* of the *Italian Concerto*

mm. 13–14, 37–9: No 32nds in r. h.

mm. 52–4, 56–8: 16ths and 32nds beamed in fours in l. h. Two independent voices suggested by notation of the printed version not discernible.

m. 67: Continuous beaming in l. h. ("Piano" marking absent in Scholz.)

mm. 69–72: 8th rest on first beat in upper voice missing. 8th on first beat (middle voice in printed version) beamed to next two to four 8ths in upper voice.

m. 103. Quarter B♭ in l. h. (Printed version: two 8ths B♭ – BB♭).

m. 146. All four 16ths beamed together on first beat. ("Piano" marking absent in Scholz.)

Chapter two

J. S. Bach's reception of Tomaso Albinoni's mature concertos

GREGORY G. BUTLER

Much has been made of J. S. Bach's encounter around 1713 with Antonio Vivaldi's *L'estro armonico* (published as Opus III in 1712) and it is undeniable that these concertos of the "prete rosso" exerted a strong and lasting influence on his German contemporary.[1] However, in recent studies, Jean-Claude Zehnder and Robert Hill have demonstrated the considerable importance of an Italian composer of concertos of an earlier generation, Giuseppe Torelli, for Bach's early approach to the genre.[2] In so doing they have suggested that if the importance of the Vivaldi reception has not been overestimated, it nevertheless needs to be viewed in the perspective of other important currents in concerto composition that impinged on Bach at various times throughout his career. I hope to widen that perspective still further by shedding light on Bach's later but equally important encounter with the mature concertos of Vivaldi's Venetian contemporary Tomaso Albinoni.

During his Weimar years, Bach seems to have valued Albinoni highly as a composer. Two of the Venetian composer's trio sonatas from Opus I appear in the Möller Manuscript,[3] indicating that the early sonatas of Albinoni were

1 Important archival research by Hans-Joachim Schulze has established that Bach first came into contact with Vivaldi's Opus III concertos sometime in 1713 upon receipt in Weimar of a shipment of music purchased by prince Johann Ernst during his sojourn in Holland. See Hans-Joachim Schulze, "J. S. Bach's concerto-arrangements for organ – studies or commissioned works?" *The Organ Yearbook* 3 (1972): 4–13; and "Johann Sebastian Bachs Konzertbearbeitungen nach Vivaldi und anderen – Studien – oder Auftragswerke?" *Deutsches Jahrbuch der Musikwissenschaft* 18 (1978): 80–100.

2 See Jean-Claude Zehnder, "Giuseppe Torelli und Johann Sebastian Bach. Zu Bachs Weimarer Konzertform," *BJ* 77 (1991): 33–95. Hill's findings appear in an unpublished paper given at a colloquium on the early works of J. S. Bach held at the University of Rostock in September, 1990. My thanks to the author for providing me with a typescript of this paper.

3 See Hans-Joachim Schulze, *Studien zur Bach-Überlieferung im 18. Jahrhundert* (Leipzig, 1983), 41.

known in the Bach circle, and Bach borrowed themes from Albinoni for the subjects of three of his own fugues written during the period around 1708 to 1710: BWV 946, BWV 950 and BWV 951.[4] Further, the sonatas of Opus VI served Bach as important instructional materials in his teaching of figured bass realization.[5] Although he clearly knew and esteemed the early sonatas, Bach must also have been acquainted with the early concertos of Albinoni. Bach's autograph copy of the continuo part from Albinoni's Op. II, No. 2 has survived from the Weimar period,[6] and Op. II, Nos. 4 and 5 from the same collection were arranged for organ by Johann Gottfried Walther, Bach's cousin and organist at the Stadtkirche in Weimar.[7] Given Bach's pronounced early interest in the chamber music of Albinoni, one is naturally curious as to whether this interest did not extend to encompass Albinoni's mature instrumental music as well.

In 1715 and then again in 1722, Albinoni brought out in Amsterdam collections of "Concerti a cinque," his Opus VII and Opus IX concertos respectively.[8] Each collection consists of twelve concertos, four each for solo violin, solo oboe and two solo oboes. More than anything else, Albinoni's particular approach to ritornello form sets these concertos apart. John Solie has remarked that in the concertos for one and two oboes from these two collections, "Albinoni maintained an allegiance to a ritornello form rather different . . . from that of Vivaldi,"[9] and all of the three vital features listed by Michael Talbot that distinguish Albinoni's concertos from those of his contemporaries have to do with the composer's original handling of ritornello form.[10]

A comparison of the formal plan of allegro movements in ritornello form published by the two Venetian composers strongly bears out Solie's assertion concerning Albinoni's distinct approach to ritornello form: the third movement of Vivaldi's Op. III, No. 9 (arranged by Bach for organ as BWV 972/1 during the period 1713–17) and the first movement of Albinoni's Op. VII, No. 11, a movement with a very similar modulatory scheme.

4 The themes for these three fugues are taken from Op. I, No. 12/4, Op. I, No. 3/2, and Op. I, No. 8/2. See Philipp Spitta, *Johann Sebastian Bach*, 2 vols. (Leipzig, 1873–80), 1: 425 and *Beilage* 2; and Michael Talbot, *Tomaso Albinoni: the Venetian composer and his world* (Oxford, 1990), 21.

5 A keyboard realization of the continuo part of the sonata for violin and continuo, Op. VI, No. 6 in the hand of Heinrich Nikolaus Gerber containing corrections in Bach's hand is preserved in the SBB. See Spitta, *Johann Sebastian Bach*, 2: 125ff. and *Beilage* 1.

6 See Hans-Joachim Schulze, *Studien*, 28.

7 These arrangements appear in Max Seiffert, ed., *Johann Gottfried Walther. Gesammelte Werke für Orgel*, Denkmäler deutscher Tonkunst 26–7 (Leipzig, 1906), 285–91.

8 For the not entirely unproblematic dating of these two prints, see Michael Talbot, *Tomaso Albinoni*, 157.

9 John E. Solie, "Aria structure and ritornello form in the music of Albinoni," *The Musical Quarterly* 63 (1977): 31.

10 Michael Talbot, "The concerto allegro in the early eighteenth century," *Music and Letters* 52 (1971): 164–5.

Vivaldi, Op. III, No. 9/3 (3/8)[11]

1–14.	–28.	–43.	–58.	–82.	–96.	–105.
R	S,R	S	S,R	S	R,S	R
I	–V,V	–vi	–iii,iii	–I	I	I

Albinoni, Op. VII, No. 11/1 (3/4)

	a	b	c	d	e	f	g	h	i	j
	1–21.	–44.	–75.	–84.	–100.	–107.	–123.	–143.	–175.	–185.
	R	S,R	S	R	S	R,S	S	S,R	S	R
	I	I	I,–V	V	–vi	vi,–iii	–I,I	I	I	I

In the outer movements of the concertos of Albinoni's Opus VII, the form is greatly extended to produce the following basic major-key scheme: (a) a lengthy opening ritornello in the tonic beginning with a distinctive and sharply profiled musical idea; (b) a period in the tonic beginning with a single phrase for the soloist(s) accompanied by the orchestra (often using the same material as the first phrase of the ritornello) followed by one or more phrases for ripienists alone almost always repeating either the antecedent phrase or the cadential portion of the consequent phrase[12] from the opening ritornello; (c) a solo period beginning in the tonic with a repetition of the opening phrase of the soloist(s) but continuing and modulating to the dominant, or alternately (as in Op. VII, No. 8/1 diagrammed below), beginning with a solo phrase modulating to the dominant followed by the cadential portion of the opening ritornello in the dominant; (d) a slightly abbreviated version of the opening ritornello, now in the dominant; (e) a solo period beginning in the dominant and passing through the tonic on the way to the sub-mediant; [(f) an optional solo period beginning in the sub-mediant and proceeding to the mediant]; (g) a short solo phrase leading back to a slightly abbreviated version of the opening ritornello in the tonic; (h) a reprise of period b, and/or (i) a varied reprise of period c in which the second solo phrase, instead of modulating to the dominant remains in the tonic; (j) a coda for soloist(s) and ripienists. The other two highly individual features of Albinoni's mature ritornello form cited by

11 In my structural diagrams arabic numerals followed by periods indicate the ends of musical periods, in virtually every case marked by a conclusive full close. The capital letters R and S refer to the ritornello (either in its entirety or a portion thereof) and to the solo sections respectively. Upper case and lower case Roman numerals refer to major and minor tonalities respectively and when preceded by a dash, to the modulation to a given tonality.

12 I avoid the terminology adopted by most Bach scholars for the tripartite segmentation of the ritornello, *Vordersatz – Fortspinnung – Epilog*, in favor of the terminology more universally adopted by music theorists, antecedent phrase and consequent phrase. I do so because I believe it more clearly reflects the actual structure of these periods, clearly articulated as they are into two phrases, most often by a half close. In my division then, antecedent phrase is the equivalent of *Vordersatz* while consequent phrase includes both *Fortspinnung* and *Epilog* segments.

Talbot are clearly in evidence in this movement as well: his tendency to restate the opening ritornello in its entirety in the course of the movement rather than to break it up into smaller fragments, and his clear demarcation of the individual periods that are strongly articulated by cadences and often by rests in all parts.[13]

What for Vivaldi occupies seven periods spread out over 105 measures is extended by Albinoni to occupy ten periods in a movement almost twice as long. This extreme expansion manifests itself first and foremost in the precisely balanced, massive tonic blocks at the beginning (mm. 1–75) and end (mm. 111–85) which in themselves account for about five-sixths of the movement. In the Vivaldian model, this tonic framing material accounts for only slightly more than a third of the movement. The middle section in Albinoni's scheme, although it explores the sub-mediant and mediant tonalities as does Vivaldi's parallel section, is brief, even cursory, accounting for only about one sixth of the movement. What is more, the middle section's tonally unstable periods, characterized by extensive use of sequence, are relatively short compared to those of the outer blocks. Albinoni's modulation back to the tonic is not really a modulation at all but rather an abrupt shift effected by a short link. With Vivaldi, the parallel section is proportionately much longer, accounting for fully half of the movement and the modulation back to the tonic is spun out in an independent period that is the longest and most complex in the movement. Vivaldi generally modulates from one tonal center to another at which point he may (mm. 14–28, 43–58) or may not (mm. 28–43) extend the tonal goal in a short *tutti* phrase, whereas Albinoni most often extends the tonal goal, either in independent periods or long tonally stable phrases at the conclusion of modulatory periods. All of these structural procedures greatly inflate the ritornello form adopted by Albinoni.

In general, the most striking difference in the two models is the more dynamic, continuous, through-composed structure of the Vivaldian scheme in which the music modulates rapidly to a new tonal center and then thrusts immediately forward to another. In the Albinonian plan, tonic harmony is prolonged almost endlessly in the opening and closing multi-period complexes and new tonal centers are drawn out, resulting in a more static, ritornello-dominated structure punctuated by large *tutti* blocks. The large framing tonic blocks, in conjunction with the reprise of the first two periods at the beginning of the concluding tonic section, result in a rounded binary structure that contrasts strongly with Vivaldi's unitary, through-composed plan.

13   See Talbot, "Concerto allegro," 164.

Based on his comparative study of Albinoni's approach to ritornello form in the concertos for one and two solo oboes from Opus VII and Opus IX and in his operatic arias from the same period, Solie concludes that Albinoni "considered concertos with oboes a species apart." They were, Solie argues, "vehicles for a solo instrument, as arias are vehicles for the voice, in a way that does not remind us of Albinoni's other concertos: that these works were composed on the model of the motto aria seems beyond dispute."[14] The presence of the solo *Devise* periods,[15] Albinoni's tendency to restate the opening ritornello in its entirety or only slightly abbreviated in the course of a movement, the brief middle section, the varied reprise of the introductory tonic block at the end of the movement in Albinoni's formal scheme and the overtly vocal writing for the solo oboe(s) support Solie's conclusion.

Following Solie's lead, in his discussion of Albinoni's approach to ritornello form in these concerti, Talbot draws particular attention to the close parallels between Albinoni's treatment of the solo oboe and that of the voice in his arias.

Like the voice, the oboe is excluded from the initial ritornello. It almost invariably enters, at the start of the second period, with a briefly stated solo motto (Riemann's *Devise*), allowing the strings to complete the period with a reference back to the ritornello . . . Then follows a period equivalent to the first vocal period in an aria: the oboe takes up its motto again and this time continues to a cadence in a new key. At this point the strings interpose a short ritornello in that key, usually condensing the opening ritornello in some way. From this point onwards the close correspondence to an aria disappears.[16]

Concerning the relationship between the solo motto and the antecedent phrase of the ritornello, Talbot notes that "whereas in some movements the contrast is striking, in others the solo motto apes the ritornello note for note."[17]

Arthur Hutchings, in referring to the mature concertos of Albinoni, has remarked: "The best outside movements of his [Albinoni's] later concertos are remarkably like some of those by Bach, who benefited from the study of his over-punctuated lines."[18] Among those allegro movements in ritornello form in Bach's Brandenburg Concertos, two stand out for their close, indeed striking adherence to the Albinonian approach to ritornello form outlined above: the third movement of the First Brandenburg Concerto BWV 1046/3 and

14   Solie, "Aria structure," 45–6.
15   As early as 1961, Arthur Hutchings noted that Albinoni was unique in employing the vocal *Devise* in the opening solo period of his allegro ritornello concerto movements. See Arthur Hutchings, *The Baroque Concerto* (London, 1961), 47.
16   Talbot, *Tomaso Albinoni*, 165.
17   *Ibid.*, 166.
18   Arthur Hutchings, "Concerto," *New Grove*.

the third movement of the Sixth Brandenburg Concerto BWV 1051/3. I would submit that these movements show clear signs of having been written under the influence of the concertos for one and two oboes of Albinoni's Opus VII.

A number of the allegro movements from the Opus VII concertos show an interesting variant of the normal Albinonian approach to ritornello form outlined above, one adopted by J. S. Bach. In this variant scheme the opening A section is tonally closed. After period (c), the partial statement of the opening ritornello in the dominant, period (d) is eliminated and in its place Albinoni inserts one or two additional periods. In the most condensed version (No. 9/3; No. 11/1; No. 11/3) there is a modulation back to the tonic and then immediately to the submediant in the same period. In a slightly more expanded variant (No. 6/1) each of these modulations is allotted its own period while in its full expansion (No. 8/1) Albinoni inserts a slightly varied restatement of the opening ritornello in the tonic between these two modulatory periods. This fully expanded version approaches most closely the A section of Albinoni's da capo arias, and with one important difference, this is the same scheme adopted by Bach in the A section of BWV 1051/3, a ritornello movement in da capo form.

Albinoni, Op. VII, No. 8/1 (mm. 1–39)

1–8.	–14.	–20.	–27.	–31.	–39.
R	S,R	S,R	S	R	S
I	I	–V,V	–I,I	I	–vi

Bach, BWV 1051/3 (mm. 1–53)

1–8.	–14.	–22.	–32.	–37.	–45.	–53.
R	S,R	S,R	S	S,R	R	S,R
I	–V,V	–V/V,V	–I,I	I	I	vi

In both movements, periods 2 and 3 constitute paired *Devise* periods that have almost the same proportions. In both, solo variants on the antecedent phrase of the opening ritornello are followed by discrete segments of the ritornello itself. It is clear from this feature in common that Bach here was not adapting the formal structure of his own da capo aria with its single *Devise* period but Albinoni's characteristic double *Devise*. Further, in his da capo arias, Bach invariably restates at least a portion of the opening ritornello in a separate period in the dominant after the *Devise* period, whereas here, after stating the consequent phrase to conclude the second *Devise* period, he modulates back to the tonic immediately in the following period, just as in the Albinonian model. The only departure from the model is the extra period in Bach's A section inserted between the fourth and fifth periods. This inserted period is a slightly abbreviated recapitulation in the tonic of the second *Devise* period (mm. 15–22), normally the penultimate period in Albinoni's ritornello scheme. As in later allegro concerto movements in da capo form, Bach seems to be treating the A section not as the strict counterpart of the parallel section in the da capo aria but rather as a complete concerto movement in miniature.

Because of the attenuation of strong thematic and textural contrasts the First, Third and Sixth Brandenburg Concertos are generally considered by Bach scholars to have been written before Bach began to apply Vivaldian ritornello procedures in his own allegro concerto movements.[19] However, Hans-Joachim Schulze has noted that for the Second, Fourth and Sixth Brandenburg Concertos, source variants are conspicuously lacking.[20] He quite logically interprets this as a strong argument against any extended period of time having elapsed between the composition of the works and their entry into the dedicatory score of March 24, 1721, and suggests that they represent a relatively late stage in the history of the collection. Further, in a recent study, Michael Marissen, focusing on relationships between structure and scoring, has suggested that the first movement of the Sixth Brandenburg Concerto can be best understood when viewed as a "sophisticated response to formal possibilities presented by Vivaldi's new concerto style" even though on the surface it resembles an old-fashioned ensemble work of Bach's.[21] The results of my analysis would tend to buttress both Schulze's and Marissen's arguments by suggesting a considerably later dating for the work than that proposed by other Bach scholars.[22]

The third movement of the First Brandenburg Concerto BWV 1046/3 may have had as its model a specific movement from one of Albinoni's Opus VII concertos: the first movement of Op. VII, No. 9.

Albinoni, VII,9/1 (C)

1–8.	–14.	–21.	–24.	–33.	–43.	–50.	–56.	–62.	–68.
R	S,R	S	R	S	R,S	R	S,R	S	R,S
I	I	I,–V	V	–vi	–ii,–IV,IV	–I,I	I	I,–I	I

---

19   See in particular Martin Geck, "Gattungstraditionen und Alterschichten in den Brandenburgischen Konzerten," *Die Musikforschung* 23 (1970): 139–52.

20   See Hans-Joachim Schulze, "Johann Sebastian Bachs Konzerte – Fragen der Überlieferung und Chronologie," in *Beiträge zum Konzertschaffen Johann Sebastian Bachs*, ed. Peter Ahnsehl, Karl Heller and Hans-Joachim Schulze, *Bach-Studien* 6 (Leipzig, 1981), 15.

21   See Michael Marissen, "Relationships between scoring and structure in the first movement of Bach's Sixth Brandenburg Concerto," *Music and Letters* 71 (1990): 494–504.

22   In a study on the concertos of J. S. Bach presently in preparation I argue on formal-structural grounds that Bach composed the first movement of the Sixth Brandenburg Concerto at the same time as at least two other concertos of his that clearly demonstrate the influence of Vivaldi's new concerto style.

Bach, BWV 1046/3 (6/8)

1–17.	–30.	–40.	–53.	–63.	–70.	–83.	–97.	–108.	–124
R	S,R,S	S,R,S	R	S	R	S	R,S,R,S	S,R,S	R
I	I,V	V	V	–vi,–iii	iii	–ii,–IV	–I,I	I	I

It has been remarked that the opening ritornello of BWV 1046/3 is the only one in the entire set that includes a true sequential progression in its consequent phrase.[23] This is only one of a number of features that mark this as an Albinonian ritornello. The antecedent phrase here, as in the opening ritornello of Albinoni's movement, consists of an ascending arpeggio figure leading to an emphatic half-close on the downbeat that is underscored by the vehement melodic gesture of a descending fifth. In this way, the antecedent phrase is clearly articulated from the consequent phrase, which begins with an extended sequential complex. This complex begins with a long sequential progression descending by step relatively quickly with two sequential units per measure and concludes with a different sequential progression that moves at half the speed with only one sequential unit per measure. The cadential portion of the consequent phrase consists of a rising broken arpeggio outlining dominant harmony culminating in a strong melodic cadential formula. The tonic resolution is extended and repeated at the lower octave in both ritornellos by a similar cadential extension.

Whereas in BWV 1051/3 periods 2 and 3 constitute a double *Devise* that closely parallels one of the variants found in Albinoni's Opus VII concertos, in BWV 1046/3 Bach has expanded and fused the two *Devise* periods.

Bach, BWV 1051/3. Periods 2 and 3 (mm. 9–22)

9–12,	13–14.	15–18,	19–22.
S	R	S	R
I–V	V	V–V/V	V

Bach, BWV 1046/3. Periods 2 and 3 (mm. 17–40)

17–20,	21–24,	25–30:	30–34,	35–38,	38–40.
S	R	S	S	R	S
I	I	V–V/V	V	V	V

In BWV 1046/3, his second period constitutes a *Devise* in which the solo entry (the motto), although it closely resembles the antecedent phrase of the

23 See Laurence Dreyfus, "J. S. Bach and the status of genre: problems of style in the G-minor sonata BWV 1029," *The Journal of Musicology* 5 (1987): 60 n. 8. I do not mean to suggest here that Dreyfus's *Vordersatz – Fortspinnung – Epilog* ritornello structure originated with Albinoni and not with Vivaldi but rather that certain details in his treatment of that generic structure, details that appealed to Bach, are specifically the product of Albinoni's particular approach.

opening ritornello, is not merely a diminution of it as in BWV 1051/3. Further, this is a Bachian *Devise*, not an Albinonian one. It consists not of two phrases as in the Albinonian model, but as in Bach's arias, of three phrases. Its companion *Devise* period does not begin with a repetition of the solo motto but rather with a solo phrase that continues and concludes the modulatory process begun in the preceding *Devise* period. In this adaptation, the resulting structure is much more dynamic and continuous. The ritornello phrase of period 2 does not present the tonally closed concluding portion of the consequent phrase of the opening ritornello, but rather restates the tonally open antecedent phrase, already given in a varied form in the opening solo motto.

The third solo phrase, without modulating, jumps off from the half close that concludes the antecedent phrase, beginning immediately on the dominant, and settles down after a weak full close on the dominant of the dominant. In this way there is no strong articulation between the two periods as in the Albinonian model. Instead, the two are fused and we plunge forward carried by the continuing solo, now in the dominant, to a half close in that key. Each phrase from the beginning onward is thus tonally open: there is no strong resolution prior to that which concludes the third solo phrase of period 2. The result is a subtle and gradual consolidation of the dominant carried out over the space of twenty-four measures and not simply confined to the last phrase of period 2 as in the more tonally static Albinonian scheme. Bach would appear to be moving toward a single *Devise* in which opening and closing short tonally stable solo-ritornello pairs of phrases flank a lengthy, tonally unstable solo progression.

At this point, in period 4, Albinoni introduces an altered form of the concluding portion of the consequent phrase of the opening ritornello, whereas Bach states the consequent phrase verbatim in its entirety. Bach's period 4 thus serves in some sense as a completion of a full statement of the ritornello in the dominant already initiated in the second phrase of period 3 and interrupted by the solo third phrase that concludes that period. On the larger structural scale, it represents the fulfillment of an expectation aroused once the full ritornello has been stated at the outset of the movement by the numerous statements of the antecedent phrase alone both in its varied version in the solo motto and its literal form in ritornello fragments.

Normally, the B sections of Albinoni's allegro concerto movements in da capo form conclude in the mediant, less often in the submediant. In one movement, Op. VII, No. 9/1, the B section concludes in the subdominant. The B sections of Bach's allegro concerto movements, too, like his arias, generally conclude in one of the mediant-related keys. The one exception among the concerto movements is BWV 1046/3, where – as in the first movement of Albinoni's Op. VII, No. 9 – the B section ends in the subdominant. This exceptional feature of the tonal planning in both movements suggests that Albinoni's movement may well have served as a formal model for BWV 1046/3. As noted above, one of the most striking formal contrasts between the concertos of Vivaldi and Albinoni has to do with the extreme brevity of the latter's B sections. In fact, although Solie does not include this feature in his comparative study of Albinoni's da capo arias and his mature concertos, formally the B sections in the two genres are not remarkably different. The B section of BWV 1046/3 is proportionately short, and there is a brief but dramatic *tutti* link back to the tonic in the concluding section of the movement, features that also point to Albinoni's habitual approach.

The formal feature that most closely links Bach's handling of ritornello form in BWV 1046/3 and that of Albinoni in his mature concertos is the clear recapitulation, here of both *Devise* periods, at the beginning of a lengthy concluding tonic complex. Unlike Albinoni, Bach does not begin this section with a statement of the antecedent phrase of the opening ritornello, probably because he has already stated it three times in the course of the movement and will state it three more times before its close. Another difference lies in Bach's restatement of the opening ritornello to conclude the movement in place of Albinoni's coda.

There is a further eccentric detail of Bach's scoring that is so particular to Albinoni and specifically to the concertos of Opus VII and IX, that it can distinguish those of Bach's concertos written after his first encounter with Albinoni's Opus VII concertos. Talbot remarks that "one is immediately struck by the intricacy of the contrapuntal interweaving between the [solo] oboe and the first violin," and he cites a long passage from Op. IX, No. 8 that "shows to perfection the subtleties of this relationship."[24] In BWV 1046/3 this same detail of scoring in which a second solo instrument emerges from the ripieno to join the solo violino piccolo in an intricate, sometimes extended, contrapuntal interweaving over basso continuo appears prominently on no fewer than four occasions. Bach further takes advantage of the richer scoring available to him so that not only does the Violin I (mm. 74–80) embroider the solo phrase with its counterpoint, but so also do both Horn I (mm. 30–5, 98–102) and Oboe I (mm. 54–60). (Extended obbligato accompaniments of this particular type appear nowhere else in the Brandenburg Concertos.) This feature suggests that Bach composed BWV 1046/3 after encountering Albinoni's Op. VII

24 Talbot, *Tomaso Albinoni*, 186–8.

concertos. Based on the foregoing structural and stylistic analyses, this movement would seem to have been composed at about the same time as, or slightly later than BWV 1051/3.

Schulze postulates a protracted history for BWV 1046.[25] In the earliest stage (possibly preceded by an even earlier layer) Bach produced the Sinfonia BWV 1046a – movements 1, 2 and Menuet and Trio I/II of BWV 1046 – to serve as the instrumental introduction and conclusion for a reperformance of "Was mir behagt, ist nur die muntre Jagd" BWV 208 on February 23, 1716. The violino piccolo parts for movements 1 and 2 give evidence of having been transposed *ad hoc* and included only at the time Bach entered the work in the dedicatory fair copy. Movement 3, the only true solo concerto movement in BWV 1046 and the only movement originally scored for violino piccolo, would thus seem to have been composed only subsequently as a second stage. This was in turn followed by the composition of, or the inclusion of the already existing Polonaise (without violino piccolo) and the revision of the scoring of Trio II without violins and with oboe. The final stage is represented by the version in the dedicatory score with the violino piccolo part added in movements 1 and 2. Thus, BWV 1046/3 represents a later layer of composition than BWV 1046/1 and 2. Klaus Häfner, in his recent study on parody procedures in Bach's vocal music, has suggested that BWV 1046/3 in its original version served as the opening sinfonia to the secular cantata "Heut ist gewiß ein guter Tag" BWV Anh. 7 written for December 10, 1720, for which the music has been lost.[26]

Is there any way of pinpointing the likely source of Bach's encounter with Albinoni's Opus VII concertos? In the fall of 1717, when Bach traveled from Weimar to Dresden for his abortive confrontation with Louis Marchand, the crown prince of Saxony had recently returned from a sojourn of more than a year in Italy, much of it spent in Venice.[27] One of the musicians from the Dresden court who had accompanied the crown prince on his travels, Johann Georg Pisendel, the *Konzertmeister*, had forged close ties not only with Vivaldi, but also, significantly, with Albinoni.[28] During his time in Venice, Pisendel prepared traveling manuscripts of at least one of the concertos of Albinoni's recently published collection, his Op. VII, No. 10, which he brought back to

---

25 See Schulze, "Konzerte," 17–18.
26 See Klaus Häfner, *Aspekte des Parodieverfahrens bei Johann Sebastian Bach* (Laaber, 1987), 423–4.
27 For an account of this trip, see Moritz Fürstenau, *Zur Geschichte der Musik und des Theaters am Hofe der Kurfürsten von Sachsen und Könige von Polen*, vol. 2 (Dresden, 1862), 85.
28 Albinoni dedicated a sonata for violin and basso continuo to Pisendel, Dresden, Sächsische Landesbibliothek, Mus. 2199–R–1. See the fascimile with commentary by Michael Talbot, *Tomaso Albinoni, Sonate B-dur für Violine und Basso Continuo, Musik der Dresdener Hofkapelle*. Autographen und Singuläre Abschriften, ed. Ortrun Landman (Leipzig, 1980).

Dresden.[29] The *Kammeroboist* of the Dresden Hofkapelle, Johann Christian Richter, was also among the crown prince's musical entourage during the Italian tour of 1716–17 and he can be expected to have taken more than passing interest in the concertos for one and two solo oboes of the same collection, although no manuscript copies of these survive in Dresden. Thus, Bach could certainly have come in contact with copies of certain concertos from Albinoni's Opus VII during his stay in Dresden. Whether he in turn made copies of works he encountered in Dresden that accompanied him when he moved from Weimar to Cöthen soon after is difficult to ascertain.

Alternatively, it seems likely that during Bach's trip to Berlin early in 1719 to take delivery of the new Mietke harpsichord for the court *cappelle* at Cöthen he acquired prints, and perhaps manuscripts as well, of the latest chamber works in circulation at the time. Certainly, the considerable sums for bookbinding paid between July 1719 and May 1720 suggest that Bach was busy buying, copying, and/or composing music while in Berlin and also perhaps, after his return.[30] Albinoni's Opus VII concertos may well have been among any acquisitions of printed music. Again the sources offer no concrete evidence. It seems unlikely, however, that Bach came in contact with Albinoni's Opus VII much before the fall of 1717, given the collection's relatively recent publication date and the rate of transmission of Amsterdam prints to Central Europe.

One of the outer movements of another concerto by Bach takes as its point of departure a movement from Albinoni's later Opus IX collection of 1722 in a much more obvious way. The work in question is the Concerto for Harpsichord and Strings in E Major BWV 1053, which may originally have been scored for solo oboe or oboe d'amore and strings.[31] Its three movements were subsequently reworked as movements for obbligato organ in two cantatas written during the fall of 1726, the first and second as movements 1 and 5 of "Gott soll allein mein Herze haben" BWV 169 for the 18th Sunday after Trinity (October 20), and the third as movement 1 of "Ich geh und suche mit Verlangen" BWV 49 for the 20th Sunday after Trinity two weeks later. A comparison of the third movement of BWV 1053 with the parallel movement of Albinoni's Op. IX, No. 3, his Concerto for Two Oboes and Strings in F Major is most revealing. Both movements have the same time signature, the fast 3/8 of the Italian sonata finale, and the same rhythmic configuration combining characteristics of the French *passepied* with the Italian *giga*. Both opening

29 See Talbot, *Tomaso Albinoni*, 161.
30 See Friedrich Smend, *Bach in Köthen* (Berlin, 1951), 18 and 151 n. 21.
31 In a recent article Bruce Haynes has called into question the hypothesis that the original version was scored for the regular oboe. See Bruce Haynes, "Johann Sebastian Bachs Oboenkonzerte," *BJ* 78 (1992): 31–3 and 42–3.

ritornellos begin with an upbeat figure featuring a descent from dominant to tonic followed by a rapid conjunct ascent in sixteenth notes back up to the dominant (Example 2.1).[32] The momentum generated by this upward rush carries the melody up in a broken triad through an octave. In Bach's adaptation, this broken triadic ascent is compressed into the space of a single measure whereas in the model, by repeating notes, the same progression is spread over three measures. In both movements, the antecedent phrase closes with the same figure, a rapid conjunct descent in sixteenth notes through a sixth down from the dominant to arrive at the leading tone on the downbeat.

Although the sequential opening sections of the consequent phrase are perhaps not so striking in their similarity, both feature at the outset a slower sequential descent through a third. The concluding cadential portions, though, are uncannily similar. Both begin with a scalar rush up in sixteenth notes from dominant through to the leading tone after which both follow the same general melodic outline right to the cadence. Bach strategically displaces the final upward leap of a fifth. After a climactic rest, he telescopes the conjunct descending fifth in sixteenths within the cadence itself instead of following the cadential resolution as in his Albinonian model. Everything is tighter, more compact, more rhythmically explosive in Bach's recasting.

Bach's movement, like BWV 1051/3, is cast in da capo form, but in its formal structure it more strongly reflects the procedure adopted in his da capo arias than does the earlier movement. Nevertheless it draws on elements adapted from the Albinonian approach to ritornello form, sometimes altered and refined, here not in the movement as a whole, but just as in BWV 1053/1, in the A section (mm. 1–137).

Bach, BWV 1053/3 (mm. 1–137)

1–19.	–43.	–61.	–79.	–108.	–125.	–137.
R	S,R,S	R	S,R,S	R,S	R	R
I	I,–V	V	I	I	I	I

Here, Albinoni's periods (b) and (c), the double *Devise*, have been reduced to a single *Devise* period, an evolutionary line of development pointed to earlier in periods 2 and 3 of BWV 1046/3. Less strictly adhering to the Albinonian

---

32 Note that I do not quote from the opening ritornellos in Example 1. In Albinoni's Op. IX, No. 3/3, the ritornello evolves from one statement to another, expanding to reach its full dimensions only in this restatement rather late in the movement. In BWV 1053/3, the second statement of the ritornello in the dominant is given because Bach reserves the melodic figure that extends the cadential resolution in Albinoni's ritornello at mm. 213–14 for the obbligato harpsichord part in the second ritornello. The harpsichord has no obbligato role in the opening ritornello.

approach to ritornello form, and more in keeping with the normal procedure in his da capo arias is Bach's short, melodically independent solo motto phrase that opens period two and that overlaps with the following statement of the antecedent phrase of the ritornello. Note that Bach states the antecedent phrase of the opening ritornello here just as he had done previously in period 2 of both BWV 1046/3 and BWV 1051/3. This is of decisive importance, for instead of tonal closure and termination of the period at this point, the harmonic progression remains open throughout.

Instead of moving back to the tonic and presenting a repetitive and tonally static statement of the solo *Devise*, Bach pushes on immediately with the concluding solo modulatory phrase. The result is a concise, streamlined and dynamic structure that prolongs the tonic of the opening ritornello through its first two phrases and retains the strong sense of forward motion and modulatory drive inherent in the second period of the Albinonian double *Devise*. The solo phrase that closes period 2, like the motto solo entry, is rather free and not dependent melodically on motivic material derived from the ritornello as in the two movements from the Brandenburg Concertos referred to earlier. The modulation to the dominant in this case is less extended, more direct. Period 3 here consists of the whole of the opening ritornello in the dominant rather than just the consequent phrase as in BWV 1046/3, a detail that represents not only an expansion of his earlier approach and that adopted by Albinoni, but that is closer to his practice in the da capo arias from the early Leipzig years.

From this point onward, Bach departs from the model of the da capo aria, as does Albinoni. The remainder of the A section (mm. 61–137), as in the concluding section of Albinoni's movement, consists of a massive block of tonic harmony. The first of the four periods that constitute the concluding tonic complex is a rather free variant of all but the cadential portion of the consequent phrase of the opening ritornello, concluding instead with an extended solo cadential approach. In a sense, then, this period constitutes a non-modulatory counterpart to the concluding two phrases of the *Devise* period, an incomplete, non-literal tonic recapitulation of the *Devise* period in keeping with Albinoni's period (j), a literal recapitulation.

The following period begins with a repetition of slight variants of the antecedent phrase of the opening ritornello at different pitch levels that is strikingly similar to the beginning of the parallel period in the Albinonian model, period (i) (Example 2.2). Perhaps the clearest borrowing from Albinoni's scheme and the most striking feature of this concluding tonic complex is the lengthy coda (mm. 125–37) in which, as in the model, the consequent phrase of the

Example 2.1a   T. Albinoni, Concerto for Two Oboes and Strings, Op. IX, No. 3/3, mm. 197–203 and 209–14

Example 2.1b   J. S. Bach, Concerto for Harpsichord and Strings BWV 1053/3, mm. 42–6 and 58–61

Example 2.2a   T. Albinoni, Concerto for Two Oboes and Strings, Op. IX, No. 3/3, mm. 121–31

Example 2.2b   J. S. Bach, Concerto for Harpsichord and Strings BWV 1053/3, mm. 78–86

ritornello figures prominently. This concluding coda is unique among Bach's concerto movements.

One might argue that in this and his other concerto movements in da capo form, Bach was simply transferring the formal structure of his da capo arias from one genre to the other. However, such is not the case. My research on, and structural analyses of Bach's earlier allegro concerto movements indicate that the evolution of this formal type was a gradual process of experimentation in adapting and integrating elements drawn not only from the aria but from sonata, concerto, fugue and dance. Further, although the first three periods in BWV 1053/3 correspond rather closely to the parallel periods in Bach's da capo arias, in those periods that follow, this genre recedes in importance as formal and structural model while that of the concerto comes prominently to the fore. Moreover, as I have taken pains to stress, Bach views the A section of this movement not simply as a literal parallel to the A section of a da capo aria, but as in BWV 1051/3, much more abstractly as a condensation or miniaturization of an entire concerto movement, a concept underscored even more clearly by an analysis of the A section of the first movement of BWV 1053.[33] Finally, both in its proportions and compositional working-out, the B section is only nominally influenced by the parallel section in the da capo aria.

With reference to general aspects of style in Albinoni's Opus IX concertos, Michael Talbot has drawn attention to certain details of scoring such as the presence of the soloist(s) in the ritornellos after the first.[34] Instead of simply doubling the first violin part, they continue with obbligato soloistic figuration. In this way Albinoni achieves a greater richness of harmony and scoring than his contemporaries. This detail of scoring is clearly in evidence in BWV 1053/3, most notably in the highly florid obbligato accompaniment of the soloist in the consequent phrase of the statement of the ritornello in the dominant at mm. 47–61 (Example 2.1).

The evidence presented above suggests that Bach modeled the opening ritornello of BWV 1053/3 on Albinoni's Concerto for Two Oboes and Strings in F Major, Op. IX, No. 3 and adopted certain formal and stylistic features from it. The original version, BWV 1053a, then, would have been composed sometime between Bach's encounter with Albinoni's concerto sometime after its publication in 1722 and the 18th Sunday after Trinity (October 20) 1726, when BWV 169 was performed for the first time. It is highly unlikely that

---

33   In the A section of BWV 1053/1 after period 3, the repetition of the opening ritornello in the dominant, Bach inserts a highly condensed, clearly articulated middle section (mm. 37–47) that explores the submediant and mediant keys.

34   See Talbot, "Concerto Allegro," 164.

Bach could have come in contact with Albinoni's Opus IX concertos while still in Cöthen so soon after their publication in Amsterdam. Further, Bach's heavy involvement in cantata composition up until the spring of 1725 may have severely limited his compositional activities in the area of instrumental music.

Is there any way of pinpointing the date of composition of BWV 1053a? The likely scoring of the work may offer a clue. Although especially difficult extended parts for obbligato oboe, oboe d'amore or oboe da caccia appear periodically in the cantatas of the early Leipzig years, they do so for relatively short periods of time, three or four Sundays at most. And so it is striking that between June 16 and November 10, 1726, a period of almost five months, Bach wrote more than a dozen and a half church cantatas that contain especially elaborate and often difficult parts for obbligato or solo oboe (d'amore, da caccia). During the entire period, there are only four cantatas with no extended obbligato or solo movements for oboe or oboe d'amore. (See Table 2.1.)

During the four and a half months between the 3rd Sunday after Epiphany and Trinity Sunday, 1726, Bach had written little in the way of vocal church music. Rather, he had performed the music of other composers. The period just prior to Trinity Sunday from Exaudi through Whitsuntide is a complete blank. And so his return to cantata composition during the Trinity period would seem to mark some sort of rekindling of the fires of creativity as he embarked on *Jahrgang* IV, and the presence of a particularly fine oboist in Leipzig during this period may have been an important contributing factor in this burst of creative energy. Symptomatic perhaps of the departure of the oboist in question is Bach's return to his more usual style of writing for oboes, doubling in pairs at the third or sixth, that suddenly reappears in the cantata for the 22nd Sunday after Trinity, "Ich armer Mensch, ich Sündenknecht" BWV 55. The talents of the resident oboist in question may well have surpassed those of Johann Caspar Gleditsch and Johann Gottfried Kornagel, Bach's regular oboists from the ranks of the *Stadtpfeifer* about whom he remarked rather disparagingly in his "Short But Most Necessary Draft" of August 23, 1730.[35]

It is possible that the musician in question was a traveling professional or a recently arrived university student or pupil of Bach's but the name of the player of the obbligato and solo oboe parts is unimportant. What is significant here is Bach's unusual, concentrated interest in the oboe during the second half of the year 1726 – a period during which the movements of BWV 1053a were reworked as cantata movements. The fact that the third movement of this concerto was modeled on a concerto for two solo oboes by Albinoni certainly

---

35 "Discretion forbids me to offer an opinion on their competence and musicianship. I will merely remark that some of them are *emeriti* and others not in such good *exercitium* as formerly." *Dok* I/22; *BR*, 121.

Table 2.1. *Cantatas from Trinity, 1726 with extended parts for solo or obbligato oboe(s)*

Date	Occasion	Text	BWV	Description
16.6	Trinity	Gelobet sei der Herr, mein Gott	129/4	Aria: Ob d'amore solo, A, Bc
23.6	1 p. Trin.	Brich dem Hungrigen dein Brot	39/3	Aria: Ob obbl, Vn. solo, A, Bc
24.6	St. John	Joh. Ludwig Bach		cantata 17
30.6	2 p. Trin.	?		
2.7	Visitation	Joh. Ludwig Bach		cantata 13
7.7	3 p. Trin.	?		
14.7	4 p. Trin.	?		
21.7	5 p. Trin.	Siehe, ich will viel Fischer aussenden	88/3	Aria: Ob d'amore I, II obbl, S, str
28.7	6 p. Trin.	Vergnügte Ruh', beliebte Seelenlust	170/1	Aria: Ob d'amore, V I *all'unisono* A, str
4.8	7 p. Trin.	Es wartet alles auf dich	187/5	Aria: Ob solo, S, Bc
11.8	8 p. Trin.	Es ist dir gesagt, Mensch	45	No obbl or solo Ob
18.8	9 p. Trin.	?		
25.8	10 p. Trin.	Herr, deine Augen sehen	102/3	Aria: Ob solo, A, Bc
25.8	B'day: von Flemming	Verjaget, zerstreuet, zerrüttet, ihr Sterne	249b/1, 2,9	Chorus: Ob I,II obbl; Adagio: Ob solo, str; Aria: Ob d'amore, A
26.8	Inaug. new Town Counc.	Ihr Tore zu Zion (?)	193/1, 3,5	Chorus: Ob I,II obbl; Aria: Ob obbl, S, str; Aria: Ob solo, A
1.9	11 p. Trin.	Joh. Ludwig Bach		cantata 15
8.9	12 p. Trin.	Geist und Seele wird verwirret	35	No obbl or solo Ob; 1,5: cf. BWV 1059/1,3
15.9	13 p. Trin.	Joh. Ludwig Bach		cantata 16

22.9	14 p. Trin.	Wer Dank opfert, der preiset mich	17/1	Chorus: Ob I, Vn I *all'unisono*
29.9	15 p. Trin./ St. Michael	Es erhub sich ein Streit	19/3	Aria: Ob d'amore I,II obbl, S, Bc
6.10	16 p. Trin.	Wer weiß, wie nahe mir	27/1	Chorus: Ob I,II obbl
13.10	17 p. Trin.	Wer sich selbst erhöhet	47/4	Aria: Ob obbl, Vn, B, Bc
20.10	18 p. Trin.	Gott soll allein mein Herze haben	169	No obbl or solo Ob; 1,5: cf. BWV 1053/1,2
27.10	19 p. Trin.	Ich will den Kreuzstab gerne tragen	56/1, 3	Aria: Ob, Vn I *all'unisono*; Aria: Ob solo, B, Bc
31.10	Reformation	Gott der Herr ist Sonn und Schild(?)	79/2	Aria: Ob. solo, A, Bc
3.11	20 p. Trin.	Ich geh' und suche mit Verlangen	49/4	Ob d'amore obbl 1: cf. BWV 1053/3
10.11	21 p. Trin.	Was Gott tut, das ist wohlgetan	98/3	Aria: Ob solo, S, Bc

adds weight to the hypothesis that it was scored with the sonority of the oboe in mind. It is certainly not inconceivable that BWV 1053a was written for our mystery oboist not all that long before Bach's recasting of its outer movements for obbligato organ in BWV 35.

It is possible that it was this, or another visiting oboist who brought the concertos for one and two oboes of Albinoni's Opus IX to Bach's attention, but this is speculation. Beginning in early 1725 Bach had begun to travel at more regular intervals than during his first eighteen months in Leipzig – to Weissenfels, to Cöthen, almost certainly to Merseburg, and, perhaps most importantly, to Dresden. He could have encountered Albinoni's latest concerto collection at any one of these courts, but given its earlier close connection with Albinoni, Dresden, which Bach visited during the fall of 1725, would seem to be a likely venue for such an encounter.

However, there is evidence that seems rather to point in the direction of Weissenfels. The ritornellos to three of the movements in "Kommt, eilet und laufet" BWV 249 (*Easter Oratorio*), a parody of the secular cantata "Entfliehet, verschwindet" BWV 249a, which Bach performed for the birthday of Duke Christian of Saxe-Weissenfels on February 23, 1725, show close parallels to one another. The detail that links the opening ritornellos of BWV 249/1, 3 and 9 most clearly is the use of the same characteristic sequential passage immediately following the fanfare-like antecedent phrases. These sequences, either in reduced solo scoring or involving concertato interjections, in every case trace the same harmonic progression: V7/ii–ii–V–I. This specific feature does not occur in any of the ritornellos to arias in cantatas composed during the pre-Lenten period up to Estomihi but does make its appearance in the cantatas written after Easter, most notably in the Sinfonia to the cantata "Am Abend aber desselben Sabbats" BWV 42/1 (mm. 2–5). What I am suggesting is that Bach encountered and assimilated these particular details of harmony and scoring in the ritornello around the time of his sojourn in Weissenfels during the last week in February of 1725. If so, they would provide us with a chronological marker helping to identify concertos written at this time or later.

In looking for the possible model for these ritornellos, one is led immediately to the ritornellos in the allegro movements of Albinoni's Opus IX concertos. The opening movement to the Concerto for Two Oboes and Strings Op. IX, No. 9 offers a particularly striking example (Example 2.3). Here, the relatively short, fanfare-like antecedent phrase of mm. 1–2 is followed in mm. 3–5 by precisely the same sequential progression as that noted above, and just as in the ritornellos of Bach, in reduced scoring, here for Violin I, Violin II and Viola *Bassetgen*. Bach's ritornello (mm. 33–40) concludes, as does Albinoni's (mm. 10–11), with a recapitulatory statement of the opening fanfare motive. The foregoing evidence further suggests that Bach's reception of Albinoni's Opus IX concertos may date to the period of Bach's visit to Weissenfels during the latter half of February, 1725.[36]

The *terminus ante quem* for the composition of BWV 1053a, October 20, 1726, falls during the period of the Michaelmas Fair. Is it not conceivable that this original version of the concerto was written for the guest appearance of our visiting oboist on the program of one of the *extraordinaire* concerts of the Collegium musicum, quite possibly under the direction of Bach himself?[37]

36 Because of the very similar structure of their opening ritornellos along with other details of form and style, in my study referred to above, I have also included the Concerto for Violin and Strings in E major BWV 1042 and the "Gloria in excelsis Deo" BWV 232¹/4 as part of a concerto complex I believe to have been composed at about the same time.

37 There is evidence that suggests that Bach may have been actively involved in the activities of the Collegium some time before he assumed its direction in April, 1729. See Andreas Glöckner, "Johann Kuhnau, Johann Sebastian Bach und die Musikdirektoren der Leipziger Neukirche," *Beiträge zur Bachforschung* 4 (1985): 23–32.

Example 2.3a   T. Albinoni, Concerto for Two Oboes and Strings, Op. IX, No. 9/1, mm. 2–6

Example 2.3b   J. S Bach, *Easter Oratorio* BWV 249/1, mm. 13–24

Whatever the case, a dating to the second half of 1726 is in keeping with the advanced formal handling of da capo concerto form in this concerto, the only one, incidentally, in which both of the outer movements of a concerto by Bach are cast in this form.

It appears from the foregoing, then, that the mature concertos of Albinoni were an important factor in Bach's approach to the genre throughout the decade of the 1720s. Albinoni was certainly not the only influence on Bach's concertos from this period but he must, I believe, be counted among the chief

influences. His extended opening ritornellos, his use of formal and structural elements derived from the aria and his decidedly vocal style of writing for the soloist seem to have appealed to Bach. If these surface details of style were important for Bach's changing approach to the concerto, then Albinoni's highly individual approach to ritornello form must be seen as having been absolutely crucial.

My findings, if they bear up under close scrutiny, obviously have implications for the chronology not only of the concertos I have linked with the mature concertos of Albinoni, but of Bach's concertos as a whole. Largely under the enduring and pernicious influence of Heinrich Besseler's chronology, and even despite the warning bells sounded in recent years by Bach scholars, the view that those concerto movements adapted by Bach in his Leipzig cantatas are of Cöthen, or even Weimar origin is still pervasive. And even though many rightly take issue with this shortsighted view, they imply strongly that those concertos not written before Bach's move to Leipzig date from the time of his taking up the direction of the Collegium musicum in the spring of 1729. Bach's compositional activity during the period of over half a decade in between, particularly the early years from 1723 to 1725 (perhaps because of the long shadow cast by the new Bach cantata chronology), is often wrongly viewed as a sort of dense knot of cantata composition from which chamber music is virtually excluded. What Robert Marshall has so persuasively argued is true of the sonata during this period, I would in turn maintain is equally true of the concerto.[38] Even if Bach was preoccupied with one genre, it was certainly not to the exclusion of all others, for this questing and inquisitive mind was ever open to new impulses, no matter what the genre, no matter what the source.

38   See Robert L. Marshall, "J. S. Bach's compositions for solo flute," in *The music of Johann Sebastian Bach: the sources, the style, the significance* (New York, 1989), 201–25.

Chapter three

J. S. Bach and G. F. Kauffmann: reflections on Bach's later style

JOHN BUTT

The name of Georg Friedrich Kauffmann (1679–1735) appears intermittently in Bach research. While he has sometimes been acclaimed as one of the very best of Bach's contemporaries – especially when it was once believed that Bach himself performed Kauffmann's vocal works, because Bach's copyists prepared some of the surviving manuscripts[1] – he is somewhat stigmatized as one of the "also-rans" for Bach's post at the Leipzig Thomasschule. Given that the town council ranked him below Bach, it is easy to assume that he was not as adept or modish as the likes of Telemann and Graupner, candidates who were preferred even to Bach.[2] Kauffmann has also been associated with Bach in certain other respects: his music was known to Johann Gottfried Walther and Johann Tobias Krebs, both of whom were in close contact with Bach;[3] Bach also sent his eldest son, Wilhelm Friedemann to study with Kauffmann's colleague J. G. Graun in Merseburg (*c*. 1727).[4] Kauffmann's vocal works were indeed performed in Leipzig, though probably not under Bach's direction. Not only is there evidence for at least one such performance prior to Bach's arrival, but also for several

---

1   Joshua Rifkin, "Kauffmann, Georg Friedrich," *New Grove*. The involvement of Bach's copyists has since been elucidated by Andreas Glöckner, "Neuerkenntnisse zu Johann Sebastian Bachs Aufführungs-kalender," *BJ* 67 (1981): 43–75, esp. 65–6; and "Leipziger Neukirchenmusik 1729–1761," *Beiträge zur Musikwissenschaft* 25 (1983): 105–12. The copyists concerned were working for Carl Gotthelf Gerlach, having left Bach's service; thus the Kauffmann pieces were performed in the New Church under the direction of Gerlach.

2   For a detailed study of the candidates and appointment procedure, see Ulrich Siegele, "Bachs Stellung in der Leipziger Kulturpolitik seiner Zeit (Fortsetzung)," *BJ* 70 (1984): 7–13.

3   See Hermann Zietz, *Quellenkritische Untersuchungen an den Bach–Handschriften P801, P802, P803*, Hamburger Beiträge zu Musikwissenschaft 1 (Hamburg, 1969); and Stephen Daw, "Copies of J. S. Bach by Walther and Krebs: a study of the Mss P801, P802, P803," *The Organ Yearbook* 7 (1976): 31–58.

4   Rifkin, "Kauffmann."

under Carl Gotthelf Gerlach at the New Church in Leipzig during the early 1730s.[5]

Furthermore, Kauffmann's serial publication of organ chorales, *Harmonische Seelenlust*, as the first substantial printed collection of such pieces for many years, must have had some impact on Bach.[6] Indeed, given that J. G. Walther claimed that J. S. Bach had recommended publication of his variations on "Allein Gott in der Höh sei Ehr" to the Leipzig engraver J. G. Krügner, it is quite possible that the cantor (who had published the first part of his own *Clavier-Übung* with Krügner) had also encouraged the Kauffmann project.[7] The findings of Christian Ahrens show that Kauffmann's series was not completed until May 1740 (and posthumously, at that), and this may partly explain why Krügner did not complete the engraving of the third part of Bach's *Clavier-Übung*, which was transferred to Balthasar Schmid in Nuremberg around the beginning of 1739. Perhaps Krügner intended Bach's collection as a sequel to Kauffmann's, but was thwarted by the protraction of the latter. Although Krügner had complained of the lack of buyers for Kauffmann's print in 1736, the size of the newspaper advertisements and the number of sales agents for each of the twelve installments seem to have been considerable. Ahrens sees the Kauffmann series as the first of a long list of well-advertised publications reflecting a "neue Gusto" in public taste, one that demanded music catering to the amateur in particular.[8]

These various points of contact lead to justifiable speculations about Bach's relationship with Kauffmann: as Peter Williams has suggested, Bach himself may have seen the third part of his *Clavier-Übung* as a sequel to, or even improvement on Kauffmann's project.[9] That some of Kauffmann's settings might also have inspired Bach's publication of the modish "Schübler" chorales

---

5   See Glöckner, "Neuerkenntnisse zu Johann Sebastian Bachs Aufführungskalender," 64–6; and "Leipziger Neukirchenmusik 1729–1761," 105–12. Hans-Joachim Schulze notes that Kauffmann's cantata "Unverzagt, beklemmtes Herze" was performed in Leipzig just prior to Bach's arrival; *Studien zur Bach-Überlieferung im 18.Jahrhundert* (Leipzig, 1984), 122.

6   Rifkin's statement in *New Grove* that this was the first publication of this kind since Scheidt's *Tabulatura nova* contains an element of truth, but should be qualified: Pachelbel, Buxtehude and Vetter all published a small number of chorale settings for organ.

7   *Johann Gottfried Walther. Briefe*, ed. Klaus Beckmann and Hans-Joachim Schulze (Leipzig, 1987), 195. See also Gregory Butler, "Leipziger Stecher in Bachs Originaldrucken," *BJ* 66 (1980): 9–26. Peter Williams, in *The Organ Works of J. S. Bach*, vol. 3 (Cambridge, 1984), 30, also infers that Bach may have recommended the *Harmonische Seelenlust* for publication.

8   Christian Ahrens, "J. S. Bach und der 'neue Gusto' in der Musik um 1740," *BJ* 72 (1986): 70. Ahrens notes that the collection was issued in twelve installments. Examination of the exemplar in the British Library, shelf number e.1148., shows the signature "Krügner Sc. Lipsice" at the bottom of pages 1, 9, 19, 29, 39, 49, 59, 69, 79, 89, 118 (the last verso). Presumably the eleventh issue began on page 99, and the final issue ran from page 109 to page 118.

9   Williams, *The Organ Music of J. S. Bach*, 3: 281, notes to vol. 2, 177.

has also been suggested by Williams.[10] Furthermore, the relationship between Kauffmann's "Komm, heiliger Geist" and Bach's setting of "Valet will ich dir geben" BWV 736 has led to speculation that Bach may have composed the latter setting late in the Leipzig years, under the influence of Kauffmann's setting.[11]

Certainly the direct comparison of the works of any two composers can easily fall prey to the Scylla of the spurious on the one hand and the Charybdis of the tautological on the other. So often do proposed similarities seem to clutch at motivic straws or at concordances that merely reflect the conventions of a shared style.[12] However, at the very least, these conventions can be re-examined and fresh comparisons might reveal more of the background against which each composer worked. This study examines the validity of claims that Kauffmann's publication might have provided some of the impetus for Bach's *Clavier-Übung* of 1739 and the "Schübler" preludes some ten years later. Moreover, it extends the examination beyond these to the remaining, third publication of organ music, the *Canonic Variations on "Vom Himmel hoch"* BWV 769. The results suggest that a study of Kauffmann's work contributes significantly not only to our understanding of the background of these three publications but also to our picture of Bach's late compositional activity as a whole.

The title page to the third part of Bach's *Clavier-Übung* stands out from the other three volumes in the series with its specification of two distinct levels of readership: "Denen Liebhabern, und besonders denen Kennern von dergleichen Arbeit" ("To amateurs/lovers and particularly to connoisseurs of such work"). While the second half of this statement might, in part, have been inspired as a response to the Scheibe affair,[13] there is a close parallel here with the title page of Kauffmann's publication: "Allen höhen und niedern Liebhabern des Claviers" ("To all high and low lovers of the keyboard"). It was certainly customary at this time to use such dedications, but most publications pander specifically towards the "Liebhaber."[14] Perhaps Kauffmann, nearing the end of his life (he died before the project was half-finished) wished to display the art he had acquired over a lifetime to its fullest extent. This encyclopedic tendency may thereby have provided an impetus not only for *Clavier-Übung* III but also for much of Bach's activity during the last decade of his life. Indeed, the reported title of Kauffmann's lost (or unwritten) treatise points to a somewhat

10　Williams, *The organ music of J. S. Bach*, vol. 2 (1980), 107; vol. 3, 65.

11　Williams, *The organ music of J. S. Bach*, 2: 284–5.

12　For an admonitory homily, see Walter Emery, *Notes on Bach's organ works: a companion to the revised Novello*, vol. 1 (London, 1952), 36–7. See also the introduction to his edition, *G. F. Kauffmann: Harmonische Seelenlust, selections* (London, 1958).

13　See David Humphreys, *The esoteric structure of Bach's Clavierübung III* (Cardiff, 1983), 78–84.

14　Ahrens, "J. S. Bach und der 'neue Gusto,'" 70–1.

pedagogical figure, one who was clearly conversant with the tradition of German compositional theory in his specification of both "old and new" styles of composition.[15]

Superficially, Bach's *Clavier-Übung* III and Kauffmann's *Harmonische Seelenlust* have much in common: both comprise chorale settings for organs with and without pedals (Kauffmann specifies their utility for organists in "Städten und Dörffern"). Furthermore, both contain works in the oldest and newest idioms available to composers of the time: on the one hand, Kauffmann and Bach frequently use "modern," so-called galant gestures, such as sighing and triplet figures, and a light, melodic texture; on the other, both composers write examples in the *stile antico*, pieces which seem specifically to allude to the austere counterpoint of the late Renaissance era.[16] Indeed, Kauffmann suggests a distinction between two types of counterpoint in his introduction to *Harmonische Seelenlust* analogous to that in his theoretical work: "Der Modus oder Art und Weise ist / vierdtens, Contrapunctus fractus & floridus: Davon der erste etwas seriös, jedoch lebhafft / der andre aber ziemlich munter / jedoch nicht wilde / sich erzeiget" ("The *Modus* or manner is, fourthly *Contrapunctus fractus & floridus*, of which the first tends to be somewhat serious, but lively, while the second is rather more vigorous, but not wild").

Parallels between the two composers' styles can most strikingly be discerned in the texture of the short settings. Bach's counterpoint in certain works of the *Clavier-Übung* III is sometimes regarded as being rather dense, obscure, if not slightly awkward in places.[17] Kauffmann's settings are similarly compact and often seem somewhat indigestible (compare Kauffmann's second setting of "Erschienen ist der herrliche Tag" and Bach's setting "Christ, unser Herr, zum Jordan kam" BWV 685). The combination of imitative counterpoint, a dense texture and an unpredictable – or at least capricious – succession of note lengths that makes the much-maligned "Allein Gott in der Höh sei Ehr" BWV 675 so distinctive, might owe something to Kauffmann's idiom, for example, his setting of "Nun ruhen alle Wälder."

15 Johann Gottfried Walther, *Musicalisches Lexicon* (Leipzig, 1732), 336: "eine ausführliche Einleitung zur alten und neuen Wissenschafft der edlen Music . . . die General- und Special-Regulen der Composition mit alten und neuen Stylo."

16 The recent illuminating study by Gregory Butler *(Bach's Clavier-Übung III. The making of a print. With a companion study of the Canonic Variations on Vom Himmel Hoch BWV 769* [Durham, N. C. and London, 1990]), surprisingly contains little reference to Kauffmann. However, Butler's discovery of three other specific outside influences (Hurlebusch, Krieger and Walther, 4–13) at least suggests that Bach was not averse to assimilating contemporary influences with this publication, and that he was perhaps purposely building on recent models.

17 Williams, *The organ music of J. S. Bach*, 2: 181: "There is an unconventional, even at times strange, quality about the counterpoint of much of *Clavierübung III*."

Although Kauffmann's publication is not so tautly structured overall as Bach's collection (perhaps his death prevented the collection from being presented in an orderly manner) there are significant parallels in local instances. Kauffmann's sequence of five manualiter settings of "Nun komm, der Heiden Heiland" (see Example 3.1a/b) may have inspired Bach's smaller "Kyrie" cycle BWV 672–4. Although the latter do not employ the cantus firmus technique of Kauffmann's settings – instead they present a free paraphrase of each successive line of the chorale – the similarity of motives and rhythms in the pieces in compound time is difficult to ignore. Compare, for instance, the leaps of a fourth to a syncopation in Kauffmann's *Vivace* setting of "Nun komm, der Heiden Heiland" (mm. 3, 4, etc.) with the opening of Bach's "Christe, aller Welt Trost" BWV 673; likewise the neighbor-note figure opening Kauffmann's *Alio modo* version of the same chorale with Bach's "Kyrie, Gott Heiliger Geist" BWV 674.

Example 3.1a   G. F. Kauffmann, "Nun komm, der Heiden Heiland," mm. 1–6

Example 3.1b   G. F. Kauffmann, "Nun komm, der Heiden Heiland," *alio modo*, mm. 1–4

Sometimes a notational similarity might point to a connection between the two collections. The concise subject of Kauffmann's short fughetta on "Wir glauben all an einem Gott" (Example 3.2a) is liberally marked with staccato strokes in the original print and this immediately invites parallels with Bach's fughetta on "Allein Gott in der Höh sei Ehr" BWV 677 (Example 3.2b) where a similar marking is a unique instance in a Bach composition of this type. Further points of similarity are the close succession of short-breathed entries, the touch of chromaticism just beyond the mid-way point, and, most

Example 3.2a   G. F. Kauffmann, "Wir glauben all an einen Gott," mm. 1–3

Example 3.2b   J. S. Bach, "Allein Gott in der Höh sei Ehr" BWV 677, mm. 1–3

Example 3.3a   G. F. Kauffmann, "Wir glauben all an einen Gott," end

Example 3.3b   J. S. Bach, "Allein Gott in der Höh sei Ehr" BWV 677, end

particularly, the use of the tonal answer (i.e., the second fugal entry of each setting) as a means of ending both pieces (with no closing fermata; see Example 3.3a/b).

Kauffmann was perhaps the first to introduce popular galant gestures systematically into organ chorales. Moreover, Bach's self-consciousness in following the fashions of the day in certain settings in *Clavier-Übung* III is difficult to deny. Although elements such as slurred "sighing" figures could have been gleaned from virtually any modish works of the day, it may well be that Kauffmann's combining of triplets with duple values in "Durch Adams Fall" and "Wenn wir in höchsten Nöten sein" influenced Bach's in "Vater unser im Himmelreich" BWV 682 and particularly in the Kauffmannesque "Allein Gott in der Höh' sei Ehr" BWV 675. This rhythmic feature becomes particularly characteristic in Bach's later works (e.g., *Well-tempered Clavier* II and the 3-part Ricercar from the *Musicalisches Opfer*).

Kauffmann's participation in the galant style has justifiably been recognized, but he has never been portrayed as an apologist of the so-called *stile antico*.[18] Nevertheless, the titles of his composition treatise and the *Harmonische Seelenlust* suggest that Kauffmann was indeed interested in keeping the old style alive and was part of that minor renaissance of which Bach and Fux are the most renowned promoters. The tell-tale sign of the stricter style – the half-note tactus – is readily evident in seven of the chorale settings: "Christus, der uns selig macht" looks almost like an exercise in two-part, fifth-species counterpoint; "Es ist das Heil uns kommen her" is less strict, with its disjunct motion in quarter-notes, but it displays the same array of "fundamental figures" and occasional chromatic motion that are found in Bach's larger "Kyrie" settings, BWV 669–71. Kauffmann's two settings of "O Lamm Gottes unschuldig" (Example 3.4) are almost as pure examples of the ancient style as any of Bach's in *Clavier-Übung* III. Indeed the caption "à 3 per imitationes" for the second half of the longer setting suggests that Kauffmann wished to draw attention to the contrapuntal rigor of the piece. Furthermore, the emphasis on imitation intensifies the latter half of the piece in a manner similar to Bach's "Kyrie, Gott Heiliger Geist" BWV 671 and the "Credo" of the Mass in B Minor. Finally, the group of three settings on "Vater unser im Himmelreich," which consists of a fugue followed by two two-part settings (with the cantus firmus above in the first, below in the second setting) draws immediate comparison with Bach's larger "Kyrie" cycle (BWV 669–71).

Certain musical features place Kauffmann in the eighteenth century – the occasional quick resolution of suspensions and two dominant sevenths in the first "Vater unser" – but it seems unlikely that he could have written in this style without some considerable study of music from at least a century before. At the very least, this study suggests that the *stile antico* was a viable method of composition in the 1730s, that the public of "Liebhaber" appreciated a small

18 The term was investigated and defined by Christoph Wolff, *Der stile antico in der Musik Johann Sebastian Bachs* (Wiesbaden, 1968).

Example 3.4   G. F. Kauffmann, "O Lamm Gottes unschuldig," mm. 1–9

dose of "pure" music with its galanteries. Perhaps Bach in his final years made a particular effort to publicize himself as a learned contrapuntalist because he felt he had failed in the modern style, and took the next best option.[19] Most likely Bach took comfort from the sprinkling of *stile antico* pieces in the *Harmonische Seelenlust* and included four in his own *Clavier-Übung* III.

This survey of contrapuntal pieces in the old style naturally leads to a consideration of Bach's late published works that he purposely designed to demonstrate his prowess in counterpoint. Can any parallels be found between Kauffmann's work and Bach's *Canonic Variations on "Vom Himmel hoch"* BWV 769? Immediate attention should be drawn to the closing measures of BWV 769 in its printed version: here all the lines of the chorale are sounded together in a dazzling array of contrapuntal artifices. The fourth of Kauffmann's settings of "Nun komm, der Heiden Heiland" (Example 3.5) is only five measures long but likewise combines all the lines "Totum in parte," with the first line held in longer notes in the upper voice, the other three heard in close succession below. Even if this miniature was not a direct influence on Bach, it is inconceivable that Bach would not have noticed and admired it.

Strict canon at the octave is represented in the *Harmonische Seelenlust* with the setting of "Wir Christenleut" that, with its cantus firmus in the pedal, greatly resembles Bach's first variation on "Vom Himmel hoch." Of course, the setting of "Wir Christenleut" is now known to be the composition of J. G. Walther, but whether Bach knew of its true attribution is immaterial here. There seem to be no other chorale settings with fully canonic accompanying

---

19   This is, in effect, one of the main points in Ahrens, "J. S. Bach und der 'neue Gusto.'"

Example 3.5 G. F. Kauffmann, "Nun komm, der Heiden Heiland," *Totum in parte*

Example 3.6 G. F. Kauffmann, "Ein feste Burg ist unser Gott," mm. 1–3

Example 3.7 G. F. Kauffmann, "Herzlich Lieb hab ich dich, o Herr," mm. 1–3

voices between Bach's "In dulci jubilo" BWV 608 ("Orgelbüchlein") and the *Canonic Variations*, so the Kauffmann publication may have been a significant influence on Bach's decision to compose – and indeed to publish – the *Canonic Variations*.

Another relationship between the "Orgelbüchlein" and the *Canonic Variations* is the imitative descending-scale head-motive of "Christe du Lamm Gottes" BWV 619, a gesture that also opens the *Canonic Variations*. Five Kauffmann settings also begin with a prominent descending scale,[20] two in particular proceed with a texture similar to that opening "Vom Himmel hoch:" the second setting of "Ein feste Burg" and "Herzlich lieb hab ich dich, o Herr" (Examples 3.6 and 3.7). This figure was clearly a popular device of the time and it would be short-sighted to suggest that its prominence in the *Harmonische*

---

20 "Ein feste Burg – Alio modo"; "Herzlich lieb hab ich dich, o Herr"; "Nun danket alle Gott"; "Nun ruhen alle Wälder"; "Puer natus in Bethlehem."

Example 3.8   G. F. Kauffmann, "Vom Himmel hoch," mm. 1–3, 13–16

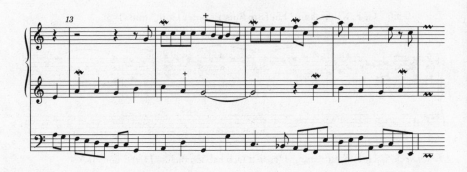

Example 3.9   J. S. Bach, *Canonic Variations on "Von Himmel hoch"* BWV 769, variation 5, mm. 7–8, 14–15

Seelenlust led Bach directly to use it to open the canonic variations; but it probably played some part in his compositional decision.

It seems more than likely that Bach was directly influenced by one piece from the *Harmonische Seelenlust*; Kauffmann's setting of "Vom Himmel hoch" itself (see Examples 3.8 and 3.9). Although the head-motive was part of the common motivic vocabulary of the day,[21] another point of concordance is the

---

21   See Walter Emery's discussions referred to in n. 12. In addition to the obvious parallels with the subject of Bach's fugue BWV 541 and the first chorus of the cantata "Ich hatte viel Bekümmernis" BWV 21,

Example 3.10   G. F. Kauffmann, "Man lobt dich in der Stille," mm. 1–6

"walking" pedal bass that is also found in the final variation in the printed version of BWV 769. At two points the settings show striking similarities: Kauffmann, m.13 and Bach, mm.7–8; Kauffmann, mm.15–16 and Bach, mm.14–15. In the latter Example the pedal is identical for nine notes and syncopations accompany the chorale line. Although it is unlikely that Bach was consciously copying Kauffmann in this piece, it is highly probable that he had unconsciously absorbed the style and gestures of the earlier setting.

In turning finally to the relationship between Kauffmann's chorales and Bach's "Schübler" print, it should first be stressed that Bach was not chiefly publishing fresh compositions here, but transcriptions of chorale settings from cantatas. Nevertheless it is possible that the style of the Kauffmann pieces influenced Bach's choices, because so many of the *Harmonische Seelenlust* chorales adopt a similarly bold melodic style, common in instrumental works but so new to the organ. The rounded ostinato subject of Kauffmann's "O heiliger Geist" has much in common with that of Bach's "Meine Seele erhebt den Herren" BWV 648 and Peter Williams has suggested that "Man lobt dich in der Stille" (Example 3.10) of Kauffmann already has the "characteristic form and melody" of the "Schübler" type.[22] Given these resemblances, it may well be that some of Kauffmann's settings – like Bach's – derived from concerted works.

Indeed, Klaus Hofmann has already suggested – observing the figured bass in "Herr Gott, dich loben alle wir" – that Kauffmann may have transcribed the

---

both the head-motive and the walking-bass line find further analogues in Bononcini's *Il trionfo di Camilla*, and Handel's *Acis and Galatea*; see Winton Dean, "Handel and Bononcini: another link?" *The Musical Times* 131 (1990): 412–13.

22 Williams, *The organ music of J. S. Bach*, 2: 107.

six settings with solo oboe in the *Harmonische Seelenlust* from cantata movements involving cantus firmus and instrumental obbligato.[23] A figured bass is hardly necessary – and is, indeed, most unusual – in an original work for organ with fully notated musical lines. Moreover, one of the settings for organ alone, "Man lobt dich in der Stille," is also liberally marked with figured bass numerals. These two preludes appear on pages 84 and 86 respectively in the original print and thus come from the latter part of the publication, published after Kauffmann's death. Perhaps they came from a common source, either a cantata score or a direct transcription thereof, in which Kauffmann – or his wife, who took over the project – forgot to omit the figured bass.

However, the detailed registrations for "Herr Gott, dich loben alle wir" may suggest that the composer had already prepared it for the organ version. Furthermore, J. G. Walther's manuscript copy of "Herr Gott" contains the registrations (but omits the figured bass). If, as has often been thought, Walther's copy predates the printed version, this would suggest that the piece was an organ piece prior to the publication of *Harmonische Seelenlust*, thus weakening the case for its instrumental origins. However, Stephen Daw has suggested that this copy was, in fact, made after the print was published, something which would conveniently account for Walther's omission of the figured bass and retention of the registrations.[24]

In his preface, Kauffmann advises that the oboe employed for the cantus firmus in six of the settings be placed "as if it were a stop on the organ" and remarks that "pieces are being played in this fashion here" (presumably in Merseburg) to great acclaim.[25] The earliest documented use of organ with obbligato instrument is that of Johann Bernhard Bach (cousin of Johann Sebastian) at St. George's Church, Eisenach. However, Kauffmann's are the earliest extant organ works with an obbligato instrument and were clearly influential in a vogue that reached its peak with the compositions of Johann Ludwig Krebs.[26] Krebs is a further link between Kauffmann and Bach because his father, Johann Tobias Krebs, was the copyist of an unpublished fantasia by Kauffmann, and both father and son were pupils of J. S. Bach.[27]

23 *Georg Friedrich Kauffmann. Sechs vierstimmige Choralbearbeitungen für Oboe und Orgel*, ed. Klaus Hofmann (Stuttgart, 1970).

24 Daw, "Copies of J. S. Bach by Walther and Krebs," 35–6.

25 Preface to *Harmonische Seelenlust*: "So wäre . . . wohl gethan / wenn die Oboe so gestellet werden könte / daß es liesse / ob wäre es ein Register in der Orgel, welches die Sache um so viel angenehmer machen würde; Denn auf dergleichen Weise sind dieselben allhier tractiret worden / welches zur guten Nachricht melden sollen."

26 For further information on the genre, see *Johann Ludwig Krebs: Collected works for organ and solo instrument*, ed. Hugh McLean (Sevenoaks, 1981), preface.

27 J. T. Krebs's copy of the "Fantasia" is found in SBB Mus. ms. Bach P801.

One final point that might suggest instrumental origins is the awkwardness of the pedal parts in certain settings. Whereas Bach will often simplify a fugal subject for pedal performance (e.g. BWV 543, fugue; BWV 526/3, Allegro) Kauffmann often makes no allowances: the bass line of "Es spricht der Unweisen Mund wohl" (Example 3.11) requires much sixteenth-note movement. This part is not unequivocally to be played in the pedal, however; indeed its highest note is the top e' seldom found on pedal-boards of the time. Thus it is conceivable that the pedals should play the tenor cantus firmus instead. "O Gott, du frommer Gott" requires similar passages in the bass (and here there is no option but to play them in the pedals) and there is uncompromising imitation between manual and pedal parts, something which could point towards an instrumental origin. Admittedly, some of the galant pieces for oboe and organ by J. L. Krebs also have demanding pedal parts, particularly fast scalar movement (e.g., Fantasia in F minor) – and these are certainly original works for organ – but Krebs may well have taken courage from Kauffmann's publication here.

Example 3.11   G. F. Kauffmann, "Es spricht der Unweisen Mund wohl," mm. 19–20

Only five of Kauffmann's vocal works survive, so it is not surprising that none contain the chorale settings that may have served as models for the organ works. However, the closing chorale setting in the Visitation cantata "Nicht uns, Herr, sondern deinem Namen gib Ehre" belongs very much to the same world as the more galant organ chorales (Example 3.12; compare, for instance, "Man lobt dich in der Stille," in the same key and meter, Example 3.10), showing, at the very least, that Kauffmann did not greatly differentiate the styles of his organ and concerted works.

Kauffmann's transcriptions for organ – particularly his compositions in instrumental style for organ – fill a significant gap in our knowledge of German organ style in the early eighteenth century. First, Bach and Walther instigated what must have been a revolutionary advance in the formal and motivic

Example 3.12   G. F. Kauffmann, cantata "Nicht uns, Herr, sondern deinem Namen gib Ehre," ritornello of concluding chorale, mm. 1–11

structure of keyboard writing with their transcriptions of instrumental concertos. Then Bach virtually invented the organ concerto with his experiments with organ obbligatos in the third cycle of Leipzig cantatas. And at some stage in his career – perhaps long before the *Harmonische Seelenlust* was planned – Kauffmann experimented with instrumental cantus firmus parts and probably adapted chorales from cantatas. Presuming that the publication of works in this idiom generated considerable general interest, it seems all the more likely that Bach's "Schübler" chorales were intended to respond to market demand. Bach may thus have left a large part of the preparation to a copyist, as Christoph Wolff has suggested.[28]

A further point about Kauffmann's publication can be drawn from its registrations. All point to a colorful, somewhat exotic palette, foreign to the chorus-based specifications of "Werkprinzip" organs of northern Germany – to many, the "classical" Baroque organs. Organs of the Bach era in both Thuringia and Saxony (where Kauffmann also worked) similarly show a trend towards colorful solo stops, often designed to mimic orchestral sounds. Moreover, Kauffmann,

28   Christoph Wolff, "Bachs Handexemplar der Schübler-Choräle," *BJ* 63 (1977): 120–9.

in his preface to *Harmonische Seelenlust*, instructs the organist to perform slurred passages in imitation of violin bowing.[29] Bach similarly tended to add instrumentally inspired articulation marks in his organ works during the last two decades of his life.[30] The "instrumentalization" of the organ by Kauffmann and Bach can thus be viewed as part of a larger trend in the field of organ building, composition and performance, one that inevitably led the organ into competition with other instruments, ultimately to its disadvantage.

Virtually every feature of Bach's late style is predated, or at least shared, by Kauffmann's *Harmonische Seelenlust*. Parallels are found in the adoption of both ancient and modern styles and in the development of the keyboard idiom itself. It is not certain how many of the Kauffmann pieces Bach knew before the publication of *Harmonische Seelenlust*, but it is striking that the similarities between the two composers emerge only in Bach's later works. The parallels might help us to understand the background to Bach's compositional activity in his later years, and to appreciate that his publications reflect the fashions of the age as much as his oft-presumed desire to provide public documentation of his artistic prowess.

29 Preface to *Harmonische Seelenlust*: "die Passagen, welche oben mit einem Bogen bedeckt seyn, nicht eben geschwind; wohl aber etwas gezogen / und gleichsam / wie mit dem Bogen auf der Violin, müssen heraus gebracht werden."
30 John Butt, *Bach interpretation* (Cambridge, 1990), 164–79.

Chapter four

The variation principle in J. S. Bach's Passacaglia in C minor BWV 582

YOSHITAKE KOBAYASHI

Recognizing the construction of a musical composition is an essential prerequisite of a better understanding of the work. It has often been stressed that the construction of many of J. S. Bach's compositions is strongly architectural. In large-scale works of a cyclical character (for example, the *Goldberg Variations* BWV 988, the *Canonic Variations on "Vom Himmel hoch da komm ich her"* BWV 769, and the motet "Jesu, meine Freude" BWV 227) this matter of architecture is a central concern. In such works, one often encounters a symmetrical construction, and for this reason Bach's music is often compared with Baroque architecture.

We owe to Christoph Wolff the discovery and convincing explication of the ordering principles in Bach's music transmitted in original printed editions.[1] In another study, Wolff attempted to demonstrate an architectonic construction of Bach's Passacaglia for organ BWV 582 as well.[2] Since then, any number of commentators have offered competing opinions about the Passacaglia, some of them mutually contradictory. Not all of these interpretations can be called scholarly; some of them rest in part on speculation.[3] Among the non-speculative analyses those of Wolff and Siegfried Vogelsänger are most compelling and deserve summary here.

---

1 Christoph Wolff, "Ornungsprinzipien in den Originaldrucken der Werke Bachs," in *Bach-Interpretation*, ed. Martin Geck (Göttingen, 1969), 144–67.

2 Christoph Wolff, "Die Architektur von Bachs Passacaglia," *Acta Organologica* 1969: 183–94; English version, "The architecture of the Passacaglia" in Christoph Wolff, *Bach: essays on his life and music* (Cambridge, Mass., 1991), 306–16, 427f.

3 For example, Piet Kee, "Die Geheimnisse von Bachs Passacaglia," *Musik und Kirche* 52 (1982): 165–75; 235–44; 53 (1983): 19–28. Michael Radulescu's conclusion that the construction of the Passacaglia is in the form of a cross is also not logically convincing; "On the form of Johann Sebastian Bach's Passacaglia in c minor," *The Organ Yearbook* 1980: 95–103.

Wolff categorizes the twenty variations over the ostinato bass in the Passacaglia according to five criteria: (1) position of the theme in the texture; (2) variation of the theme; (3) motivic working-out in rhythmic/melodic and harmonic dimensions; (4) contrapuntal technique; and (5) number of voices. According to this scheme, the variations can be divided into seven groups, the fourth of which forms an axis of symmetry:

[Variations]	1–2	3–5	6–9	10–11	12–15	16–18	19–20
[Segment]	I	II	III	IV	V	VI	VII
[No. of vars.]	2	3	4	2	4	3	2

At first glance, this result is logical, and there is nothing to be said against the individual arguments for these groupings, considered on their own merits. There remains the question, though, whether Bach really intended this construction, and further whether the listener can perceive it. To put it another way: are the variations that make up a group really so strongly bound together that the ear of an analytically informed listener can follow this architecture with the help of the above diagram?

It is hardly possible to reach a unanimous consensus on this question. For Siegfried Vogelsänger, for example, the symmetry Wolff finds is not sufficiently thorough-going.[4] Vogelsänger claims to find an architecture that contains several levels, as the following diagram shows:

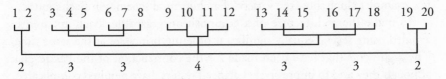

Vogelsänger's criteria for this grouping are multi-layered, and sometimes difficult to follow, for example, his claim that variations 10 and 12 belong together.[5]

The numerous previous attempts to group the variations in the Passacaglia and thus to uncover the architecture of the work have led to widely differing results, making clear how difficult such undertakings are.[6] In light of the

4 Siegfried Vogelsänger, "Zur Architektur der Passacaglia J. S. Bach*s*," *Die Musikforschung* 25 (1972): 40–50.

5 Vogelsänger, "Zur Architektur der Passacaglia," 41.

6 The literature includes, in addition to the items in notes 2, 3 and 4, Werner Tell, "Das Formproblem der Passacaglia Bachs," *Musik und Kirche* 10 (1938): 102–12; Siegfried Vogelsänger, "Passacaglia und Chaconne in der Orgelmusik," *Musik und Kirche* 37 (1967): 14–24; Karl Geiringer, *Johann Sebastian Bach. The culmination of an era* (New York, 1966), 227–8.

large number of competing opinions, one begins to have doubts, and on reflection has to wonder whether Bach really had a symmetrical structure in mind at all. Have we been chasing a phantom? The proposed architectonic schemes have consistently been impressively presented, if they are also consistently in disagreement. They are so beautiful – almost too beautiful – that I cannot escape the impression that in research up to now, attractive analytical goals have first been established, and a path to them searched out after the fact. Characteristically, the defenders of symmetry suspect each other of having made up their minds beforehand about particular groupings favorable to their schemes. It would thus seem to be high time for an unbiased – even "blind" – analysis of the work, one whose results are not predetermined.

The Passacaglia is a variation composition; this is not at issue here. But there are various structural principles by which a variation composition can be composed. Further, it goes without saying that a composer can structure individual works according to different principles and from different points of view. Bach was no exception in this regard. The *Goldberg Variations* are organized on the principle of an increasing interval of canonic imitation. The *Canonic Variations on "Vom Himmel hoch"* follow different ordering schemes in the printed and autograph versions: the print is laid out according to a principle of increase (in the complexity of canonic technique), the autograph according to a principle of symmetry (with the high point in the middle).[7] Strong axial symmetry is to be found, for example, in the motet "Jesu, meine Freude." These few examples alone show the variety of architectural schemes in Bach's music.

To make the architecture of a composition graspable, Bach apparently avoided using several equally significant ordering principles at the same time. The arguments that have been made for the construction of the Passacaglia, although they lead to impressively balanced results, have required complicated, many-branched arguments, because their authors have worked with several principles at once. And this creates particular problems when one tries to follow these visually compelling and architectonic models by ear. This raises the question of whether the Passacaglia might not be governed by some single overarching constructive principle. I approach this question in the remarks that follow, avoiding the tendency to analyze one variation harmonically, another contrapuntally, and so on. The purpose here is to determine whether the composition can be analyzed consistently with respect to only one parameter.

To do so, we need to examine not so much the composition as the various parameters, such as harmony, counterpoint, motives, rhythm, number of

7   See Wolff, "Ornungsprinzipien in den Originaldrucken."

voices, and instrumental technique, asking whether one of these is so apt that it can stand as the sole analytical tool. The answer is "no" for all these musical parameters with one exception: rhythm. Because rhythm comes to play such a significant role in the genre of the variation – one thinks, for example, of Brahms's variations – it seems surprising that it has not sufficiently been taken into account in connection with Bach's Passacaglia. Perhaps the image of Bach as a contrapuntist has contributed to this tendency and has led the search astray, especially in this work, in which so many contrapuntal niceties are to be found.

Let us first address the problem of the rhythmic relationship of the variations to each other. The results of this rhythmic analysis may be summarized here beforehand: simply put, there is an ever more complex rhythm in this work, manifested as well in gradually decreasing note values. This process is best followed through the theme and each of the variations. It is worth following the variations in some detail, because the process by which they unfold and the way in which they relate to each other are critical to understanding the architecture of the composition.[8]

The ostinato **theme**, played monophonically at the opening, consists of half and quarter notes; the penultimate note is a dotted half, and these longest notes begin the work with the calmest motion. **Variations 1 and 2** are characterized by a syncopated rhythm, in which quarter notes and dotted eighths with sixteenths predominate. The sixteenth notes here do not yet contribute to the acceleration of motion, but rather content themselves merely with a kind of ornamental function as anticipations; they have no role in the overall harmonic structure. The slow-moving middle voices, consisting mostly of suspensions, are dominated by syncopations: ♪♩ or ♪♩ .

The first two variations share their broad rhythms, and in this sense the second is a repetition of the first and thus represents an emphasis of its sedate quality. To avoid a simple repetition, Bach shapes the second variation differently in melody and harmony. A similar procedure – repetition of a rhythmic model with changes in other elements – will be seen later in variations 10–11 and 19–20.

In **variation 3**, walking eighth notes determine the rhythmic events, and in **variation 4**, the eighth-note stepwise motion is enlivened by anapestic or dactylic rhythmic figures (♫♩ or ♩♫).

The rhythmic structure of **variation 5** remains the same as in the previous variation, with a difference that lies in the leaping motion of the sixteenths. Despite the unchanged rhythmic values, this represents a true variation, in that

---

8   The distribution of variations in paragraphs in the following discussion is not meant to imply any structural grouping.

the sixteenth notes are clearly set off because of the interval of their leaps and made audible by Bach's staccato indication. In contrast to variation 4, the rhythmic process here spreads to the ostinato bass, making this variation even livelier.

Two rhythmic elements dominate **variation 6**: rising stepwise motion in three sixteenth notes and complementary rhythms. In **variation 7**, the flow of stepwise sixteenth-note motion is continued, now in groups of seven rising sixteenths and often in two voices at a time. In **variation 8**, the stepwise motion consists of substantially more than seven sixteenth notes; the sixteenth notes are presented here in at least two – sometimes even three – upper voices simultaneously. The predominant rhythmic configuration in **variation 9** is identical with that in variation 6. This variation is clearly differentiated by the leaps of a third in sixteenths, a rhythmic motion now also taken up by the ostinato bass. Bach has thus rhythmically intensified unchanged note values by the same means he used to increase intensity from the fourth to the fifth variation.

Variations 10 and **11** present a *perpetuum mobile*, with unbroken sixteenth notes in the soprano (variation 10) and in the alto range (variation 11). The two variations stand in a loose double-contrapuntal relation to each other, in that a voice exchange places the ostinato theme in the soprano in variation 11. The goal of this contrapuntal device presumably lies not in the presentation of this technique *per se*, but rather in the extension of the unbroken motion without resorting to simple repetition.[9] In variation 11, the doubled length of the constant sixteenth-note motion, achieved by rhythmic repetition, intensifies the character of the *perpetuum mobile*.

Until now, Bach has presented simple rhythmic paradigms with ever-smaller note values in duple meter. This ever more lively motion temporarily reaches its limits in variations 10 and 11, and is intensified again only with the introduction of triplets in variation 17. The rest of the Passacaglia is concerned primarily with the combination and variation of previously introduced rhythmic paradigms.

In **variation 12**, a group of three eighth notes is combined with a running figure of sixteenths (eighth notes from variation 3, sixteenths from various previous variations). The sixteenth-note motion here shows a new, falling stair-step figure, also taken up by the ostinato bass. The brisk motion in the bass emphasizes the heightened "turbulence" of this variation. Complementary rhythmic elements (dominant in variations 6 and 9) and syncopated elements (characteristic of variations 1 and 2) are merged in **variation 13**. The ostinato

---

9 Strictly speaking, this is not true double counterpoint, because the middle voice in variation 10 disappears in variation 11, and the ostinato theme is configured somewhat differently in each of the two variations.

theme, now in the alto range, also takes part in this process. The complementary rhythm is occasionally interrupted by the combination of two voices in sixteenth-note motion.

Variation 14 and the following two variations have something in common: they are all based on broken chords in sixteenth notes. In **variation 14**, the rising broken chord supports a counter melody that moves in the opposite direction. The ostinato theme is combined with the chord; more strictly, the theme is integrated into it. If one follows the "hidden" theme, a new rhythmic paradigm emerges in addition to the running sixteenth notes: ♩ ♪ ♪ ♪ ♪ ♪ ♪

In **variation 15**, in contrast to the previous variation, the broken chords appear without a counter melody and always directed upwards. The ostinato theme is similarly integrated into the chords, yielding yet another new rhythmic scheme: ♪ ♪ ♪ ♩ ♪ ♪ ♪

This variation, because of its monophonic texture, represents a counterpart to the first appearance of the ostinato at the beginning of the composition; the theme appears there in the longest notes, here in the smallest duple values. The broken chords from the two previous variations form, in **variation 16**, an acciaccatura-like arpeggio with suspensions drawn from variations 1 and 2. The notes of the broken chords flow towards their goal, the third beat of the measure, where their energy is dammed up. This and the following eighth-note chords stop the flow of sixteenth notes. Thus, the rhythmic feature of this section is defined by a continuing struggle between the two competing forces of the horizontal sixteenth-note motion and the vertical chordal eighth notes.

In **variation 17**, the diminution process reaches the smallest note values in the Passacaglia by the introduction of triplet eighth notes, and thus also the fastest motion in the piece. This variation is related to variations 4 and 5 inasmuch as the triplets may be viewed as deriving from the anapestic or dactylic figures of those earlier sections. The two upper voices move mostly in parallel, occasionally in contrary motion. The dactylic paradigm is paramount, too, in **variation 18**, albeit here combined with the syncopations characteristic of the first two variations. At least two (in a few places all) of the upper voices move homorhythmically.

The two final variations are intimately connected. **Variation 19** incorporates the rhythmic model of variations 1 and 2 (syncopations) and 13 (rhythmically complementary exchange of quarter and sixteenth notes). The motivic unit has to be regarded as comprising one quarter note and four syncopated sixteenth notes tied to it, making up essentially a 2/4 measure. Taken together with the ostinato bass, this rhythmic complex conceals a latent hemiola structure. The dominance of the bass theme prevents this from coming to the fore, however.

Variation 20 is the pinnacle of the rhythmic complexity. Here, the previous variation is *de facto* doubled vertically in the following complex way: the two upper voices from the previous variation are exchanged in the manner of double counterpoint, so that the original tenor melody now appears in the soprano I range and the original soprano melody in the tenor.[10] Because the new tenor melody is displaced a quarter note earlier – to the left in the score – it now moves in parallel with soprano I. Further, it is imitated by soprano II, and soprano I by the alto, at the distance of a quarter note, so that the imitating voices also move in parallel.[11] The two pairs of voices thus alternate quarter-note and sixteenth-note motion, and produce a rhythmic structure that can be characterized as complementary in pairs. The latent hemiola structure of the penultimate variation is retained. Occasionally, and particularly at the end of this final variation, all four upper voices move in simultaneous sixteenth notes, apparently to emphasize this last high point of the composition.

This way of considering the composition reveals more or less close connections between certain variations, but from these connections there emerges no strict symmetrical grouping. The fact that certain variations refer to earlier ones plays a more secondary role; the by and large gradual increase in rhythmic complexity that characterizes the work overshadows other details. Each variation unfolds with increasing tension according to its own rhythmic dynamic, and each rhythmic paradigm is anticipated and announced in the setting of the last note of the previous statement of the ostinato. The further the diminution process proceeds, the more complex and lively the rhythmic appearance becomes.[12] From this point of view, the monophonic presentation of the ostinato at the beginning makes particular sense.

That rhythm is the governing variation principle does not rule out the possibility that certain variations are also the product of variation of harmonic, contrapuntal or other musical elements, of course. These elements provide a palette of colors, not an architectonic structure.

The question of what conception governs the variations in the Passacaglia can now be answered simply: the principle of growth. This means that the high point of the work's tension is reached only at the end after a gradual build-up,

---

10   The static voice in the alto range, which first functions as harmonic filler and then takes part in the rhythmic activity of the second half, is not included in the contrapuntal complex.

11   The first note of the third note from the top in m. 163 may well represent an error in the secondary copies that transmit the work. A strict imitation would require e♭' here, not c'.

12   That systematic thinking about rhythmic values is reflected in Bach's music is illustrated in the cantata "Weinen, Klagen, Sorgen, Zagen" BWV 12. In BWV 12/1, the note values that underlie each of the parts are halved from bottom to top in the manner of mensural music: quarter notes in the continuo, eighths in the violas, sixteenths in the violins, and thirty-seconds in the oboe. See Alfred Dürr, *Die Kantaten von Johann Sebastian Bach mit ihren Texten*, 5th edn. (Munich and Cassel, 1985), 350.

and not in the middle, as is suggested by a symmetrical architectural model. Here I am in agreement with Peter Williams, who, commenting on the analyses of Wolff, Vogelsänger, Klotz and Radulescu, concludes that "all the groupings [in these analyses] are suspect."[13] A symmetrical structure and the sense of stasis that results from it[14] are nowhere to be found in our view of the piece. In contrast, the dynamic of development – one can hardly speak of a static metamorphosis – so characteristic of the genre of variation, is one of the most conspicuous features of Bach's Passacaglia.

The principle of growth is, in whatever form, not the exclusive characteristic of a Romantic esthetic, as Werner Tell would have it,[15] but is to be found often in the Baroque. In any event, the organizational principle of the work does not necessarily have to agree with the outline of its registration in performance; the growth in rhythmic and metrical complexity is independent of the sounding volume. The increase in volume achieved by a full registration toward the end of the Passacaglia indeed seems justified, but does not rule out some rise and fall along the way. A variation work requires nothing less than an equally varied registration.

As one can see from the foregoing arguments, in the Passacaglia Bach worked according to a particular conception underpinned by a single, thoroughgoing principle. Previous analyses have worked with several principles. Despite the aesthetically impeccable schemes these analyses present, they are difficult to perceive with the ear. In contrast, the rhythmic development demonstrated above, notwithstanding its complexity, can be followed aurally by any musically trained listener. That Bach worked according to a particular principle does not mean, however, that he applied it schematically or mathematically exactly. He permitted himself certain liberties and exceptions that should not be perceived as weaknesses of conception, but rather that lend the work variety and individuality.[16]

---

13 *The organ music of J. S. Bach*, vol. 1 (Cambridge, 1980), 265. Williams questions all attempts at grouping on the one hand, but on the other hand suggests no new formal principle for Bach's Passacaglia.

14 See Wolff, "Die Architektur von Bachs Passacaglia," 190.

15 "Das Formproblem der Passacaglia Bachs," 103f.

16 In this regard the Passacaglia is no exception. In the composition of fugues, too, Bach was no more schematic or orthodox. It should be added here that the companion fugue to the Passacaglia is outside the scope of the present essay. This is not to say that the Passacaglia should be considered entirely independently of the fugue, but their connection is a matter for a further investigation.

Chapter five

Forms and functions of the choral movements in J. S. Bach's *St. Matthew Passion*

ULRICH LEISINGER

Johann Sebastian Bach's *St. Matthew Passion* BWV 244 has been described as a "kaleidoscopic panorama of the rich and multi-faceted repertoire of forms in late Baroque vocal music." More than any other work by Bach (or one of his contemporaries), the *St. Matthew Passion* comprises "practically the entire repertoire of forms in sacred and secular vocal music of the Baroque."[1] The recitatives and arias fulfill a single and well-defined function: the recitatives, based on chapters 26 and 27 of the Gospel according to St. Matthew, present a narration of the passion story; the arias on poetic texts by Christian Friedrich Henrici (Picander) are inserted into the plot as reflections on the meaning and importance of the passion story for the listener. The choral movements, however, belong to various genres, each of which has its own traditions and is defined by its own structure and function: *turba* choruses, chorales and free choral movements.

It is evident, though, that the idea of the *St. Matthew Passion* as a "kaleidoscopic panorama" necessarily has its shortcomings. The question remains open: how does a conglomeration of diverse types of movements achieve cohesiveness and unity? Indeed, unity is a basic requirement for calling the *St. Matthew Passion* one of the "greatest artistic monuments of mankind."[2]

The exceptional position of the *St. Matthew Passion* is partly caused by Bach's use of double chorus. Although dialogues that allow for an antiphonal writing are often found in librettos of the time, Bach was apparently the first to

I would like to thank my dear wife Ina and my colleague Noël Bisson (Harvard University) for kind assistance in preparing the English version of my paper.

1 Christoph Wolff, "Musical forms and dramatic structure in Bach's *St. Matthew Passion*," *Bach* 19, no.1 (1988): 6.
2 *Ibid.*

extend the idea of writing for double chorus to the whole passion. Two accidental reasons may have facilitated Bach's decision. For liturgical reasons, the oratorio passion ends with the burial of Jesus; the events at the sepulcher are reserved for the liturgy of the service on Easter Sunday. The oratorio passion is therefore closely linked to the subject matter of funeral music. In fact, two of Bach's passions, the *St. Matthew* and *St. Mark Passions*, are related by means of parody to Leipzig funeral compositions.[3] Bach used double choruses in funeral motets during his Leipzig years.[4] As at least two of them almost directly preceded the *St. Matthew Passion*, a link to this older tradition is very likely.

From Bach's "Entwurf einer regulirten Kirchenmusik" (1730) we learn that he usually had to split up the performance forces at hand to provide both the St. Nicholas and the St. Thomas church with music for regular services.[5] As only one Good Friday Vespers service with figural music took place alternating annually between the two main churches, he was able to count on at least twice the number of singers for his performances of oratorio passions. Since the first *Kantorei* (usually responsible for the church music at St. Thomas) and the second *Kantorei* (from the St. Nicholas church) may be regarded as independent teams, it must have been a special attraction for the composer to make use of them as separate groups in a polychoral piece instead of merely increasing the volume of one chorus by doubling the number of singers per part.

In this essay, I will address these two most distinctive features of Bach's *St. Matthew Passion:* its use of a double chorus and its mixture of a wide variety of musical types. As to the first feature, Bach chose to employ a double chorus not just for practical reasons, but as a reflection of personal artistic ambitions relating to his duties and experiences in Leipzig. Further, his use of a double chorus connects closely with eighteenth-century ideas about polychoral writing and its possibilities. Bach's use of a double chorus is also intimately tied up with the second major feature of the work, its "kaleidoscopic" variety, especially in choral movements, and the problem of unity that variety presents.

Bach's decision to compose the St. Matthew Passion

For the Lutheran of Bach's time, Good Friday and Easter Sunday were undeniably the most important events of the ecclesiastical year. In the Leipzig St.

---

3 See BC III, D 3 and D 4. It is worth mentioning here that Johann Ludwig Bach in Meiningen wrote a funeral piece with double choruses for Duke Ernst Ludwig in 1724, although we have no hint that Johann Sebastian Bach was familiar with this composition when planning the *St. Matthew Passion*. For a discussion of the work see Klaus Hofmann, "Forkel und die Köthener Trauermusik Johann Sebastian Bachs," *BJ* 69 (1983): 115–18.

4 "Der Geist hilft unsrer Schwachheit auf" BWV 226 and "Komm, Jesu, komm" BWV 229.

5 *Dok* I/22 and 180. Bach was obliged to provide four churches (St. Thomas, St. Nicholas, Neue Kirche, St. Peter) with singers, but he usually had no more than about thirty capable choir boys.

Thomas church, a large-scale oratorical work on the subject of the passion story, a setting of the Gospel of St. Mark by Johann Kuhnau, was first performed on Good Friday, 1721. This work was repeated after the composer's death in 1722.[6]

In 1724, the Leipzig city council granted the St. Nicholas church, the second of the main churches, the right to celebrate the Good Friday Vespers every other year. It seems, however, that Bach, who had taken over the *Thomaskantorat* in mid-1723, considered the St. Thomas church better suited for the Good Friday Vespers than the St. Nicholas church, at least for practical reasons. Records for the annual passion in Leipzig are unfortunately incomplete, but they indicate that Bach scheduled the performances of his own works for St. Thomas whenever possible during the first decade of his tenure at Leipzig and that he tended to fulfill his obligations in the Nikolaikirche with smaller and less demanding works by other composers.[7]

A look at the history leading up to the *St. Matthew Passion* may be helpful in better understanding Bach's ambitious undertaking. The *St. John Passion* BWV 245 was repeated with minor changes the year after its completion, on March 30, 1725.[8] Scholars have discussed Bach's revisions extensively, and much effort has been devoted to a search for possible aesthetic motivations. However, the far more astonishing fact that the piece was immediately repeated has hardly been considered worth attention.[9] Taking into account J. S. Bach's desire to fulfill his duties with his own compositions that were new (at least to Leipzig) during the first years of his stay, it appears strange that he chose to repeat a work that was known to the audience almost in its entirety for the most important feast day. It is also remarkable that the performance materials from 1724 – with the exception of some extra copies of ripieno parts – were no longer available in the spring of 1725. Arthur Mendel[10] explained the loss of the complete set of parts convincingly by proposing that Bach might have lent the material to a person outside of Leipzig.[11] This loan of a set of parts indicates

6 *Dok* II/180. In the Leipzig Neukirche a passion oratorio was performed in 1717. See Andreas Glöckner, *Die Musikpflege an der Leipziger Neukirche zur Zeit Johann Sebastian Bachs*, Beiträge zur Bach-Forschung 8 (Leipzig, 1990), 147.

7 The most extensive list is in Alfred Dürr, *Die Johannes-Passion von Johann Sebastian Bach* (Munich, 1988), 141.

8 See BC III, 985 and 988.

9 An exception is Hans-Joachim Schulze, "Bemerkungen zum zeit- und gattungsgeschichtlichen Kontext von Johann Sebastian Bachs Passionen," in *Johann Sebastian Bachs historischer Ort*, Bach-Studien 10 (Wiesbaden and Leipzig, 1991), 203.

10 NBA II/5 KB, 69 (Alfred Dürr).

11 A similar situation is to be found with two other works written in 1724, the cantata "Wer da gläubet und getauft wird" BWV 37 for Ascension Day (first produced on May 18, 1724) and the Sanctus BWV 232[II] (Dec. 25, 1724). If these sets of parts were given away jointly it must have happened some

clearly that someone desired to perform the piece in 1725. Bach was apparently not yet planning a second performance of the *St. John Passion* for the Lent season at the time that he lent the materials. Rather, Bach must have decided very late to repeat the *St. John Passion*, in any case so late that there was no possibility of calling back the materials. For this reason, a nearly complete set of parts had to be written anew.

This observation leads to the question of which work Bach originally intended for the Good Friday service in 1725. Bach was obviously thinking about a composition of his own. Otherwise he could easily have taken Reinhard Keiser's *St. Mark Passion* (even as a last-minute substitute for another project that he was unable to realize) as he owned a complete set of parts from his years in Weimar. A performance of this work did take place in 1726, and it was far less of an effort to adapt this piece to Leipzig standards than to recopy the whole *St. John Passion* and substitute several of its arias.[12] Not until 1727 did Bach present to the people of Leipzig new passion music of his own composition. From Bach's point of view, all previous performances of his passion music had suffered from inconvenient circumstances: the 1724 performance took place in a church that had too little space for the musicians to be set up properly and, in 1725, an "old" work had to be repeated.[13] Therefore, it seems plausible that the *St. Matthew Passion* was carefully planned to make up for these failures, and the work surely exceeded all expectations.

Structural decisions in the planning of the passion

The overall structure of an oratorio passion is basically determined, because the biblical text was an essential part of the liturgy and was expected to be given according to one of the gospels.[14] The insertion of non-biblical texts did not necessarily allow for an individual interpretation of the passion, since many texts of the time share the same theological motives and implications. Nevertheless,

time between Christmas, 1724 and Good Friday, 1725. It is known only that Count Sporck in Bohemia received the parts of the *Sanctus* (Dok I/183a). It is difficult, however, to imagine what use he could have made of an oratorio passion that was not suited for the Roman Catholic liturgy.

12 For lack of documentary evidence, it is difficult to speculate on which of his own works Bach may have been planning to perform in 1725. We may think of a performance of the lost Weimar passion (BC III, D 1). It is unlikely that Bach would have considered a setting of Picander's passion oratorio *Erbauliche Gedanken auf den Grünen Donnerstag und Charfreytag* (see Philipp Spitta, *Johann Sebastian Bach*, 2 vols. [Leipzig, 1873–1879], 1:335ff. and 873ff.) as this text is not suited for liturgical purposes.

13 As the second version of the *St. John Passion* is apparently nothing more than a convenient last-minute substitute, it is no wonder that Bach did not regard the changes as real improvements, and restored the original version for later performances.

14 Changes such as interpolations from other gospels or omissions of sentences are restricted to insignificant details.

even after the decision to present a passion according to St. Matthew had been made, there remained important decisions – either for the pastor, the librettist, or the composer – that were of consequence for the overall impression of the oratorio passion. Most of these decisions concern choral movements, and include the choice and placement of chorale stanzas, the question of additional movements as a frame for the biblical plot, and – in the case of a bipartite passion music – the position of the sermon, which was clearly conceived as the center-piece of the Good Friday service.

The text of the *St. Matthew Passion* printed in the second volume of Picander's *Ernst-Scherzhaffte und Satyrische Gedichte* (Leipzig, 1729) contains only two of the chorale texts.[15] These are artfully interwoven into free poetry. It seems likely that J. S. Bach himself was responsible for the choice and appropriate insertion of the remaining stanzas. The chorales are traditionally interpreted as the ideal voice of the congregation, demonstrating that the passion story is of immediate importance to the participants in the service. This view is strongly supported by the observation that Bach incorporated the vast majority of the chorales into the presentation of the biblical text instead of linking them to the "individual" reflections as presented in the arias.

For one major group of chorales, Bach relates choral stanzas and biblical text by textual parallels. This connection strengthens the impression of a congregational response to the reported events. For Bach the correspondence of certain words seems to have been of greater importance than the use of hymns that are explicitly destined for the Lent season.[16] Similar procedures may be observed in many other passion compositions of the eighteenth century.

With another group of chorale settings, we find Bach using several stanzas of three chorales, most notably "O Haupt voll Blut und Wunden." No fewer than four stanzas of this chorale are included in the earlier version of the work. A fifth chorale setting makes use of the same melody but with another poem. In contrast to the first group of chorales, no literal textual associations can be observed for most of these chorale insertions, and one wonders whether or not the melody is here of greater importance than the text. For the revision of 1736, Bach added another stanza of "O Haupt voll Blut und Wunden." He entered the text incipit of stanza no. 2 "Es dient zu meinen Freuden" first but

---

15 Pp. 101–12. The two chorales are no. 1 ("O Lamm Gottes unschuldig") and No. 19 ("Was ist die Ursach' aller solcher Plagen"). For a facsimile of the whole, see NBA II/5 KB, 73–8.

16 See the pairs of movements: nos. 9e–10 (keyword: "bin ichs?" – "Ich bins"; nos. 14–15 ("Hirte"); nos. 24–25 ("so geschehe dein Wille – "Was mein Gott will, das gscheh allzeit"); nos. 28–29a ("verließen" – "Jesum laß ich nicht"); nos. 31–32 ("falsche Zeugnis" – "falsche Tücken"); nos. 36d–37 ("wer ist's, der dich schlug?" – "Wer hat dich so geschlagen"); nos. 53c–54 ("sein Haupt" – "O Haupt"; "speieten" – "bespeit"); nos. 61e–62 ("und verschied" – "Wenn ich einmal soll scheiden").

decided then to use yet another text ("Ich will hier bei dir stehen").[17] A repetition of the music of no. 15 one half-step lower seems to have been Bach's main concern in this instance. The decision to use one single chorale melody at various places seems to be a characteristic of Leipzig passion compositions, but is rarely found elsewhere.[18]

The predominant role of "O Haupt voll Blut und Wunden" for the *St. Matthew Passion* culminates in the stanza "Wenn ich einmal soll scheiden" (No. 62) that immediately follows the evangelist's report of the death of Jesus. The placement of this chorale stanza at this point is not unusual – Bach had already done so in his Weimar arrangement of Keiser's *St. Mark Passion*. In Bach's *St. Matthew Passion*, however, this chorale is carefully prepared by its prior appearances. In "Wenn ich einmal soll scheiden," Bach combines the two main principles of the chorale settings in the *St. Matthew Passion:* on the one hand, it rounds off the series of chorales that are characterized by textual associations; on the other, it is indisputably the culmination point of his settings of "O Haupt voll Blut und Wunden," as the complexity of the harmonic language increases with every new appearance. It would surely be an oversimplification if one claimed that the setting of "Wenn ich einmal soll scheiden" is the essence of Bach's chorale writing in the *St. Matthew Passion*. But Johann Christoph Friedrich Bach must have had such an idea in mind when he chose his father's chorale setting as the opening movement of his own oratorio *Der Tod Jesu* on a text by Karl Wilhelm Ramler in 1769.[19]

Bach and his librettist Picander provided the biblical story as narrated by St. Matthew with a large-scale framework that reflected the bipartite structure of the work with the sermon as its liturgical center: each part of the *St. Matthew Passion* begins and ends with choral movements. Judging from the anonymous *St. Luke Passion* BWV 246, which Bach chose to perform in 1730 and again around 1745, it becomes clear that this is no characteristic feature for the oratorio passion as a musical genre.[20] The *St. Luke Passion* starts with a large opening chorus, but neither the beginning of the second part nor the end of each part is set off conspicuously.

17 BC III, 1047.
18 Examples from the Leipzig area are a pasticcio passion performed by Bach's son-in-law Johann Christoph Altnickol in Naumburg and the arrangement of Hasses '*I pellegrini al Sepolcro* for the Good Friday liturgy by the Thomaskantor Johann Friedrich Doles. See Ulrich Leisinger, "Hasses 'I pellegrini al sepolcro' als Leipziger Passionsmusik," *Leipziger Beiträge zur Bach-Forschung* 1 (Hildesheim, in press).
19 Hannsdieter Wohlfarth, *Johann Christoph Friedrich Bach* (Berne, 1971), 245 n. 32.
20 See BC III, D 6. The oratorio passions by Georg Philipp Telemann in Hamburg, which according to a note by Johann Mattheson were also regularly conceived as bipartite works until 1755, confirm that Bach's passion settings are the exception rather than the rule. See Johann Mattheson, *Plus Ultra*, vol. 3 (Hamburg, 1756), 656–7, and Hans Hörner, *Gg. Ph. Telemanns Passionsmusiken* (Borna-Leipzig, 1933), 77–9.

It has often been observed that the simple chorale no. 29a "Jesum laß ich nicht von mir" used at the end of the first part in the early version of the *St. Matthew Passion* can hardly be regarded as an equal counterpart to the monumental opening chorus, the opening duet with chorus of the second part and the final unit of the work consisting of the recitative no. 67 "Nun ist der Herr zur Ruh gebracht" and the aria for chorus no. 68 "Wir setzen uns mit Tränen nieder." The insertion of the chorale fantasia "O Mensch, bewein dein Sünde groß" in the later version has been explained metaphorically as the replacement of a weak pillar of the monumental work by a more adequate one.[21] A closer look at the libretto reveals, however, that the disturbed balance of the early version may instead have been due to a necessary change to Picander's original conception. Picander's print contains mainly his own poetic texts. Here, the end of the first part bears the instruction "Als Jesus gefangen worden" ("after Jesus' capture") and consists of the pair of movements "So ist mein Jesus nun gefangen" and "Sind Blitze sind Donner in Wolken verschwunden" only.[22] It is not difficult to imagine what an enormous effect this savage chorus would have made had it come at the very end of the first part. From the librettist's point of view this pair of movements, no. 27a and no. 27b, would provide a solid fourth pillar for the overall architecture that is often claimed to be missing, because it parallels in its structure the pair of movements no. 67 and no. 68 at the end of the second part.

However, Picander apparently did not consider that the two scenes that form the end of the first and the opening of the second parts in his plan cannot simply be split up. These scenes – Peter with the sword and the flight of the disciples – are linked in Matthew's Gospel by an extended speech by Jesus. It is significant that no reference to the biblical text appears in Picander's libretto to give a clue as to how the biblical text and the free poetry were to be distributed in this section. From the printed text alone it is not even clear whether recitative no. 28, Jesus' speech, belongs to the first or second parts of the passion. These biblical verses were an important passage of the passion story, and could not simply be suppressed. It would have been no solution, however, to add them to the second part of the work. This would only have shifted the problem to the beginning of the second part, which then would have started with a recitative instead of a large-scale choral movement.[23] Picander's conception for

21   Emil Platen, *Die Matthäus-Passion von Johann Sebastian Bach* (Cassel and Munich, 1991), 160f.
22   For a facsimile see NBA II/5 KB, 75.
23   Furthermore, we must not overlook the fact that the distribution of the biblical text was not completely left to the discretion of the poet and the composer. The pastor most likely made the final decision as to the placement of the break between the two parts. Extending the first part through the words "then all

the end of the first part, which looks enormously convincing in the printed libretto, does not work out because the poet did not sufficiently take into account the fitting in of the biblical text.

Bach's use of a double chorus

The use of double chorus is implied in the libretto in most of the arias with chorus and in the movements framing the two parts of the passion. These movements obviously have structural functions: Picander has chosen to use dialogues at key points of the work and at culmination points. The use of double chorus in the *St. Matthew Passion* is certainly the most conspicuous feature indicating Bach's extraordinary ambitions. Though this idea is emphasized in a great deal of the literature, authors only rarely elaborate on it.[24] Otto Brodde offers a possible theological interpretation of polychoral music.[25] He proposes three main perspectives: (1) polychoral writing as a transformation of the principles of antiphony; (2) polychoral writing as an artful use of the performing space with symbolic significance; (3) polychoral writing as a realization of ideas and imaginations of divine music. Although Brodde is mainly referring to seventeenth-century music, these concepts are also appropriate for J. S. Bach's time.[26]

As far as I know, only Ján Albrecht has tried to classify the polychoral movements of the *St. Matthew Passion*.[27] He distinguishes four types of movements, each based on its own traditions. Type I comprises those movements in which Chorus II interrupts the continuous flow of Chorus I with short responsorial invocations (e.g., nos. 27a and 60). Type II may be understood as an inner monologue, most often in the form of an antiphonal alternation (nos. 19, 20, 67). The aim of movement Type III is an effective representation of actions and dialogues (e.g., no. 30). Type IV enriches the sound of the full ensemble by introducing an element of contrast (nos. 1 and 27).

the disciples forsook him, and fled," obviously allows for a very specific interpretation of the passion story in the sermon.

24 For instance, Friedhelm Krummacher ("Mehrchörigkeit und thematischer Satz bei Johann Sebastian Bach," *Schütz-Jahrbuch* 1981, 39–50) completely dismisses the *St. Matthew Passion* from his discussion of Bach's technique of double choruses, because in his opinion Bach's writing for double chorus is fully developed only in the eight-part motets.

25 Otto Brodde, "Theologische Konzepte in mehrchöriger Musik," *Schütz-Jahrbuch* 1981, 7–11.

26 Despite a promising title ("Die theologische Bedeutung der Doppelchörigkeit in Johann Sebastian Bach's 'Matthäus-Passion,'" in *Bachiana et alia Musicologica. Festschrift Alfred Dürr zum 65. Geburtstag*, ed. Wolfgang Rehm [Cassel, 1983], 275–86), Lothar and Renate Steiger do not succeed in explaining the significance of Bach's use of double chorus from a theological point of view.

27 Ján Albrecht, "Die Entwicklung der Mehrchörigkeit bis zu ihrer Anwendung in Bachs Werk," in *Johann Sebastian Bach: Weltbild, Menschenbild, Notenbild, Klangbild*, ed. Winfried Hoffmann und Armin Schneiderheinze (Leipzig, 1988), 175–9.

The use of double chorus is discussed extensively in a surprisingly little-known treatise from the eighteenth century. Friedrich Wilhelm Marpurg devotes ten pages of his *Anleitung zur Singecomposition* (1758) to aspects of composing polychoral pieces.[28] He offers a thorough classification of compositions for "equal" or "unequal" forces and supports his explanations by well-chosen examples.

Two (or more) equal choruses can be used in a monologue-like fashion when presenting the same text, or as a dialogue with different texts. As an example for a monologue between two equal choruses Marpurg quotes from a psalm setting by Johann Friedrich Agricola. An example from the *St. Matthew Passion* would be the movement "Sind Blitze sind Donner in Wolken verschwunden" (No. 27b).[29] Marpurg defines unequal forces as a communication taking place between the whole chorus and individuals who may or may not belong to the same chorus, or when different genres are combined within a movement (aria or recitative with chorus, chorus with chorale).

In his classification, Marpurg separates those movements that contain recitatives.[30] An example from the *St. Matthew Passion* is movement no. 19 ("O Schmerz"). Here, a chorale movement ("Was ist die Ursach aller solcher Plagen") is embedded in the recitative. Both layers are completely independent musically and could stand by themselves. Using a high and exaggerated range for the tenor and a register unusually low for Bach for the chorale melody, the composer increases the tension further.[31] The Daughter of Zion describes the events in an exaggerated manner; the Faithful confess their sins that made Jesus' sacrifice inevitable. Marpurg mentions explicitly that recitatives in settings for unequal choruses are sometimes distributed among all four soloists.[32]

Several of Picander's poetic texts are dialogues for unequal forces in Marpurg's terminology and are marked in the printed libretto as exchanges between the Daughter of Zion and the Faithful. Bach sets these texts as arias (or recitatives) with chorus, the opening chorus being a remarkable exception. The allegorical Daughter of Zion from the Song of Songs is traditionally interpreted as the bride of Christ and is hence used as a symbol for the Christian church. Unlike many of his contemporaries, Bach obviously did not understand the Daughter of Zion as a *dramatis persona*, but rather as an ideal voice, capable of being represented by different human voices.

28 Friedrich Wilhelm Marpurg, *Anleitung zur Singekomposition* (Berlin, 1758), 104–15.
29 Dialogues between equal forces are not found in the *St. Matthew Passion*.
30 Marpurg, *Anleitung zur Singekomposition*, 114–15.
31 Bach usually sets chorale movements significantly higher than the melodies found in contemporary hymnals.
32 Marpurg, *Anleitung zur Singekomposition*, 115. Cf. *St. Matthew Passion* no. 67 "Nun ist der Herr zur Ruh gebracht."

In the aria with chorus no. 27a ("So ist mein Jesus nun gefangen"), the two ensembles work on completely different levels. The two soloists resign themselves to Jesus' arrest; the chorus, however, attempts to interfere by crying that he be left unmolested. The Baroque doctrine of affections does not allow for the representation of two antithetical human passions at the same time. By the use of two ensembles, the soloists of the first chorus vs. the full second chorus, Bach overcomes this limitation. The motive of protest is continued in the extraordinary chorus no. 27b "Sind Blitze, sind Donner in Wolken verschwunden" that immediately follows. A glance at the *St. John Passion* may give us a hint for an interpretation of this pair of contrasting movements: Peter is the one who is drawn back and forth between the affects of furious rage and resignation.

One of Marpurg's quotations is the text of the aria with chorus "Eilt, ihr angefochtnen Seelen" from the famous passion text by Barthold Heinrich Brockes. The aria with chorus "Eilt, ihr angefochtnen Seelen" in the *St. John Passion* is based on Brockes's text, and Brockes's aria also apparently inspired Picander in the aria with chorus no. 60 "Sehet, Jesus hat die Hand, uns zu fassen, ausgespannt" from the *St. Matthew Passion*. Marpurg dismisses the Brockes text as a "childish" example that is not worth imitating "as the otherwise unemployed chorus bursts in with clumsy short questions."[33] However, the simple fact that he cites a poetic text almost fifty years old at all demonstrates the text's seminal role and its enormous impact on the conception of librettos in eighteenth-century passion music.

In the *St. Matthew Passion*, the arias with chorus nos. 27a and 60 belong (together with the opening movement) to the same type: an aria punctuated by short questions and invocations from the chorus. Recitative no. 59 ("Ach Golgatha") describes the insults that Jesus is suffering and raises the question of the significance of the crucifixion. The answer is given in the following aria with chorus no. 60 ("Sehet, Jesus hat die Hand, uns zu fassen, ausgespannt"): Jesus spreads his arms to grasp and redeem his people. The interpretation that Jesus' spread arms on the cross are open to embrace the Faithful is often found in contemporary passion sermons. The short questions of the chorus are rhetorical and, indeed, do not really contribute to the plot. Rather than dismissing the movement as – in Marpurg's words – a "childish" example, we should try to interpret this type of movement theologically: the call "come, come" is not unheard – the Faithful have perceived it. Note also that the

---

33 Marpurg, *Anleitung zur Singekomposition*, 111: "Ein, wegen der ungeschickten kurzen Fragen, womit das sonst nicht weiter beschäfftigte Chor beständig hereinplatzet, nicht nachzuahmendes kindisches Exempel ist das folgende . . ."

traditional sequence of statements by the Daughter of Zion and the Faithful become simultaneous events in Bach's composition.[34]

Marpurg devotes special attention to the idea of embedding a chorale into a poetic text. He cites several examples from passion oratorios by Carl Heinrich Graun including *Der Tod Jesu* (1755).[35] As the last and most complex of all texts he includes, astonishingly, "an example taken from a passion of the late Capellmeister Bach," quoting the whole text of the opening chorus of the *St. Matthew Passion*. Marpurg holds the combination of chorale and free poetry in high esteem. Nevertheless he remains suspicious about the interrupting questions: "The short incomplete questions, *whom, as what, what, where?* of the otherwise unemployed chorus sound undoubtedly somewhat brutal and should not be imitated in any poetry intended for a musical setting."[36] Marpurg's mention of the *St. Matthew Passion* in 1758, which apparently has not been discussed before, is a welcome document of a still mostly unknown history of reception of Bach's passions before their legendary revival around 1830. Furthermore, Marpurg's discussion of different types of double choruses provides us with a well-reasoned eighteenth-century vocabulary that can be applied successfully to the choral movements of the *St. Matthew Passion*.

Unity in variety and the idea of perfection

There is no doubt that in the *St. Matthew Passion*, J. S. Bach intentionally combines the most diverse types of movements. Bach uses chorale settings, compositions on biblical texts as well as on free poetry. At the same time, we recognize the composer's efforts to unify the piece. Interrelationships between different movements of the same type are easily observed.[37] Furthermore, the biblical text, the story of the passion of the Savior, guarantees continuity and coherence, as all other musical events are related to this biblical narration.[38]

34 See Wolff, "Musical forms and dramatic structure," 15.
35 *Ibid.*, 112–14.
36 *Ibid.*, 113–14: "Ein viertes Exempel aus einer Paßion vom sel. Herrn Capellmeister Bach. [text of *St. Matthew Passion* no. 1] . . . Die kurzen abgebrochnen Fragen: *wen, wie, was, wohin?* klingen ohne Zweifel bey dem nicht weiter beschäfftigten Chore, etwas brutal, und sind in keinem Singgedichte nachzuahmen." Marpurg's quotation of the text of the opening chorus is apparently not based on a score of the *St. Matthew Passion*, as Johann Sebastian Bach inserted the word "selber" in line 13 (see NBA II/5 KB, 104). It comes very close, however, to the libretto in the hand of Johann Friedrich Agricola attached to the score SBB Am.B. 6 and 7, that – unlike the Picander print – explicitly gives the name of the composer (for a facsimile see, NBA II/5a, xiii–xiv [Alfred Dürr]). Marpurg's quotation apparently establishes at least a date *post quem non* for Agricola's textbook.
37 There are, for example, striking similarities between the following movements: nos. 58b ("Der du den Tempel Gottes zerbrichst") and 58d ("Andern hat er geholfen") and nos. 36b ("Er ist des Todes schuldig") and 36d ("Weissage uns, Christe").
38 The oratorio passion is epic, not dramatic, in nature. This is emphasized by Johann Gottfried Krause,

Here an observation first made by Christoph Wolff and developed by Hans-Joachim Schulze is enlightening.[39] In the *St. John Passion* the biblical text may be regarded as the skeleton of the work: all free poetic texts and the chorales can be interpreted as insertions into the coherent and musically completely self-sufficient realization of the narration. Because Bach used different insertions for every performance of the *St. John Passion*, this work shows a certain tendency towards a pasticcio. In the *St. Matthew Passion*, however, Bach's setting of Picander's texts is not just inserted into but is closely interwoven with the biblical narration. This treatment of the text leads to an overall structure in which every movement has its specific place and function and cannot easily be replaced by any other movement. The unity of the *St. Matthew Passion* is therefore based on more than just the idea of a continuous biblical plot.[40] This brief discussion of the choral movements in the *St. Matthew Passion* makes it clear that two contradictory principles, the idea of unity and the idea of variety, seem to struggle for predominance.

The phrase "unity in variety" nowadays sounds vague if not meaningless. However, it must be regarded as a meaningful approach for an evaluation of the quality and significance of a work of art from the first half of the eighteenth century. Although the concepts were certainly not new, the philosophical writings of Gottfried Wilhelm Leibniz (1646–1716) attest for the first time to the idea that the seemingly incompatible fundamental ideas of unity and variety can be reconciled.[41]

It must suffice here to state that for Leibniz and his followers, unity in variety is far more than a practical rule.[42] The idea of unity in variety is a

---

Von der musicalischen Poesie (Berlin, 1752), 474–5. Consequently, a continuity of the narration rather than of the dramatic actions is a basic requirement.

39   Schulze, "Bemerkungen zum Kontext," 205–6.

40   The question of how the tonal arrangement of the work contributes to its unity has generated much controversy. See, for instance, Friedrich Smend, "Zur Tonartenordnung von Bachs Matthäus Passion," *Zeitschrift für Musikwissenschaft* 12 (1919–20): 336–41; Eric Chafe, *Tonal Allegory in the Vocal Music of J. S. Bach* (Berkeley and Los Angeles, 1991), 391–423; Nicolas Schalz, "Die Matthäus-Passion oder zu Bachs widerständiger Aktualität," in *Johann Sebastian Bach. Die Passionen*, Musikkonzepte 50/51, (Munich, 1986), 3–85.

41   Ulrich Leisinger, *Leibniz-Reflexe in der deutschen Musiktheorie des 18. Jahrhunderts* (Würzburg, 1994), 131–9.

42   The philosophical dimension of the idea of unity in variety can be presented here only in an extremely abbreviated version, based on Leibniz's *Monadology* (1714) and his *Principes de la nature et de la grâce* (1714). For Leibniz, simple substances, the monads, can be found in all existing things. The monads owe their existence to the grace of God who created them as completely self-sufficient entities. Monads do not have parts, so every monad is a unity. But they have a variety of inner characteristics, the so-called perceptions, caused by continuous changes within the monad. So every monad is unity and variety at the same time. The perceptions of every monad are linked by a pre-established harmony with the perceptions of all other monads. Hence every monad is a living mirror of the universe. The variety of perceptions are reflections of the one universe. Therefore, there is not only variety in the unity (perceptions within the monad) but also unity in the variety (the whole universe is mirrored in every single monad).

fundamental concept of metaphysics; it is indicative of the best possible order of the universe. If music is understood as an imitation of nature or as a symbol for divine order in the world, then unity in variety necessarily becomes an aesthetic postulate. Leibniz's ideas were promoted with fervor by many, including Christian Wolff in Halle and Johann Gottsched in Leipzig, two of the most influential figures in intellectual life in protestant Germany. Lorenz Mizler and Johann Abraham Birnbaum were two devoted followers of Leibniz–Wolffian metaphysics closely related to J. S. Bach.

The correspondence conducted by Leibniz and Christian Wolff show most clearly the enormous impact of the principle of unity and variety.[43] In a letter dated October 3, 1714, Wolff asked for a definition of perfection. Leibniz answered briefly in an undated letter: "The perfection about which you ask is the degree of positive reality . . . so that something more perfect is something in which more things worthy of observation [*notatu digna*] are found." In a letter of May 18, 1715, Leibniz explained this in more detail:

When I say that something in which more is worthy of observation is more perfect, I understand general observations or rules, not exceptions, which constitute imperfections. The more there is worthy of observation in a thing, the more general properties, the more harmony it contains . . . You also see from this how the sense of harmony, that is, the observation of agreements [*consensus*] might bring forth pleasure, since it delights perception, makes it easier, and extricates it from confusion. Hence, you know that consonances please, since agreement is easily observable in them . . . Agreement is sought in variety, and the more easily it is observed there, the more it pleases; and in this consists the sense of perfection. Moreover, the perfection a thing has is greater, to the extent that there is more agreement in greater variety, whether we observe it or not. Therefore, this is what order and regularity come to.

Leibniz ends his letter with an emphatic statement:

[P]leasure is the sensation of perfection. Perfection is the harmony of things, or the state where everything is worthy of being observed, that is the state of agreement [*consensus*] or identity in variety; you can even say that it is the degree of contemplatibility [*considerabilitas*]. Indeed, order, regularity, and harmony come to the same thing . . . Hence, it also follows quite nicely that God, that is, the supreme mind, is endowed with perfection, indeed to the greatest degree; otherwise he would not care about the harmonies.[44]

---

43 Carl Immanuel Gerhardt, *Briefwechsel zwischen Leibniz und Wolf* (Halle, 1860). The relevant passages are selected and translated into English in Roger Ariew and Daniel Garber, *G. W. Leibniz: Philosophical Essays* (Indianapolis and Cambridge, 1989), 230–4. All quotations here are from this translation.

44 Although the letters between Leibniz and Christian Wolff were not published until 1860, the ideas discussed here were widely disseminated in both Leibniz's and Wolff's writings. Most influential were Leibniz's *Monadology* and *Principes de la nature et de la grâce* and the so called German Metaphysics by Christian Wolff, *Vernünfftige Gedanken von Gott der Welt und der Seele des Menschen* (1720). All three works were often reprinted during the eighteenth century.

We can now attempt an interpretation of the *St. Matthew Passion* by means of these criteria. The great variety of musical forms and genres in Bach's *St. Matthew Passion* can easily be explained by the concept of perfection as unity in variety in the Leibniz–Wolffian sense: the musical genres can be understood as a realization of the "general observations or rules." Each new genre included in the work does not endanger the unity of the whole; rather, it contributes to the work's perfection. The combination of genres, as demonstrated in the arias with chorus or the aria with chorale adds more "general properties" and "more harmony" to the work. A movement like the opening chorus, with its ingenious combination and union of diverse texts (Song of Songs, chorale, eighteenth-century poetic models) and musical sources (double chorus, both monologue and dialogue in Marpurg's terms, and a chorale tune), abounds in "things worthy of observation" but is nevertheless controlled. It is complex but still ordered.

Bach's writing for double chorus fits into this conceptual frame without difficulty. The highly differentiated settings of the crowd choruses explore the inherent possibilities of the four- to eight-part motet style. Antiphonal writing (as discussed with regard to movement no. 20) enables the composer to express more than one affect in a single movement. Furthermore, the writing for double chorus can be seen as a symbol for the divine and pre-established harmony. Leibniz develops this idea in a letter to Antoine Arnauld that surely remained unknown to Bach.

Finally, using a comparison, I would like to say, that the harmony between the body and the soul is similar to different orchestras or choirs that – separated one from another – play their parts or sing and that are disposed in such a manner that they can not hear or see each other, but nevertheless perfectly harmonize if everyone is just following his part. Whoever hears them all at once will detect a miraculous harmony that is even more astonishing as if they had some connection one to the other.[45]

It is tempting to apply this imaginative metaphor to a movement like "Sind Blitze, sind Donner in Wolken verschwunden" where the seemingly unrelated phrases of the two choruses add up to a harmonious whole.

In light of these metaphysical ideas, Bach's revision of the *St. Matthew Passion* in 1736 can be understood as an even stronger realization of Leibniz–Wolffian ideas of perfection. Bach separates the two choruses physically by splitting the *basso continuo* part in two, one for each chorus.[46] The independence of the choruses adds further variety within the unity of the harmonic frame. Replacing the simple chorale no. 29a "Jesum laß ich nicht von mir" by the

---

45   Undated letter (1687) to Antoine Arnauld. My translation from Carl Immanuel Gerhardt, *Die philosophischen Schriften von Gottfried Wilhelm Leibniz*, 7 vols. (Berlin, 1875–90), 2: 95.
46   NBA II/5 KB, 113.

grandiose multifaceted chorale fantasia no. 29 "O Mensch, bewein dein Sünde groß" supports the unity of the work as it is a counterpart almost equal in rank to the opening chorus – and yet fundamentally different.

A well-known eighteenth-century report from J. S. Bach's circle allows us to interpret his works in Leibniz–Wolffian terms. Johann Abraham Birnbaum refers to the mastery of Bach's polyphony when he defends the composer against the criticism of Johann Adolph Scheibe:

Where the rules of composition are most strictly observed, there without fail order must reign . . . It is certain, by the way, that the voices in the works of this great master of music work wonderfully in and about one another, but without the slightest confusion. They move along together or in opposition, as necessary. They part company, and yet all meet at the proper time. Each voice distinguishes itself from the others by a particular variation, although they often imitate each other. They now flee, now follow one another without one's noticing the slightest irregularity in their efforts to outdo one another. Now when all is performed as it should be, there is nothing more beautiful than this harmony . . . Now, the greater the art is – that is, the more industriously and painstakingly it works as the improvement of Nature – the more brilliantly shines the beauty thus brought into being.[47]

The implication is evident: the more variety found in a work, the greater its perfection. The remark that in the *St. Matthew Passion* "Bach – in a rather systematic manner – integrates an unprecedented maximum of the compositional types and forms of his day" points in the same direction.[48]

I would like to stress that no documentary evidence can be presented that Johann Sebastian Bach ever possessed or read any of Leibniz's or Wolff's treatises.[49] The Leibniz–Wolffian argument about the role of unity in variety must, however, be regarded as a commonplace in protestant Germany during the first half of the eighteenth century. Thus, it may help us to evaluate the enormous complexity of the *St. Matthew Passion* as a realization of the ideal of perfection from the point of view of Bach and his contemporaries.

47 *Dok* II/409; *BR*, 244. Without reference to Leibniz and Christian Wolff, the concept of perfection and the present quote are briefly discussed by Christoph Wolff in "'Die sonderbaren Vollkommenheiten des Herrn Hofcompositeurs.' Versuch über die Eigenart der Bachschen Musik," in *Bachiana et alia Musicologica, Festschrift Alfred Dürr zum 65. Geburtstag*, ed. Wolfgang Rehm (Cassel, 1983), 358f.
48 Wolff, "Musical forms and dramatic structure," 6.
49 It is characteristic that no evidence has ever been presented for the often-repeated claim that Bach was familiar with Leibniz's short fragment "Von der Weisheit" (C. I. Gerhardt, *Die Philosophischen Schriften von Gottfried Wilhelm Leibniz*, vol. 7, "Fragment E," 86–90). The statement was most likely first made by Walter Blankenburg, "J. S. Bach und die Aufklärung," in *Bach-Gedenkschrift 1950*, ed. Karl Matthäi (Zurich, 1950), 26, then repeated, for example, by Hans Heinrich Eggebrecht, "Bach und Leibniz," in *Bericht über die wissenschaftliche Bachtagung der Gesellschaft für Musikforschung, Leipzig* (1950), ed. W. Vetter and E. H. Meyer (Leipzig, 1951), 442, and by David Goldman, "Der Wissenschaftler Johann Sebastian Bach," *Ibykus* 4 (1985), 14. A similar but vaguer statement can be found in Robin A. Leaver, *Bachs theologische Bibliothek* (Neuhausen-Stuttgart, 1983), 2. Leibniz's essay was, however, not disseminated in manuscript during the eighteenth century and it remained unpublished until 1838 (G. E. Guhrauer, *Leibniz's Deutsche Schriften*, vol. 1, [Berlin, 1838], 420–6).

Chapter six

The theological character of J. S. Bach's *Musical Offering*

MICHAEL MARISSEN

The Cross alone is our theology.

Martin Luther, commentary on Psalm 5:12[1]

The complicated transmission problems of the print of J. S. Bach's *Musical Offering* BWV 1079, dedicated in 1747 to King Frederick II ("the Great") of Brandenburg-Prussia, have occasioned an enormous amount of scholarly speculation about the way the collection was put together and the possible significance of its ordering. Substantial progress on the first question was made about twenty years ago in research by Christoph Wolff, who published new findings based on a close examination of the technical features in each of the (fragmentary) surviving exemplars of Bach's print.[2] Wolff demonstrated that none of the previously suggested orderings for the *Musical Offering* could be supported by the early documents. He proposed a new ordering of the various fascicles of Bach's print but suggested that it probably had little if any significance for thinking about or performing the collection.

For encouragement and criticism in completing this essay, I would like to thank Gregory Butler, Eric Chafe, Eugene Helm, Robert Marshall, Daniel Melamed, Joshua Rifkin, David Schulenberg, and Jeanne Swack.

1   See Alister E. McGrath, *Luther's Theology of the Cross* (Oxford, 1985), 1, 152, 167, and 169. Luther's commentary on Psalm 5 appeared in vol. 3 of the sixteenth-century Wittenberg Edition of his collected works (various printings), which, according to Robin A. Leaver, *Bachs theologische Bibliothek* (Neuhausen-Stuttgart, 1983), 64, formed part of Bach's extensive theological library.

2   Christoph Wolff, "Der Terminus 'Ricercar' in Bachs Musikalischem Opfer," *BJ* 53 (1967): 70–81 (updated in Wolff, *Bach: essays on his life and music* [Cambridge, Mass, 1991], chapt. 25); "New research on Bach's *Musical Offering*," *The Musical Quarterly* 57 (1971): 379–408 (updated in *Essays*, chapt. 18); NBA VIII/1 KB (1976); "Überlegungen zum 'Thema Regium'," *BJ* 59 (1973): 33–8 (updated in *Essays*, chapt. 25).

Wolff assumed that Bach's print had been produced entirely by Johann Georg Schübler. His reconstruction was consequently called into question by Wolfgang Wiemer's discovery that two members of the Schübler family of Zella were responsible for preparing the print.[3] In light of Wiemer's work, I have argued elsewhere that Bach probably arranged the various pieces in the *Musical Offering* by genre (two fugues–sonata–ten canons) and that the final product from the Schübler brothers essentially reflected this arrangement.[4] Close study of the print, along with evidence from secondary manuscripts of the collection and contemporary letters describing it, suggests that the layout of the complete print corresponded to the description found in a 1747 Leipzig newspaper advertisement: "[The *Musical Offering*] consists of 1.) two fugues, one with three, the other with six obbligato parts; 2.) a sonata for transverse flute, violin, and continuo; 3.) diverse canons, among which [wobey] is a *fuga canonica*."[5]

In the present essay, I propose to show that the *Musical Offering* assumes an increasingly theological character as it moves from genre to genre (fugues – sonata – canons). This interpretation conflicts with previous views of the collection, the majority of which locate themselves on a continuum between two extreme positions. The first, advanced most forcefully by Friedrich Blume and still widely accepted among scholars, holds that this music – in particular, its canons – is "abstract": it explores "pure" issues of form, was not really meant to be performed, and is nonreferential.[6] The other, advanced by Ursula Kirkendale and widely accepted among performers, holds that the music is loaded with significance: it was meant, as declared in Bach's preface, to glorify its dedicatee, and, accordingly, the collection was organized in such a way that it takes on the classical form and content of a detailed rhetorical argument.[7] Blume's view has been partly discredited, as some scholars have, for example, taken seriously the clear performance indications in the print: the sonata is printed in separate parts rather than in score; Canons 2 and 8 specify scorings; Canons 2–3, 6, and 8–10 provide articulation markings; and Canons 2, 4, and 6–9 provide trills.[8] Kirkendale's view has been questioned too, but her

---

3   Wiemer, *Die wiederhergestellte Ordnung in Johann Sebastian Bachs Kunst der Fuge* (Wiesbaden, 1977), 40–3. New research in progress by Gregory Butler shows that the print represents the work of three Schübler brothers.

4   Michael Marissen, "More source-critical research on J. S. Bach's *Musical Offering*," *Bach* 25, no. 1 (1994): 11–27.

5   The advertisement was unknown to scholars before the 1970s, when it was published in Wolff, "New research on Bach's *Musical Offering*," 399.

6   Blume, "J. S. Bach," *MGG.*

7   Kirkendale, "The source for Bach's *Musical Offering*: The *Institutio Oratoria* of Quintilian," *Journal of the American Musicological Society* 33 (1980): 88–141.

8   Wolff, NBA VIII/1 KB, 118. Wolff goes on to show that the various contrapuntal lines in the canons with unspecified scorings correspond to normal eighteenth-century flute, violin, and keyboard ranges

critics have focused more on the form of her argument than its general import, pointing out that the proportions of a rhetorical oration are completely distorted in the suggested sequence for Bach's movements.[9]

Like Kirkendale, I believe Bach's music does carry referential meanings. But in light of the collection's strange prefatory language and rubrics, predominantly old-fashioned musical style, and oftentimes almost funereal *Affect*, Bach's stated intention of glorifying Frederick the Great appears incomprehensible if "glorification" is understood in the conventional manner. Bach's music seems to project rather different notions of glory. Far from elevating or shedding radiance and splendor on Frederick, the *Musical Offering* promotes a biblical understanding of glory – the idea of "glorification through abasement," a view tied up with Luther's "theology of the cross" as opposed to the "theology of glory." In the end, then, Bach's collection could act as a sort of general argument not just for different forms and styles of music – Bach's high baroque counterpoint rather than the galant homophony of the Prussian court – but for decidedly different world and life views from those promoted by French enlightenment thinkers like Frederick.

Before exploring musical details of Bach's *Musical Offering* and their contribution to the collection's increasingly theological character, it is worth considering some of the historical background for the meeting of these two figures. The private appearance on May 7, 1747 of J. S. Bach, church musician in Saxony, at the court of Frederick the Great, King in Prussia, is the most extensively documented event in Bach's otherwise unglamorous career. The full story has been told many times and therefore only the most relevant aspects of it will be mentioned here.[10] The normal evening concert at the Prussian court involved a series of sonatas for flute and continuo performed by Frederick and one of his accompanists (C. P. E. Bach among them), or flute concertos performed by Frederick and a group of his chamber musicians. The music was almost invariably of Frederick's or his teacher and flute maker Johann Joachim Quantz's composition.[11] The recitals were extremely strict affairs. One had to be specifically invited by the king (the audience was small, the chamber musicians typically being the only persons present who were not from the aristocracy),

(119–21). Throughout this essay, the numbering of Bach's canons corresponds to that employed in the NBA.

9   See Wolff, *Essays*, 421–3. Kirkendale's interpretation, which accepts a nineteenth-century ordering of the collection, also suffers from implausible observations on source-critical matters; see Marissen, "More source-critical research on J. S. Bach's *Musical Offering*."

10   For the entire story, see especially Hans T. David, *J. S. Bach's Musical Offering* (New York, 1945), 3–15; and Wolff, NBA VIII/1 KB, 101–10.

11   Karl Friedrich Zelter, *Karl Friedrich Christian Fasch* (Berlin, 1801), 14 and 49.

and, on pain of reprimand (possibly violent in the case of the musicians), nobody except Quantz was permitted to react in any way to the king's performances.[12] Bach's invitation by Frederick to take over one of these evening concerts, then, must be considered remarkable.

Bach was well known in professional musical circles throughout the German speaking areas of Europe not only for his abilities in composition and keyboard playing but also for his improvisations. Frederick must have been primarily, perhaps exclusively, interested in the latter, for Bach's concert apparently involved only a series of improvisations. At one point during the evening, Frederick provided Bach with a difficult theme upon which to improvise a fugue. The audience and Frederick were astonished by Bach's performance, but Bach himself was dissatisfied with his improvised fugue.[13] He apparently made known then and there that he intended "to set [Frederick's theme] down on paper in a regular [ordentlichen] fugue and have it engraved in copper."[14] Considering the typically severe atmosphere of Frederick's chamber concerts, one has to wonder what sort of an impression such an announcement, however politely expressed, would have made. For a start, it contradicts the king's own opinion of Bach's performance; moreover, it points up the higher value of thinking through and reflecting upon the demands of fugue; and, finally, it suggests the value of publishing results for others to study and contemplate.[15] In his preface to the print, Bach was fairly explicit about all of this:

Your Majesty's Self deigned to play to me a theme for a fugue upon the clavier, and at the same time charged me most graciously to carry it out in Your Majesty's Most August Presence. To obey Your Majesty's command was my most humble duty. I noticed very soon, however, that for lack of necessary preparation, the execution of the task did not fare as well as such an excellent theme demanded. I resolved therefore and promptly pledged myself to work out this right Royal theme more fully [or "more closely to perfection" – vollkommener auszuarbeiten] and then make it known to the world. This resolve has now been carried out as well as possible.[16]

12   Regarding the atmosphere of Frederick's concerts, see Ernest Eugene Helm, *Music at the Court of Frederick the Great* (Norman, Oklahoma, 1960), 28–39.

13   The leading German newspapers reported that everyone present was filled with amazement at Bach's improvisation; see *Dok* II/554; *BR*, 176. Jacob Adlung, *Anleitung zu der musikalischen Gelahrtheit* (Erfurt, 1758), described the experience as "still fresh in people's minds" (more than ten years later); see *Dok* III/693.

14   See the newspaper report in *Dok* II/554 and *BR*, 176.

15   In this connection it is worth noting that Frederick did not permit Quantz to publish his music performed in the Prussian court concerts, because these pieces were to be written and preserved only for the entertainment of the king. See Charles Burney, *The present state of music in Germany, the Netherlands and United Provinces*, vol. 2 (London, 1775), 153.

16   *BR*, 179; Facsimile ed. Christoph Wolff, *Johann Sebastian Bach: Musicalisches Opfer BWV 1079* (Leipzig, 1977), hereafter "Peters-Facsimile." This is also reproduced in David, *J. S. Bach's Musical Offering*, 6–7; NBA VIII/1, 12–3; and *Dok* I/173.

Bach's entering Frederick's chamber music rooms must really have constituted a meeting of two clashing worlds.[17] Bach was sixty-two years old. Frederick was thirty-five (i.e., younger than Bach's oldest children). Bach was middle-class, had been married twice, and had fathered twenty children. Frederick was, of course, aristocratic, had a politically arranged marriage, and had no children (a homosexual, he did not spend much time with his wife, and he did not live with her). Bach was an orthodox Lutheran, deeply interested in music and theology, who spoke and wrote German and was probably not fully comfortable with French. Frederick was strongly anti-Christian (though politically tolerant),[18] deeply interested in French enlightenment philosophy and poetry and, above all, in personal control of political power. He spoke and wrote in French and was apparently not fully comfortable with German. When Johann Christoph Gottsched once remarked to him that German poets could not expect to get any encouragement so long as the German language was too little and French too much understood among the nobility and at the courts, Frederick replied: "That is true, for from my youth I have read not a single German book, and I speak the language like a coachman; now, however, I am an old fellow of forty-six, and have no more time for it."[19]

Bach's and Frederick's views on the functions of music could hardly have been more different. Bach believed the primary purpose of music was to honor God and refresh people's minds or spirits and that music was a craft involving concentrated effort for composers, performers, and listeners. In his teachings on continuo playing, Bach remarked: "[The basso continuo makes] a well-sounding harmony to the Glory of God and to the sanctioned enjoyment of the spirit [*zulässiger Ergötzung*[20] *des Gemüths*]; the aim and final reason, as of all music, so of the thorough bass, should be none else but the Glory of God and the refreshing of the mind."[21] Frederick believed the primary purpose of music

17 The contrasting characterizations that follow have partly been drawn from Adalbert Schütz, "Zur Deutung des Musikalischen Opfers (Joh. Seb. Bach und Friedrich der Große)," in *Wort und Dienst: Jahrbuch der Theologischen Schule Bethel* 6 (1959): 170–9.

18 Regarding his views on Christianity, see Friedrich der Große, *Briefe über die Religion*, ed. Rudolf Neuwinger (Berlin, 1941); and *Theologische Streitschriften*, ed. Neuwinger (Berlin, 1939).

19 Letter of October 22, 1757 from Gottsched to Cölestin Christian Flottwell; see Gustav Mendelssohn Bartholdy, *Der König: Friedrich der Große in seinen Briefen und Erlassen* (Ebenhausen bei München, 1912), 314–8.

20 In modern German, "Ergötzen" has largely taken on the meaning "to amuse," or "to entertain." But in eighteenth-century usage, it meant "to bring about palpable joy"; see Johann Christoph Adelung, *Grammatisch-kritisches Wörterbuch der Hochdeutschen Mundart*, rev. edn. (Leipzig, 1793), col. 1894. Adelung provides several examples for its usage, mostly from the Bible, none of which has to do with entertainment or diversion. The word is used in this more edifying sense each time it appears in Bach's church cantatas.

21 Printed in Philipp Spitta, *Johann Sebastian Bach*, 2 vols. (Leipzig, 1873–1880), 2: 916. This represents Bach's wording of thoughts expressed in Friedrich Erhardt Niedt's *Musicalische Handleitung* (Hamburg, 1710–17; rev. edn., 1721).

was to entertain and divert, that music should be straightforwardly pleasant and uncomplicated, and that it should not require concentrated effort on the part of composers, performers, and listeners. While playing the flute before cabinet meetings, Frederick focused his thoughts on other things and came up with answers to difficult political problems. His flute apparently played this sort of role also on the battlefield.[22] Comparing the relative merits of various artistic and intellectual pursuits, Frederick remarked early on in his career to Ulrich, Count von Suhm, the following:

We have divided our activities [at court] into two categories. The one is useful, the other agreeable. Studying philosophy and the history of languages are among the useful; the agreeable include music, the comedies and tragedies which we stage, the masquerades and the gifts that we give each other. But the serious occupations always take precedence over the others.[23]

Against this background, then, what sort of collection did Bach compose, publish, and dedicate to Frederick? A series of two fugues, a sonata, and ten canons, all based on the king's theme – a fairly mixed bag of musical items. The more usual practice at the time was to dedicate pieces (typically six of them) in the same genre. For example, C. P. E. Bach dedicated the six keyboard sonatas now known as the "Prussian Sonatas," H. 24–9/Wq 48, to Frederick in the early 1740s. It was also the more usual practice to dedicate pieces known to be in line with the tastes of the dedicatee. It is difficult to imagine a stronger contrast in the 1740s than that between the strict style (*gelehrte Stil* – "learned" counterpoint) of Bach's *Musical Offering* and the consistently galant style (thin-textured homophony with singing melodies and relatively unobtrusive basses) of the hundreds of sonatas and concertos by Quantz and Frederick that were performed night after night at the Prussian court.

All things considered, it seems unlikely that Frederick had any real interest in studying or performing the relentlessly strict counterpoint encountered in Bach's *Musical Offering*. His personal copy evidently passed out of his library during his lifetime: this same exemplar at one time belonged to Johann Philipp Kirnberger, who died three years before Frederick.[24] Hoping to prove to Baron van Swieten that Bach's musical understanding was unmatched, in 1774 (almost thirty years after the fact) Frederick sang aloud the chromatic fugue

---

22 Georg Thouret, *Friedrich der Grosse als Musikfreund und Musiker* (Leipzig, 1898), 134, citing an unspecified letter from Frederick to Jean le Rond d'Alembert. Thouret's report seems to fit perfectly with the contents of Frederick's voluminous correspondence with d'Alembert, but I have not succeeded in locating Thouret's source.

23 Letter of October 23, 1736; Mendelssohn, *Friedrich der Große*, 73; translated in Robert B. Asprey, *Frederick the Great* (New York, 1986), 111.

24 Wolff, NBA VIII/1 KB, 61.

subject he had given to Bach, who on the spot, according to Frederick, made of it a fugue in four parts, then in five parts, and finally in eight parts![25] As enthusiastic as Frederick's assessment is, it appears nonetheless to be fully in line with his un-Bachian tastes. Frederick was evidently interested in the power of fugue as "spectacle": he may very well have found it an entertaining and exciting diversion to witness Bach improvise completely unpremeditated fugues on a difficult subject (more entertaining, say, than he would have found variations on a theme, something less harrowing because it requires less skill). Frederick was evidently not much interested, however, in fugue as composition. He gave Carl Heinrich Graun the order in the 1740s not to write French overtures, apparently in part because of his distaste for their fugal sections, and among his more than 120 surviving sonatas there is only one movement in fugal style;[26] none of Frederick's compositions is in the learned style.

Citing obscure nineteenth-century research by Georg Thouret, some scholars have reported that Frederick was in fact a great lover of learned composition.[27] Thouret's material needs to be considered carefully in context, however, since his essay is engaged in a rather ugly diatribe against "Italian superficiality and French insipidity" as compared with the "beauty, truth, and nobility" of "authentic German" music.

There is no evidence that Frederick ever acknowledged or rewarded Bach's efforts. Bach may well have known precisely what was meant by the eighteenth-century expression "für den König von Preußen arbeiten" ("to work for the King of Prussia" – i.e., to work for nothing).

Bach's Three-Part Fugue has come under a great deal of criticism, especially from Hans T. David, who found serious shortcomings in it, suggesting that it

25 See *Dok* III/790 and *BR*, 260.
26 Warren Kirkendale, *Fugue and fugato in rococo and classical chamber music*, rev. edn. (Durham, N. C., 1979), 311. Quantz's more than 100 sonatas composed for Frederick are all three-movement works in galant style without fugues; see Kirkendale, *Fugue and Fugato*, 310, and Charlotte Gwen Crockett, "The Berlin flute sonatas of Johann Joachim Quantz" (Ph.D. diss., University of Texas at Austin, 1982), 55–6. Regarding Graun's overtures, see Helm, *Music at the Court of Frederick the Great*, 144 (but cf. 200).
27 See Andreas Holschneider, "Johann Sebastian Bach in Berlin," in *Preußen, Dein Spree-Athen: Beiträge zu Literatur, Theater und Musik in Berlin*, ed. Hellmut Kühn (Reinbeck bei Hamburg, 1981), 140, quoting Thouret, "Die Musik am preußischen Hofe im 18. Jahrhundert," *Hohenzollern-Jarhbuch* 1 (1897): 56; cf. Wolff, NBA VIII/1 KB, 105. Thouret does not specify the nature of his source for Frederick's views (contrary to Wolff), but he must have gotten them from Zelter, *Karl Friedrich Christian Fasch.* Zelter (p. 48) relates an incident of Fasch's improvising a third entry into the accompaniment of a canonic passage from a flute sonata composed and performed by Frederick. Reacting to this improvisation, Frederick reportedly said (which is what Thouret quotes), "It always pleases me if I find that music is concerned with the faculty of understanding; if a beautiful piece of music sounds learned, this is as pleasant to me as it is to hear clever conversation at table."

probably represents exactly or approximately what Bach had improvised for Frederick.[28] David's dissatisfaction with the fugue centers on its lack of balance and symmetry, properties David did find for the rest of the *Musical Offering* – or at least in his symmetrical reconstruction of the collection. In light of source-critical research by Wolff and others, David's reconstruction could no longer be considered plausible, but writers have continued nonetheless to share David's sense of stylistic unease with the Three-Part Fugue.

Wolff accounted for the stylistic peculiarities of the piece by investigating alternate meanings of the word "ricercar."[29] In Bach's time, the term could refer to an improvisation (typically noncontrapuntal) in which one "searches out" themes or tests the tuning and probes the key. Principally, though, it meant a strict and highly elaborate fugue. Wolff suggested that in the *Musical Offering* print Bach used the term "Ricercar" for both the free Three-Part and strict Six-Part Fugues not carelessly but with the idea of exploring the two different types of ricercar.

Perhaps, though, this does not do justice to Bach's achievement in these pieces, particularly in the case of the Three-Part Fugue. Regarding the notion that the Three-Part Fugue represents Bach's actual or approximate improvisation for Frederick, recall that Bach had declared himself to be dissatisfied with his improvised fugue and resolved on account of the "lack of necessary preparation [that the] excellent theme demanded" to "write down on paper a regular [ordentliche] fugue." He also declared his printed results to have been worked out "as well as possible." In light of these biographical and the earlier mentioned musical considerations, it becomes much more difficult to reconcile Bach's printed Three-Part Fugue exactly (or even approximately) with the notion of improvisation. Furthermore, some of the most formulaic music within Bach's two Ricercars occurs not in the Three-Part but rather the Six-Part Fugue. The latter contains sequential episodic passages in which the fugue subject is alluded to remotely if at all (mm. 29–39, 79–83); the episodic passages in the Three-Part Fugue, in contrast, are continually marked by the learned procedures for which Bach was so well known (combination of two cells from the initial countersubject in mm. 18–22; combination of the subject's head and tail in mm. 31–7, 115–18; stretto on the tail – simultaneously in diminution – in mm. 122–4; stretto on a prominent secondary motive in mm. 150–1; and a

28 David, *J. S. Bach's Musical Offering*, 8, 30, 35, 44, 63, 134, 143, 147, 151, and 152. Similar statements were made by Spitta, *Johann Sebastian Bach*, 2:673; and, more strongly by Albert Schweitzer, *J. S. Bach* (Leipzig, 1908), 398. See also Christoph Wolff, *The New Grove Bach family* (New York, 1983), 109.

29 Wolff, *Essays*, 329–31.

close point of imitation on the initial countersubject in mm. 161–5). In other words, although there is undoubtedly a "strict-free" or "severe-loose" contrast between these two fugues in general mood, it is not so readily apparent that there is such a contrast in form or contrapuntal procedure.

In fact, taking a lead from Bach's enthusiastic disciple Friedrich Wilhelm Marpurg, we could actually exchange the strict/free designations and apply the former to the Three-Part and the latter to the Six-Part Fugue. Marpurg says that there are two kinds of "regular fugue": "strict or free." In strict fugues, the episodes frequently allude to or quote from parts of the subject and its initial counterpoint by means of division, augmentation, diminution, and contrary motion. If such a piece is worked out at length and introduces all kinds of contrapuntal artifices, it can be called by the Italian name of *Ricercare* or *Ricercata*.[30] Marpurg notes that the fugues of J. S. Bach typically conform to this style. In free fugues, the episodes mostly present material that may be related to but is not derived from the subject and its initial counterpoint. Marpurg notes that the fugues of Handel typically conform to this style. On the basis of Marpurg's discussion, then, Bach's Six-Part Fugue would more likely have been labeled "free" and the Three-Part Fugue "strict."

Nonetheless, throughout the Three-Part Fugue, Bach cultivates elements of the galant style: thinner textures, triplet figuration within music that is otherwise duple at each metric level, and "sighing" appoggiaturas.[31] Wolff focuses on the galant passages to show the breadth of Bach's stylistic interests and to make the compelling argument that this fugue is well served in performance on the fortepiano. Bach was no doubt interested in exploiting the capabilities of the relatively new instrument, but he could certainly have used much more effective means than inserting a few galant-style passages into an extended, strict high-baroque fugue. In addition to broad compositional or specific organological explanations, perhaps these passages, undeniably out of place, need further interpretation.

Each of the passages in question features rapid modulatory sequential movement in the flat direction. In mm. 38–42 the music moves from C minor to E♭ minor (transposed at mm. 87–91, where it reaches A♭ minor), and in mm. 109–18 from G minor to E♭ minor/major. Bach rarely travels so many steps away from the home key in his instrumental works. In that repertory, he mostly sticks to the tonic, dominant, subdominant keys and their relatives – what Bach's contemporary Johann David Heinichen called the "ambitus" of

---

30 Marpurg, *Abhandlung von der Fuge*, vol. 1 (Berlin, 1753), 18–20; *Dok* III/655; *BR*, 253–4. The quotation from Marpurg in Wolff, *Essays*, 330, needs to be considered in this wider context.
31 Wolff, *Essays*, 254–5.

the key.[32] In his choruses and arias, Bach much more frequently visits keys outside the ambitus, almost invariably for textual reasons. Distant tonal movement in the flat direction in Bach's church cantatas frequently expresses ideas concerning death, spiritual decay, lament, suffering, vanity, emptiness, and the like.[33] This tonal procedure and its expressive associations are found also in at least one nonliturgical keyboard work: the *Capriccio on the Departure of his most beloved Brother* BWV 992, where, in the section entitled "Is a setting-forth of various casualties that could befall him abroad," the music moves rapidly in the flat direction, well outside the ambitus, to B♭ minor. In the Three-Part Fugue from the *Musical Offering*, the rapid movement towards the flattest extremes of the tonal circle (E♭ minor and A♭ minor) where the music changes from high-baroque to galant textures appears to suggest negative associations with the lighter style. So although the Three-Part Fugue has galant elements, they are undercut by a tonal device that reinforces the piece's strict qualities.

Whereas keyboard fugues can hardly have been expected to conform to the tastes cultivated at Frederick's court, a sonata would seem, on the face of it, to be much more promising. Yet here, too, Bach's music is aesthetically at odds with its dedicatee. First of all, Bach's sonata ought to have been, like each of Frederick's and Quantz's contemporary sonatas, a galant-style work for solo flute with unobtrusive continuo or obbligato keyboard. In a performance of Bach's sonata for a Prussian court soirée, though, the flutist would not occupy visually or musically the central position, because the piece is a trio sonata in the learned contrapuntal style for flute, violin, and continuo.[34] Also, a sonata conforming to Prussian court taste would follow Giuseppe Tartini's model with three movements: Slow – Fast – Fast(er). Every one of Quantz's more than one hundred sonatas for the Prussian court is a galant-style piece in three movements, marked Slow – Fast – Fast except for six of them that are Fast – Slow – Fast.[35] Bach's sonata has four movements in the configuration Slow – Fast Fugue – Slow – Fast Fugue, and it would have been classified as a "church sonata" (*sonata da chiesa*), not a galant "chamber sonata" (*sonata da camera*).[36]

32   See Eric Chafe, *Tonal allegory in the vocal music of J. S. Bach* (Berkeley, 1991), 65–72. Whether Bach knew Heinichen's term is unknown.

33   Many of these are discussed in Chafe, *Tonal allegory*. Bach's cantatas also feature tonal arrivals outside the ambitus in the sharp direction, associated with matters like joy, forgiveness, life, redemption, and so on.

34   Although Bach published the dedication sonata as a trio sonata, he apparently also at one point envisioned, but immediately abandoned, a performance (in Leipzig?) for solo instrument and obbligato keyboard; see Wolff, NBA VIII/1 KB, 74–5.

35   Crockett, "The Berlin flute sonatas of Johann Joachim Quantz," 55–6.

36   Sonatas were categorized in this way by eighteenth-century French writers from Sebastien de Brossard to Jean-Jacques Rousseau; see William Newman, "Sonata," *New Grove*. Bach was evidently aware of

Whether or not Frederick would have classified sonatas as *da chiesa* or *da camera*, he evidently associated various sorts of contrapuntal music with the church, and, according to Charles Burney, he had a strong distaste for all music that "smells of the church." Reporting on a conversation with Johann Friedrich Agricola about some of his church compositions, Burney wrote: "he said that it was a style of writing which was but little cultivated at Berlin, as the King will not hear it . . . his Prussian majesty carries his prejudice against this kind of music so far, that when he hears of any composer having written an anthem, or oratorio, he fancies his taste is contaminated by it, and says, of his other productions, every moment, *Oh! this smells of the church* [emphasis original]."[37] It is not surprising, therefore, that among the hundreds of surviving sonatas from Frederick's library there are none that could be classified as sonatas *da chiesa*.

Bach's trio sonata, with its contrapuntal "smell of the church," could be called antigalant. This goes well beyond its surface texture. Consider, for example, Bach's treatment of galant mannerisms in the Andante, passages widely regarded as representing Bach's concessions towards Frederick's taste.[38] These excerpts can actually be considered among the least galant in the sonata. The movement does indeed open with a textbook galant-style, balanced period with parallel thirds and sixths in the upper voices and with appoggiaturas marking the phrase endings. But the gesture is immediately undermined by isolating and sequencing its various elements into overlapping phrases of irregular length; in other words, one might say the galant is "baroqued." Simultaneously, the music moves rapidly outside the ambitus to B♭ minor in the first half of the movement and E♭ minor in the second half (see the absurdly extended sequential passage of isolated appoggiaturas at mm. 20–8). As already mentioned, traveling outside the ambitus is rare in Bach's instrumental music but more common in his church music, where such movement

---

the "da camera" and "da chiesa" designations, for his musical library included pieces with these designations. See Kirsten Beißwenger, *Johann Sebastian Bachs Notenbibliothek* (Cassel, 1992). Bach was presumably familiar with the contrapuntal, four-movement Sonata in G minor labeled *Sonata da chiesa* in the *Zweiundzwanzigste Lection* of Georg Philipp Telemann's *Der getreue Music-Meister* (Hamburg, 1728), a collection in which Bach's *Canon à 4* BWV 1074, was published.

37 Burney, *The present state of music*, 91–2. Zelter, *Karl Friedrich Christian Fasch*, 46, also reports, from his conversations with Fasch, that Frederick's dislike for church music was well known and that he once said at the opera, "the music smells of the church [schmeckt nach der Kirche]!"

38 See, for example, David, *J. S. Bach's Musical Offering*, 123; Alfred Dürr, *Im Mittelpunkt Bach* (Cassel, 1988), 55; Gerhard Herz, *Essays on J. S. Bach* (Ann Arbor, 1985), 177; Holschneider, "Johann Sebastian Bach in Berlin," 141; Kirkendale, "The source for Bach's *Musical Offering*," 122; Hans-Joachim Schulze, "Johann Sebastian Bachs 'Musikalisches Opfer' – Bemerkungen zu seiner Geschichte und Aufführungspraxis," in *Zur Aufführungspraxis und Interpretation der Musik von Johann Sebastian Bach und Georg Friedrich Händel*, ed. Eitelfriedrich Thom (Blankenburg/Michaelstein, 1985), 11–5; and Wolff, NBA VIII/1 KB, 105.

in the flat direction is associated with negative topics in his texts. Bach's sonata employs this tonal procedure right at the point where galant gestures have been most clearly set up, interpreting and contradicting, rather than supporting, the galant melodic style – again, a highly "baroque" approach, similar to that taken in the isolated galant passages in the Three-Part Fugue.

In the trio sonata there are also subtler sorts of conflicts with galant sensibilities. Consider the stylistic mixtures and contradictions in the first Allegro, whose opening takes on the features of a French bourrée.[39] In bourrées the first phrase is eight beats in length, preceded by an upbeat. Beat 7 and the first half of 8 constitute the primary repose, or "thesis," whereas beat 3 and the first half of 4 provide a preliminary resting point, or secondary thesis; beats 1, 2, second half of 4, 5, 6, and the second half of 8 involve motion, or "arsis."[40] The eight quarter-note beats of Bach's mm. 1–4 accommodate this arsic-thetic description of dance steps. The description does not map onto Bach's second phrase (also four measures in length), however, which is organized by falling sequences, each two beats in duration. The third phrase is only two measures long, and it brings the movement to its first thetic arrival on the tonic.

At the point where the traits of the French bourrée begin to fall apart (mm. 5 and following), the music begins clearly to show features of Italian concerto ritornellos. Bach's concerto-style works (including many arias and some sonatas) show a predilection for a Vivaldian ritornello type containing three clearly differentiated internal divisions, now known as the *Fortspinnungstypus*. In the Vivaldian ritornello most cultivated by Bach, the first segment (*Vordersatz*) grounds the tonality with primarily tonic and dominant harmonies, ending on either the tonic or (more typically) the dominant. The second segment (*Fortspinnung*) is sequential, often marked with root movement by fifths. And the third segment (*Epilog*), whether involving further sequencing or other procedures, brings the ritornello to a satisfying close by way of a cadential gesture in the tonic.[41] This description maps neatly onto Bach's mm. 1–10 of the sonata Allegro, where mm. 1–4 are *Vordersatz*, mm. 5–8 are *Fortspinnung*, and mm. 9–10 are *Epilog*. Because the ten measures are tonally closed (i.e., begin and end in the tonic) and their subsequent quotations are immediately surrounded by episodic material, the section acts like a concerto ritornello. The

---

39 For the properties of the various dances in Bach's time, see Meredith Little and Natalie Jenne, *Dance and the music of J. S. Bach* (Bloomington, 1991).

40 This "arsic-thetic" terminology of the ancient Greeks is adopted by Little and Jenne, *Dance and the music of J. S. Bach*, 16.

41 On formulating these categories primarily in terms of harmonic properties rather than thematic ones, see Laurence Dreyfus, "J. S. Bach's concerto ritornellos and the question of invention," *Musical Quarterly* 71 (1985): 327–58.

movement could therefore also be considered what German contemporaries called a *Sonate auf Concertenart* ("sonata in concerto style").[42]

The mixture of genres becomes more complex at m. 11, however, as the flute joins in, performing the entire ritornello a fifth higher, after which the ensemble moves on with episodic material derived from the three segments of the opening. In other words, this bourrée-style, concerto-style sonata movement turns out to be a fugue, one that Marpurg would have considered a "strict fugue." At the first middle entry (some twenty-five measures later!), Bach piles on yet another genre reference. The new slow-moving bass line, presented with rhythmically more active counterpoints above it, corresponds to baroque cantus-firmus technique. This bass line is experienced less as a new countersubject than as a distinct melody that virtually overwhelms the fugue subject. The cantus firmus turns out, of course, to be the Royal Theme provided by Frederick.

Enlightenment thinkers would not necessarily have had anything against mixing features of so many genres in one work. Aestheticians did speak frequently and forcefully of the need for clarity in the representation of styles and genres,[43] and one straightforward way to effect this was to avoid combining them. But such mixtures were certainly tolerated and even encouraged so long as they were "agreeable" (that is, did not obscure or contradict each other). That is why eighteenth-century German composers could speak of the merits of combining certain elements of the French and Italian styles in their galant chamber music.[44]

They might have experienced some problems, however, with the mixture of styles in Bach's sonata. It is not difficult to imagine that "strict fugue" and cantus-firmus technique – the references closest to the surface of this music – would have been perceived as contributing to the piece's severity. The concerto and bourrée references, however, are in conflict with this *Affect*. Concertos, with their wayward episodes for soloists, are obviously much less strict than fugues and cantus-firmus pieces. But more to the point, bourrées were especially prized in the eighteenth century for their carefree character. In 1739 Johann Mattheson described its essential characteristics as: "*contentment; pleasantness* reigns; and as a result bourrées are so to speak somewhat *unconcerned, tranquil,* easy going, leisurely, and yet not at all unpleasant [emphases

42 See Jeanne Swack, "On the origins of the *Sonate auf Concertenart,*" *Journal of the American Musicological Society* 46 (1993): 369–414.

43 See Ernst Cassirer, *The philosophy of the enlightenment* (Princeton, 1951), 275–360.

44 For insightful discussions of these and related issues, see Dreyfus, "The articulation of genre in Bach's instrumental music," in *The universal Bach* (Philadelphia, 1986), 10–38; and "J. S. Bach and the status of genre: problems of style in the G-minor sonata BWV 1029," *The Journal of Musicology* 5 (1987): 55–78.

original]."[45] This was evidently Bach's basic understanding of the bourrée as well, for the texts of nearly all his cantata movements written in bourrée style speak straightforwardly of carefree, joyful, and sunny matters.[46] These associations with the bourrée conflict with the fugal and cantus-firmus styles in Bach's sonata.

The "disagreement" in this sonata movement is not limited to problems of surface *Affects*. The Royal Theme nearly drowns out the counterpoint in all the middle entries of this da capo fugue. The Royal Theme is 9 measures long, whereas the fugue subject is 10. The Royal Theme therefore enters in the second measure of the middle entries. In other words, the new counterpoint seems like the principal voice of the fugue even though its entrance does not coincide with the beginning of the expositions. If the Royal Theme destroys the sense of what constitutes the subject in this fugue, it also, more subtly, obfuscates the bourrée dance steps that had been clearly accommodated at the outset by the contours of the subject's *Vordersatz*: whereas the third strand in the middle entries supports the arsic-thetic properties of the bourrée dance steps in the *Vordersatz* segments, the Royal Theme obscures them, for its arses appear on the bourrée's theses (see, e.g., the first beats in mm. 47 and 49).

The remaining movements of the sonata also mix various genres with opposing *Affects*. The Largo features slow-moving repeated notes in the bass, a common trait in (relaxed) galant sonatas, while the upper voices move more actively, their rhythm being organized according to the properties of the (socially formidable) French sarabande, the most difficult and sophisticated of baroque dance steps (basically outmoded by the 1740s). At the same time, this highly formal dance takes on some of the syntax of the more wayward Italian concerto style without fully conforming to its tonal procedures (*Vordersatz*, mm. 1–8; *Fortspinnung*, mm. 9–13; *Epilog*, mm. 13–16; in the B section, episodes and returns of segments from the A section). The second Allegro features a highly ornamented variation of the Royal Theme as the severe chromatic subject for a dancelike but strict fugue.

If the fugues and sonata do not seem to match Frederick's tastes and interests, the canons must almost surely have represented an affront to his aesthetic ideals of musical composition. Enlightenment writers on music considered canons to be the most learned form of counterpoint. Many of them, not surprisingly,

---

45 Cited in Little and Jenne, *Dance and the music of J. S. Bach*, 226 n. 2; Johann Mattheson, *Der vollkommene Capellmeister* (Hamburg, 1739), 226.
46 See Doris Finke-Hecklinger, *Tanzcharaktere in Johann Sebastian Bachs Vokalmusik* (Trossingen, 1970), 29–31, 135, and 140–2.

had little good to say about this sort of writing, calling it unnatural, unmelodious, excessively artificial, eye-oriented rather than ear-oriented, and so forth.[47] Canons were considered completely at odds with the desire for freedom of expression in music. Mattheson went so far as to label the canon with its binding rules as a "Dictator," in relation to whom "delectable variety stands completely to the wayside."[48]

Bach does not appear to have been primarily interested in canon as a form in which to demonstrate his compositional wares. He employs canon and other forms of learned counterpoint throughout his career, most commonly in his church music, because of its association with "The Law"; this is, of course, the original meaning of the word "canon": "rule," "measuring stick," or "law." Canon and other forms of learned counterpoint in Bach's music are often tied up somehow with the number 10, by reference to biblical law (the "Ten Commandments"). For example, ten movements (every third one) from the thirty *Goldberg Variations* are pieces of learned counterpoint (a series of canons, at the unison through ninth, followed by a Quodlibet). There are ten imitative expositions in the opening chorus of the cantata "Du sollt Gott, deinen Herren, lieben" BWV 77, whose text is based on the New Testament summary of the law and whose accompaniment includes ten trumpet entries of phrases from the chorale "Dies sind die heilgen zehn Gebot" ("These are the holy Ten Commandments"), five of them in canon with the continuo.[49] And there are ten canons in the *Musical Offering*.

In this context, it becomes clearer how the *Musical Offering*, viewed as a whole,[50] takes on an increasingly theological character: learned contrapuntal keyboard ricercars and a learned contrapuntal sonata da chiesa, both employing tonal procedures uncommon in Bach's instrumental music but more familiar from his church cantatas, move to a series of ten austere canons.

What understanding of the law is Bach likely to have had, and to what purpose would the *Musical Offering* refer to the law? Luther teaches that the law has two functions, the one "civil" and the other "spiritual" or "theological."[51]

47 For a survey of eighteenth-century German writers on this topic, see Peter Schleuning, *Geschichte der Musik in Deutschland – Das 18.Jahrhundert* (Reinbeck bei Hamburg, 1984), 338–47.
48 Mattheson, *Critica musica*, vol. 1 (Hamburg, 1722), 341 nn. (a) and (c); quoted in Schleuning, *Geschichte der Musik*, 342.
49 See Herz, *Essays on J. S. Bach*, 205–17.
50 The issue of whether a collection is best performed as a whole can be separate from whether there is any value in thinking about a collection as a whole. There are instances of Bach's writing whole works that were certainly not performed at one sitting: for example, he carefully numbered the various sections in the *Christmas Oratorio* and the *Mass in B minor*. This point was made by John Butt, *Bach: Mass in B minor* (Cambridge, 1991), 21.
51 I have summarized the relevant aspects of Luther's teaching on the law from Paul Althaus, *The theology of Martin Luther* (Philadelphia, 1966), 251–73.

The first function concerns public peace and order in the present world, and it operates through God-instituted offices of government, parents, and teachers. Humans are able to fulfill these laws and therefore also God's law in its civil sense. The law has another function, however, insofar as it is not understood in its political sense but in its spiritual sense – which Luther says is its true and genuine meaning. Humanity, after The Fall into sin, simply cannot fulfill the law in its spiritual or theological sense, because doing so demands a pure heart, perfect obedience, and perfect fear and love of God – all unattainable conditions. This law is not satisfied by outward fulfillment, since after The Fall humans are essentially sinful, no matter what their actual behavior. Here the function of the law is to make us feel its power, recognize our sin, experience God's wrath, and be led to repentance (all of this is expressed clearly in the concluding verses of Luther's chorale "Dies sind die heilgen zehn Gebot"). The law, however, is not God's entire word. The gospel (i.e., "good news") stands alongside it. Law and gospel have opposite functions, even though each contains aspects of the other. The law condemns and makes us conscious of our inherent sinfulness, whereas the gospel preaches forgiveness of sins through Christ. The law leads into death; the gospel proclaims eternal life (i.e., "salvation") by Christ's redemption. The law places humans under the wrath of God (what Luther calls God's "alien work"); the gospel brings grace (God's "proper work").

Bach's ten canons in the *Musical Offering* are possibly tied up with Luther's understanding of the theological function of the law. This seems most clear from the canons that Bach provided with inscriptions. The heading above Canon 9 reads "Quaerendo invenietis," and there can hardly be any doubt that Bach is quoting Matthew 7 or Luke 11: "Quaerite, et invenietis" – "seek and you will find." That Bach attached great importance to the notion of seeking in the *Musical Offering* is also evident from his use of the term "Ricercar" for the opening fugues and from his inscription "Regis Iussu Cantio Et Reliqua Canonica Arte Resoluta," spelling out "RICERCAR" for the canons.[52]

What humans ultimately seek, to the Lutheran mind, is salvation. Luther teaches that justification cannot be attained through good works but only through faith, something itself not humanly attained but received as a gift from God. For Luther the minimum condition for justification appears to be a recognition of one's need for grace and an appeal to God's merciful bestowal of it. This is indicated, as the Reformation scholar Alister McGrath has pointed

52   In Frederick's copy, however, this acrostic appears at the opposite side, which is otherwise blank, of the first page of the Three-Part Fugue. Bach's full title admits so many possible translations that it is difficult to know exactly what it means.

out, by Luther's numerous discussions of faith and humility but also by the extremely frequent use in his writings of verbs such as "cry out," "ask," "seek," and "knock."[53] Bach's heading for Canon 9, "Seek, and you will find," should probably not be understood only (or even primarily?) as a practical musical matter, an invitation for the reader to solve the puzzle of the second voice's entry. Rather, in the context of canonic reference to the law, this inscription, quoted from the Bible, can also be further understood as a reminder of the theological function of the law: recognition of sin and the need for receiving God's grace. Abraham Calov's Bible with Lutheran commentaries (Wittenberg, 1682), Bach's copy of which survives, also interprets Matthew's "seek, and you will find" in terms of the need for receiving the gift of faith from God.

Two other canons are marked with inscriptions only in Frederick's copy of the collection. Canon 4 here reads "As the notes increase, so may the fortune of the king," and Canon 5, "As the notes ascend, so may the glory of the king." These two canons are clearly meant to be linked, for the word "king" (Regis) appears only once, between the two canons and, uniquely, in bold script, to serve as the last word for both of the inscriptions.[54] Eric Chafe has recently pointed out that these two canons show an opposition between their *Affect* and their external signs of glory.[55] In the first, the dichotomy appears between the usual significance of the majestic French overture rhythms and the unmistakably melancholy tone,[56] and in the second it appears between the evidently all-encompassing modulations and their deliberate registral finiteness.[57] Chafe concludes that Bach seems here to highlight what Walter Benjamin called the "disproportion between the unlimited hierarchical dignity with which [the monarch] is divinely invested and the humble estate of his humanity."[58]

I would like to underscore and augment Chafe's observations by focusing on a few more aspects of Canon 4 and the wording of Bach's preface to the collection. Consider first Bach's preface, which has not figured prominently in interpretive discussions of the *Musical Offering*. It is somewhat peculiar that Bach sent to Frederick a printed German preface. Courtesy, in the original sense of the word, would have required a dedication in French. It is true that

53 McGrath, *Luther's theology of the cross*, 89.
54 Fortune and glory were commonly linked; this is true, for example, for the character *Schicksal* in Bach's cantata "Angenehmes Wiederau" BWV 30a.
55 Chafe, *Tonal allegory*, 22–3, 213–15.
56 Chafe, *Tonal allegory*, 23. In the absence of any prior discussion, my students have invariably experienced these two canons as having negative *Affect*, no matter how the pieces are performed.
57 Chafe's view here contradicts Douglas R. Hofstadter, who suggests that Bach relished the idea that Canon 5 could theoretically modulate upwards *ad infinitum* to glorify the king; see Hofstadter, *Gödel, Escher, Bach* (New York, 1979), 10.
58 Chafe, *Tonal allegory*, 23; Benjamin, *The origin of German tragic drama* (London, 1977), 70.

the work, although dedicated to Frederick, was published with a wider audience in mind. But Quantz's *Versuch einer Anweisung die Flöte traversiere zu spielen* (Berlin, 1752), likewise dedicated to Frederick and also intended for a wider audience, was published in two editions, one in German and the other in French. Frederick was apparently not altogether comfortable with the German language.[59] At any rate, he certainly made himself clear on what he thought of German as a vehicle for intellectual discourse in his scathing essay of 1780, *De la littérature allemande*.[60] Not surprisingly, he saw to it that the *Societät der Wissenschaften* in Berlin continued publishing its proceedings in French after such groups elsewhere in the German states had decided on the vernacular.[61]

Several phrases in Bach's German preface suggest a theological tone for Bach's collection. The opening sentence reads: "Ew. Majestät weyhe hiermit in tiefster Unterthänigkeit ein Musicalisches Opfer . . ." ("To your Majesty, [I] consecrate herewith, in deepest submission, a *Musical Offering...*"). Compare this wording with the similar but more conventional language of the opening sentence in the preface from Quantz's flute book, lacking the significant word "Opfer" and using "widmen" for Bach's "weyhen": "Eurer Königlichen Majestät darf ich hiermit, in tiefster Unterthänigkeit, gegenwärtige Blätter widmen . . ." ("To your Royal Majesty, may I herewith dedicate, in deepest submission, these pages . . ."). On Bach's title page, the word *Opfer* (offering, sacrifice) is set dramatically larger than the rest of the text, suggesting that his choice of wording is significant. The expression "musical *offering*" may not seem so meaningful in and of itself; Bach's student Lorenz Christoph Mizler, for example, refers to serenading as a "musicalisches Opfer."[62] Linking "weyhen" with "Opfer" in a published collection of instrumental music in the late 1740s, however, must have sounded strange.[63] For Bach to write "consecrate an offering" makes his dedication "smell of the church" right from the outset. The religious import of Bach's language is also clear from similar expressions in his Calov Bible. Consider the following excerpt from Exodus 29 (text in parentheses is Calov's commentary):

59 See the quotation cited in n. 19.
60 I have relied on "An essay on German literature: its defects, their causes, and the means by which they may be corrected," in Frederic II, King of Prussia, *Posthumous works*, vol. 13, translated by Thomas Holcroft (London, 1789), 397–457. For a discussion of Frederick's essay and its broader contexts, particularly social ones, see Norbert Elias, *The history of manners*, the civilizing process 1, (New York, 1978), 10–15.
61 See Eric A. Blackall, *The emergence of German as a literary language 1700–1775*, rev. edn. (Ithaca, 1978), 109–11.
62 Mizler, *Musikalische Bibliothek*, vol. 3 (Leipzig, 1752), 607; cited in Kirkendale, "The source for Bach's *Musical Offering*," 136 n. 152.
63 My thanks to Professor Emery Snyder (Princeton University), a specialist in eighteenth-century German literature, for confirming this suspicion.

v. 37 Seven days you shall make atonement for the altar and [Bach inserts the missing word *weihen* (consecrate)] it (in the consecration [*Heiligung*] of the altar which occurred then for the first time so that in its use no sin would be committed and so that the gift of the altar itself would be consecrated [*geheiliget würde*] . . . Also in memory: God did not want offerings [*das Opfer*] brought to Him in any other place but that which was consecrated [*geweihet war*]).⁶⁴

Towards the end of his preface, Bach uses some peculiar language that seems especially significant. Bach writes: "This resolve [to work out the Royal theme] . . . has none other than this irreproachable intent, to glorify . . . the fame of a monarch [*den Ruhm eines Monarchen zu verherrlichen*]." Both "rühmen" and "verherrlichen" mean "to glorify," and neither one of these words by itself would seem particularly significant. But to use them together, the one as the object of the other, would in the 1740s have seemed linguistically odd in a secular dedication.⁶⁵ When Bach's text speaks of "glorifying the glory" of the king, it presumably refers to different notions of glory.

For help on this question, we can turn to the texts of Bach's surviving vocal works. The only instance there of "glorifying glory" is found in the opening chorus from the first version of the *St. John Passion* BWV 245. The text reads (my emphases): "Lord [*Herr*], our ruler [*Herr*scher], whose glory [Ruhm] is glorious [*herr*lich] in all the lands, show us through your Passion that you, the true son of God, have at all times, even in the most serious abasement, been glorified [ver*herr*licht]!" Like Bach's preface to the *Musical Offering*, this text links "Ruhm" with "verherrlichen." The wording "*Ruhm* . . . verherrlicht" in the *St. John Passion* was presumably adopted deliberately, for the libretto otherwise quotes Psalm 8, a well known psalm, whose text speaks of the glory of God's name ("Name," not "Ruhm").

The *St. John Passion* chorus reflects very clearly one of the central ideas in Lutheran theology, the notion that Christ's glorification as the king of humanity centers on his suffering on the cross. This is obviously not the place for a detailed consideration of Luther's "theology of the cross."⁶⁶ The only place God's glory is revealed to humans is, paradoxically, hidden in Christ's suffering on the cross; and this in turn provides a model for how

---

64 Translated in Howard H. Cox, ed., *The Calov Bible of J. S. Bach* (Ann Arbor, 1985), 406.

65 My thanks again to Professor Snyder for confirming this suspicion. To give Bach's phrase in English as "to extol the fame" might seem on the face of it to be simpler and to make more sense, but, leaving aside the question of this translation's accuracy, we would need to consider how likely it is that Bach would want to extol fame (on this point, see the quotation cited in n. 68).

66 For a general summary, see Althaus, *The theology of Martin Luther*, 25–34; for more detailed treatments, see McGrath, *Luther's theology of the cross*, and Walther von Loewenich, *Luther's theology of the cross* (Minneapolis, 1976).

humans ought to live.[67] This is why Bach's church cantatas can speak so often of our finding joy in suffering; it is also clear from a perusal of Bach's markings in his Calov Bible that the practical applications of the theology of the cross in one's daily life were of great importance to him. For Lutherans, true knowledge of God and a right ethical attitude are not separate matters but one and the same. Seeking knowledge of God through philosophical speculation is in the same category as seeking salvation through good works. Both exalt humans to the level of God, and both use the same standard for God and our relationship to God: glory and power.

Regarding human notions of glory, consider also the following passage of commentary that Bach underlined in his Calov Bible:

As soon as a little success comes to us human beings, from that moment on we want the honor [*Ehre*], and soon pride [*Ehrgeitz*] overtakes us, making us believe that I have done that myself and that the nation and the people owe me their debt and we reach for the glory [*Ruhm*] that belongs solely and purely to God.[68]

Frederick, by contrast, wrote frequently and forcefully in favor of a view very much opposed to Bach's. Consider the following example, from his remarks in a letter of September 26, 1770 to d'Alembert:

Talents no doubt ought to be distinguished, especially when they rise to supereminence. Great minds labour only for fame, and it would be treating them severely to let them always hope for, yet never enjoy, the thing of which they are in search. The penalties annexed to all ranks of mankind can only be softened by this balm, a little of which is necessary, even to the greatest men.[69]

The theology of the cross, in contrast to Frederick's views, recognizes God in Christ's suffering, and sees humans as being called to suffer, ultimately allowing God to work in them instead of seeking glory through their own acts. It is in this sense that the theology of the cross is a theology of faith: God's hidden "proper work" of grace that justifies us (the gospel) is a gift tied up with God's manifest "alien work" of wrath (the law) that makes us recognize our worthlessness and sinfulness. And so, like the law, glory might be said to have two senses, the one essentially spiritual and the other more

---

67 McGrath, *Luther's theology of the cross*, 176–81 and 191, points out that twentieth-century scholars came too strongly to emphasize Luther's notion of God's hiddenness (with the devastation of war in Europe, was God really there?). Luther believed, however, that God's glory is *revealed* within or behind its opposite: "hidden" in the cross and suffering. McGrath does not mean to suggest that the theology of the cross was anything less than central to Lutheran theology (hence the subtitle of his study: *Martin Luther's theological breakthrough*).

68 Translated in Cox, *The Calov Bible*, 424.

69 Frederic II, King of Prussia, *Posthumous works*, Vol. 11, translated by Thomas Holcroft (London, 1789), 192–3.

worldly. Bach captures this in the *St. John Passion* and in the preface to the *Musical Offering* by using for the one "ver*herr*lichen" (literally, to glorify in the sense of "to make Godlike" – to suffer) and for the other "rühmen" (to glorify in the sense of "to make known").

Bach musically represents the spiritual glorification of worldly glory in a particularly striking and straightforward way in Canon 4 from the *Musical Offering*. Here the bass line points to the French overture with its traditional baroque associations of majesty and glory. The realization of the canon, however, calls for augmentation and contrary motion. In its realization, the line becomes deregalized, because at half speed the dotted rhythms can no longer give the impression of the French overture.[70] In other words, the obvious worldly glory of the original line is spiritually glorified by the canonic realization. The music, in this interpretation, hardly needs an inscription to make its point clear to a Lutheran audience. The inscription provided only in Frederick's copy, "As the notes increase, so may the fortune of the king," in this context has a rather different meaning from what is usually suggested (namely, "Vive le roi!").[71] The melancholy *Affect* and the deregalized canonic solution link regal fortune (worldly works – glory) not to splendor, might, and fame but to the theology of the cross.

The general message of the *Musical Offering* as interpreted here would probably not have been lost on a well versed intellectual like Frederick (if he even bothered to consider in any detail Bach's music and its inscriptions), and it is unlikely that Bach would have shied away from making bold statements before a king: in his Calov Bible, Bach highlighted a passage of commentary that

---

70 Some performers (e.g., on the well-known 1970s recording directed by Gustav Leonhardt, released on various labels and formats) assimilate overdotting in the augmented voice with overdotting in the bass, so that thirty-second notes of the original voice become thirty-second notes in the augmented voice too. Bernhard Kistler-Liebendörfer, *Quaerendo invenietis: Versuch über J. S. Bachs Musikalisches Opfer* (Frankfurt, 1985), 14, also recommends this solution. One of the main reasons Kistler-Liebendörfer argues for assimilated double-dotting (and, presumably, why Leonhardt employed it) is that it softens the dissonances in a realization featuring an augmentation of the entire bass line. Bach must have meant only the first half of the bass line to be featured in the augmented realization, however, since, as few performers will have noticed from their modern editions, augmenting the entire line necessarily involves changing the 1747 print's melodic readings and rhythms. The realization works unproblematically when only the first half of the printed bass line is augmented (a solution encountered in Bach's own realizations of other augmentation canons; for the details, see Wolff, NBA VIII/1 KB, 114). I would argue that no matter which canonic realization is employed, assimilated overdotting should not be adopted, because it goes against the letter and the spirit of the augmentation and its rubric.

71 See, e.g., Kirkendale, "The source for Bach's *Musical Offering*," 107 and 110; and Lothar Hoffmann-Erbrecht, "Von der Urentsprechung zum Symbol: Versuch einer Systematisierung musikalischer Sinnbilder," in *Bachiana et alia Musicologica: Festschrift Alfred Dürr zum 65. Geburtstag*, ed. Wolfgang Rehm (Cassel, 1983), 118.

reads, "[A preacher] need not guard his mouth nor take into view gracious or wrathful lords or noblemen, nor consider money, wealth, honor, or power, shame, poverty, or harm; he need not think any further than that he says what his office demands."[72] The many printed copies of the *Musical Offering* instructed not only Frederick, however, but also Bach's fellow German musicians and friends in the ways of learned counterpoint and of the theology of the cross.[73] Bach apparently believed that in his compositional ventures he was fulfilling the commandment of the gospel's summary of the law ("love God, and love your neighbor as yourself"). According to Bach's understanding of the law, loving one's neighbors implies imparting one's God-given knowledge to them. Bach's preface to a series of organ chorales reads: "Orgel-Büchlein . . . / Dem Höchsten Gott allein zu Ehren, / Dem Nechsten, draus sich zu belehren . . ." ("For the most high God alone to glorify, and for my neighbor, from which to take instruction . . ."). Ultimately, the *Musical Offering* instructs Bach's fellow humans and honors God.

72 Cox, *The Calov Bible*, 444. For more concerning the Calov Bible and connections between Bach's instrumental music and his practical understanding of theology, see Michael Marissen, *The social and religious designs of J. S. Bach's Brandenburg Concertos* (Princeton, 1995).
73 Perhaps even the apparently conflicting formats of oblong and upright papers in the print of the *Musical Offering* play visually into this notion of the cross. This is not so far-fetched as it might initially sound. Consider that Bach highlighted in his Calov Bible a verse and its commentary describing how Old Testament priests took offerings [Opfer] and waved them back, forth, up, and down before the Lord. The commentary, remarkably, specifies that they did this "to form the cross of Jesus." See Cox, *The Calov Bible*, 406 (cf. the second paragraph of 407).

Chapter seven

A thirty-six voice canon in the hand of C. P. E. Bach

DANIEL R. MELAMED

Considering the riches to be found there, it comes as a surprise that relatively little attention has been paid to the section of Carl Philipp Emanuel's estate catalogue that lists music by "various composers," defined for the purposes of the catalogue and in the family-centered world of the Bachs as those outside the clan. The main reason people have paid attention to the listing at all is that it is a point of access to the contents of J. S. Bach's music library, in that a number of the older items that C. P. E. Bach owned can be shown to have come from his father.[1]

It is perhaps characteristic that scholars of J. S. Bach's music have sometimes seemed to regard Carl Philipp Emanuel as little more than a conduit for his father's precious legacy. But given the importance for Bach studies of the division of J. S. Bach's estate and the transmission of his music library, there is little doubt that C. P. E. Bach's catalogue is the most important document we have. This is especially true for its list of J. S. Bach's compositions, particularly the church cantatas. Scholars have been slower to take advantage of the list of music by other composers, in part because the items there are often more difficult to trace to J. S. Bach.

This section of the catalogue recently revealed an old score and a set of performing parts in J. S. Bach's hand for a late seventeenth-century motet.[2] I do not think there are more unknown J. S. Bach autographs among the pieces listed there, but any number of interesting and potentially revealing items

1 Such sources were of particular value, for example, for Christoph Wolff's study of Bach's contact with Palestrina-style counterpoint, *Der Stile antico in der Musik Johann Sebastian Bachs* (Wiesbaden, 1968).
2 Daniel R. Melamed, "Eine Motette Sebastian Knüpfers aus J. S. Bachs Notenbibliothek," *BJ* 75 (1989): 191–6.

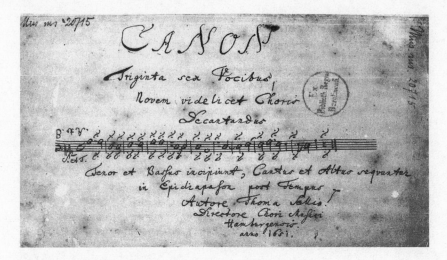

Figure 7.1   SBB Mus. ms. 20715, f.1r

remain to be investigated. One of them, a curious canon manuscript in the
hand of Carl Philipp Emanuel, suggest his interest in older repertory, in contrapuntal artifice, and in an important group of seventeenth-century theorists
and composers. These interests he surely acquired from his father, and perhaps
the older Bach was the source of the canon.

The item in question is represented by a listing in the estate catalogue that
reads "Canon Triginta sex Vocibus &c. von Thomas Sellius."[3] The entry refers
to a manuscript now in Berlin, SBB Mus. ms. 20715, measuring 41.5 x 34 cm.
and consisting of one large bifolium; on its first page, crosswise, is the following: "C A N O N / Triginta sex Vocibus, / Novem videlicet Choris / Decantandus /
[musical notation of the canon] / Tenor et Bassus incipiunt, Cantus et Altus
sequuntur/in Epidiapason post Tempus /Autore Thoma Sellio / Directore
Chori Musici / Hamburgensis. / anno 1651." [Canon to be sung in thirty-six
voices, namely nine choirs . . . tenor and bass begin, soprano and alto follow
an octave above one *tempus* later. Author Thomas Selle, cantor in Hamburg,
1651.] (See Figure 7.1.)

The exact provenance of this manuscript is not easy to trace, but I suspect
that it came to the Berlin library through the collector Georg Poelchau, who
in 1805 bought from C. P. E. Bach's estate a large quantity of similar material –
music of more historical than practical value.[4] The canon does not appear in

3 *Verzeichniß des musikalischen Nachlasses des verstorbenen Capellmeisters Carl Philipp Emanuel Bach*
   (Hamburg, 1790); facsimile edition, *The catalog of Carl Philipp Emanuel Bach's estate*, ed. Rachel W.
   Wade (New York, 1981), 88.
4 See the notes to *Dok* III/957.

the catalogues of Poelchau's collection, nor is it listed in the estate catalogue of Carl Friedrich Zelter, through whom some of Poelchau's material passed (by way of the Berlin Sing-Akademie) to the Berlin library.[5] Nonetheless, I suspect that the canon did come from Poelchau, either bound with some other item and thus not listed separately in the catalogue,[6] or indirectly, leaving Poelchau's collection before the compilation of the catalogue.

The canon manuscript is a striking document. The first page gives the work's title, attribution, and description, and a canonic notation of the composition. The last page is blank, but the inner pages present the full 36–voice realization of the canon, in nine choirs of four voices each. (See Figure 7.2.) A few errors and some details of the layout suggest that the canon's solution was worked out on the page and not copied from some other realization – more a calligraphic exercise than a musical one, given the nature of the piece. The copyist of the manuscript is Carl Philipp Emanuel Bach; as far as I know, the item's autograph status has not been noted before. I will return to the date of the handwriting and the paper on which the manuscript is written.

C. P. E. Bach's title page attributes the canon to Thomas Selle, and the canon has appeared in lists of Selle's compositions at least as early as Gerber's *Lexicon.*[7] The Selle worklists in *MGG* and *New Grove* suggest that C. P. E. Bach's copy is the only surviving source, but RISM A/I reveals a listing for a printed edition dated 1651, with a single copy recorded in the Moscow Conservatory, and we might guess that this print was the source of C. P. E. Bach's manuscript copy.[8] There is a surprise here, though: the item in Moscow is the same piece but no print. It is, rather, another manuscript copy, laid out exactly like C. P. E. Bach's. How this manuscript found its way into the RISM catalogue of printed music I do not know, but there is no evidence that the piece was ever published under Selle's name. The RISM item is a phantom.

So the Moscow manuscript cannot have been C. P. E. Bach's source; in fact, the copying almost certainly went the other way, from C. P. E. Bach's copy to the Moscow manuscript. The Moscow copy is in the hand of an anonymous scribe whose work surfaces in the Voss-Buch collection and in the circle of the

5 Poelchau's catalogue: SBB Mus. ms. theor. kat 41, 51, 56, and 61; Zelter's estate catalogue: SBB N. Mus ms. theor. 30. Poelchau did have a copy of the canon; it appears in SBB Mus. ms. 38107, which contains canons from Poelchau's library on loose sheets, some of which may once have been part of a canon collection (SBB Mus. ms. 30326) assembled by the late eighteenth-century Dresden *Capellmeister* Joseph Schuster. This copy of the canon does not appear to have been made from Mus. ms. 20715.
6 The manuscript was bound at one time, as thread holes show.
7 Ernst Ludwig Gerber, *Historisch-biographisches Lexicon der Tonkünstler,* 4 vols. (Leipzig, 1790–2) cites the manuscript copy listed in C. P. E. Bach's estate catalogue in the entry for Selle.
8 *International Inventory of Musical Sources* A/I (Cassel, 1971–), item S2762. I am grateful to Michael Ochs, Svetlana Sigida, and Howard Smither for their help in obtaining copies of this source.

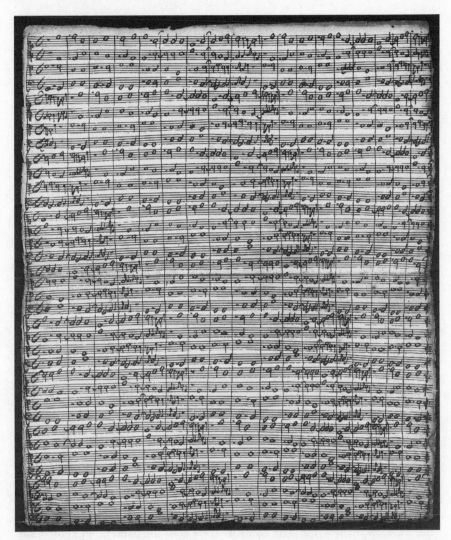

Figure 7.2   SBB Mus. ms. 20715, ff. 1v–2r

Levy and Mendelssohn families in Berlin.[9] Those families were closely associated with the Berlin Sing-Akademie, and their likely connection to the Moscow copy lends credence to my guess that the piece was known in Sing-Akademie circles and that Bach's copy passed through the hands of Carl Friedrich Zelter, presumably from Poelchau. There are also some markings on

9   Personal communication. I am grateful to Professor Kobayashi for sharing this information with me, and to Kirsten Beißwenger for her assistance.

the Moscow copy that may point to its ownership by Eduard Grell, a later director of the Sing-Akademie.[10] This second copy of the canon is thus an interesting document of Berlin musical circles in the nineteenth century, but does not have much bearing on the transmission of the work in the eighteenth century or in the Bach family, or on the attribution of the work to Selle.

If no printed seventeenth-century source of the canon attributed to Selle ever existed, where did this piece and its attribution come from? If we continue to look among sources of Selle's music, we will be disappointed, because the work is not by him at all. This 36-voice canon, one of the most celebrated pieces of its type in the seventeenth and early eighteenth centuries, is actually the composition of Romano Micheli, a polemical pamphleteer on music and composer of elaborate canons.[11] This particular canon first appeared in Micheli's *Speciminia musices* (Rome, 1633), where it is dedicated to King Louis of France, presumably a double dedication to both Louis IX (St. Louis) and Louis XIII (the reigning monarch).[12]

The canon originally carried the text "Ludovicus Rex defensor omnium Christianorum" (King Louis, defender of all Christians) to which the music of the canon is intimately connected; the notes are derived from its vowels, a *soggetto cavato dalle parole*, or, as Micheli called the technique he repeatedly claimed to have invented, a tune created *sopra le vocali di più parole*.[13] Here, the text yields:

Lu - do - vi - cus	Rex de - fen - sor	om - ni - um Chris - ti - a - no - rum
ut sol mi ut	re re re sol	sol mi ut mi mi fa sol ut
[hard hexachord]	[natural hex.]	[hard hexachord]

The reason for the mutation to the natural hexachord will become clear shortly.

Micheli's print surely represents the earliest source of the canon, but C. P. E. Bach or the person responsible for the model from which he copied almost certainly did not know the composition directly from it. This is because Bach's copy transmits a slightly different version of the canon: the first and third notes are subdivided, a change that suggests strongly an accommodation of a different text. In fact, the canon was much better known with a different text in the

10   The canon does not appear, however, in the auction catalogues of Grell's estate (Berlin: Liepmann-ssohn, 1887). My thanks to Peter Wollny for checking this for me.
11   See Charles Atkinson, "Micheli, Romano," *New Grove*.
12   I am grateful to Howard Smither for the loan of microfilms of sources of Micheli's music, and to Charles Atkinson for pointing me to them.
13   On this claim and its reception see C. Atkinson, *New Grove* and Claude V. Palisca, "Marco Scacchi's defense of modern music (1649)," in *Words and music: the scholar's view*, ed. Laurence Berman (Cambridge, Mass., 1972), 189–235.

late seventeenth and eighteenth centuries from its appearance on the frontispiece of Athanasius Kircher's *Musurgia universalis* (Rome, 1650).[14] In this
symbolic engraving, the canon carries the rubric "Canon Angelicus" and is
fitted with the text "Sanctus, sanctus, sanctus." Bach's copy transmits this
musical version of the canon, though without the "Sanctus" text or any other.

A brief aside about this illustration: much has been written about the
symbolism of Kircher's frontispiece, and about the role of the canon in that
symbolism. It must be stressed that the theological and symbolic significance of
the canon was not apparently part of the musical composition's original design.
The use of nine choirs, nine repetitions of the text, nine breves in the canon,
and the inevitably pervasive *trias harmonica perfecta* – the major triad – may
well be symbolically appropriate in the mouths of angels on the frontispiece
engraving. But all of these features derive from the original text in honor of the
King of France: from its length and from the particular vowels in its text. This
is not to say that these features might not carry symbolic value in the context of
the illustration, but their symbolism was not part of the original conception of
the piece.[15] This might well make us cautious about over-interpreting the
canon even in its new context of Kircher's illustration. At the least, we should
be careful to attribute any putative musical symbolism to the designer or
executor of the engraving and not to the composer.

In the body of *Musurgia universalis*, Kircher discusses the canon and clearly
attributes it to Micheli.[16] It thus seems unlikely that Bach or the copyist of his
model knew Kircher's text directly, given the patently false attribution to Selle
in the manuscript. Another source that can be ruled out is the abridged
German translation of *Musurgia universalis* by Andrea Hirsch (Schwäbisch-
Hall, 1662), which mentions the canon but does not reproduce the music.

The canon was apparently widely known in German musical circles, at least
in the early eighteenth century. Johann Heinrich Buttstedt cites the canon and
its appearance on Kircher's frontispiece in his discussion of the *stylus canonicus*
in *Ut, mi, sol, re, fa, la* (Erfurt, 1716), a copy of which C. P. E. Bach owned.[17]
The entry for Micheli in the *Kurtzgefaßtes musicalisches Lexicon* (2nd edn.
Chemnitz, 1749) mentions the piece, citing Kircher's authority. Kircher was,

14 Reproduced in George J. Buelow, "Kircher, Athanasius," *New Grove*.
15 On the canon and its putative symbolism, see Ulf Schurlau, *Athanasius Kircher (1601–1680) als
    Musikschriftsteller*, (Marburg, 1969), 112f; Rolf Damann, *Der Musikbegriff im deutschen Barock*, 2nd
    edn. (Cologne, 1984), 407; Walther Krüger, "Ein neunchöriger Sanctus-Kanon," *Musik und Kirche* 25
    (1955): 180–3; E. Lowinsky, "Ockeghem's canon for thirty-six voices: an essay in musical
    iconography," in *Essays in musicology in honor of Dragan Plamanac* (Pittsburgh, 1969), 155–80.
16 Pp. 583–4.
17 See Ulrich Leisinger, "Die 'Bachsche Auction' von 1789," *BJ* 77 (1991): 121.

to all evidence, apparently principally responsible for the canon's circulation in the eighteenth century.

Kircher was also partly responsible for the canon's mention in the second part of Friedrich Wilhelm Marpurg's *Abhandlung von der Fuge* (Berlin, 1754) in the section on canons.[18] Marpurg cites the "Sanctus" text of the original, credits and summarizes Kircher's resolution of the canon, and refers to the canon's composer as "Michael Romanus." This last detail confirms Marpurg's reliance on Kircher, because in the Latin text of *Musurgia universalis*, Kircher refers to the composer as "Romanus Michaelius Romanus" – Romano Michaeli, the Roman – which Marpurg interpreted incorrectly as "the Roman, Michael Romanus."

But Marpurg clearly knew not only Kircher's treatise but other sources of the canon as well, because he remarks further that the canon is generally and incorrectly attributed to Selle.[19] One must wonder what those other sources might have been. Marpurg was, of course, in contact with C. P. E. Bach in Berlin, and even reported discussing contrapuntal matters with J. S. Bach himself in Leipzig.[20] Like Johann Mattheson and Lorenz Mizler, he published examples of J. S. Bach's counterpoint, including three of his canons in the same section of the Abhandlung in which he discusses Micheli's 36-voice work.[21] It would thus not be at all surprising if the "Selle" canon sources he knew were from the Bach circle; perhaps he even saw C. P. E. Bach's copy or its model. The juxtaposition of J. S. Bach's and Micheli's canons in Marpurg's treatise is probably accidental and not indicative of transmission, but is symbolic, at least, of the possibility that Marpurg knew Micheli's canon from the Bach circle.

In sum, it is not clear by exactly what route of transmission C. P. E. Bach acquired Micheli's canon. Kircher's treatise, which transmits the version that fits the "Sanctus" text was at least an indirect source. Further, the canon's rubric in Bach's copy is close to that in Kircher's treatise, especially the large heading "C A N O N" with extra space between letters. The most important difference between Kircher's version and Bach's lies, of course, in the false attribution to Selle in the latter. At some point, apparently, someone copied the canon from *Musurgia universalis* and attributed it to the Hamburg cantor. It is not clear whether this misattribution was a simple error, an incorrect guess, or a deliberate falsehood, but Marpurg's remark implies that it was widespread in the eighteenth century.

18 P. 72f. and Tab. xxxviii.
19 "Dieses ist ein . . . Canon, welcher insgemein, wiewohl mit Unrecht, dem Thomas Sellius, ehemahligen Capellmeister in Hamburg, zugeignet wird." *Abhandlung von der Fuge*, 2: 72.
20 See *Dok* III/701.
21 On the publication of Bach's canons, see NBA VIII/1 KB (Christoph Wolff) and *Dok* III (*passim*).

Example 7.1   R. Micheli, 36-voice canon as copied by C. P. E. Bach, realization of one 4-voice choir

The notation of the canon has been changed as well in C. P. E. Bach's copy by someone who understood both musical matters and Latin. As Micheli's and Kircher's instructions explain, the canon is to be realized starting with the bass part. The tenor begins at the same time, an octave and a fifth higher, in inversion. The alto and soprano follow a whole note later (in Bach's version), an octave higher, in the same relationship to each other. (See Example 7.1.) This constitutes one complete choir; each of the other eight begins a breve later for a total of nine choirs and thirty-six voices. Unlike Micheli and Kircher, who give the bass voice and instructions for realizing the canon from it, Bach presents the inverted form (soprano) and bass parts on the same staff, the latter reading upside down, with sigla indicating roughly the entrance of the other thirty-four voices. This notation is less explicit, in that it lacks instructions for the required inversions, and emphasizes the canonic artifice of the composition.

This artifice is pretty slim in reality. The canon consists essentially of a G major triad in changing positions, with only a passing tone in the last measure of the subject (The restriction to G major chord tones explains the mutation in the middle of the solmization of the subject.) Proper partwriting, such as it is, is achieved by ensuring that there is no identical melodic motion on beats that will line up among the eighteen like-moving voices, which imitate every whole note. This is why there is syncopation at various levels in the second half of the tune: some of the melodic intervals are repeated in the course of the subject, but they are made to occur at different places in the measure so that they will never line up in the realization. This is also why there are rests in the subject;

Example 7.2   J. S. Bach, *Canon trias harmonica* BWV 1072

they are a standard dodge for avoiding parallel perfect intervals when the canon is realized.

Micheli's piece is of the type that came to be known as a *canon trias harmonica*, described by Marpurg, who illustrates it with a canon by Andreas Werckmeister and one by J. S. Bach (BWV 1072). Of the latter, Marpurg remarks that "J. S. Bach, the composer, titled this canon *Trias Harmonica*, the triad, because no other harmony is contained in it."[22] Marpurg does not print BWV 1072 in puzzle form – only in a realization – but it is clear that this canon is similar in construction to Micheli's: a musical phrase is answered at pitch every two beats, as well as in inversion, here one beat later and a fifth above. (See Example 7.2.)

We can glean more from C. P. E. Bach's manuscript itself. According to a preliminary chronology of Carl Philipp Emanuel's handwriting developed by Pamela Fox, the right-opening bass clef found throughout the realization

22   "J. S. Bach als Verfasser hat diesen Canon die Trias Harmonica, den harmonischen Dreyklang betitelt, weil keine andere Harmonie als diese enthalten ist." *Abhandlung von der Fuge*, 2: 97f.; *Dok* III/655. On BWV 1072 and the Werckmeister canon, see NBA VIII/1 KB, 30f.

is not found after 1749.[23] The manuscript's overall appearance probably rules out the early 1740s or earlier, and so the best estimate of the manuscript's preparation puts it in the mid- to late 1740s – within J. S. Bach's lifetime.

Our control over the paper C. P. E. Bach used is not so strong, but the paper of the canon apparently does not appear among his other autograph materials.[24] Merely knowing that this is a unique paper doesn't help much, except that it may be identifiable. The watermark in the paper is almost certainly the coat of arms of Schönburg; the uncertainty comes because the canon is written on a sheet of so-called *Doppelpapier*, made by pressing together two sheets of paper still wet as they were pulled from the mold. Such paper is difficult to identify because light does not pass through it very well, and because there are usually two superimposed watermarks. Within the limitations presented by this difficulty, we can say that the paper of the canon is similar to – and perhaps identical with – one used by J. S. Bach in Leipzig, apparently from the 1720s to the 1740s.[25] The nature of the composition, the secure date of C. P. E. Bach's copy in the 1740s (within Johann Sebastian's lifetime), and the suggestive paper evidence make plausible the hypothesis that C. P. E. Bach's acquisition of the canon was connected to his father. One wonders whether the similarities between the 36-voice canon and BWV 1072 are generic or whether they suggest some closer connection.

The 36-voice canon is a composition we would probably be quicker to associate with J. S. Bach's interests than Carl Philipp Emanuel's. In fact, the younger musician's interest in the piece is a little hard to fathom; according to Charles Burney, he was positively disdainful of canons:

"[W]hen our conversation turned upon *learned music*, he spoke irreverently of canons, which, he said, were dry and despicable pieces of pedantry, that anyone might compose, who would sacrifice his time to them; but it was ever a certain proof to him, of a total want of genius, in any one that was fond of such wretched studies, and unmeaning productions."[26]

Bach made this comment some twenty-five years after he copied the 36-voice canon, so his views may well have changed in the interim. Perhaps more importantly, one suspects that the kind of piece of which he speaks so disparagingly is very different from the Micheli/Selle canon he copied. C. P. E.

23 "Toward a comprehensive C. P. E. Bach chronology: *Schriftchronologie* and the issue of Bach's 'late hand,'" American Musicological Society Annual Meeting, Montréal, November, 1993. Professor Fox kindly gave me the benefit of her expert opinion on the canon manuscript in personal communication. The upside down clef in the canonic notation of the work is clearly exceptional.
24 At least none of the C. P. E. Bach scholars I have asked knows of it.
25 NBA ix/1, *WZ* [watermark] 72.
26 Charles Burney, *The present state of music in Germany, the Netherlands, and United Provinces* (London, 1775), ed. Percy A. Scholes, *Dr. Burney's musical tours in Europe*, vol. 2, *An eighteenth-century musical tour in Central Europe and the Netherlands* (London, 1959), 212.

Bach probably had in mind the trifling canons – sometimes on insipid aphoristic texts – produced in volume at the time. The 36-voice canon presumably represented something more substantial, both musically and historically. We should note that it merited an entry in C. P. E. Bach's estate catalogue. If he was indeed responsible for the compilation of the catalogue, the listing of the canon suggests that the work held the status of a "piece" for him and was not considered merely a "despicable piece of pedantry." One wonders, too, whether Emanuel Bach associated the canon with his father, and preserved and listed the work partly for that reason.

The estate catalogue listing is wrong, of course, in one important respect: the work is not by Thomas Selle. Selle (1599–1663) was educated in Leipzig at the University and possibly at the Thomasschule, and became cantor at the Johanneum in Hamburg, as C. P. E. Bach's inscription indicates. This is a post he took up in 1641, so the description of him as its occupant in 1651, the year cited in the canon manuscript, is at least plausible. The origin of this date and the attribution is obscure, although it seems more likely than not that C. P. E. Bach's source included it. The date is one year after the appearance of Kircher's treatise – the ultimate source of C. P. E. Bach's version – but how that might relate to the canon's transmission is far from clear. Perhaps Selle did have a role in the canon's transmission, entering the canon in an autograph album and ultimately ending up with the attribution of the composition.

All this might be just academic except that the attribution may well be significant even though it is wrong. The canon is not by Selle, but it was transmitted as his; C. P. E. Bach thought Selle was its composer, and so, presumably, did J. S. Bach. (Recall, too, that Marpurg thought it necessary to correct a general misattribution of the work.) Selle himself was probably not a subject of special interest, but he came from a circle that must surely have interested J. S. Bach and perhaps Carl Philipp Emanuel as well. As a musician in Hamburg, Selle represents a link – if an indirect one – to Johann Adam Reinken and Johann Theile. Together with Dieterich Buxtehude, they were not only among the most important composers of their time, but represent the most important German theoretical circle of the seventeenth century. That they were cultivators of the contrapuntal art is well illustrated in Theile's counterpoint treatise, the *Musicalisches Kunstbuch*.[27] Canons were of particular interest to them; Theile included many in the *Kunstbuch*, Selle's portrait includes one, and an elaborate canon ornaments the group portrait of Buxtehude, Reinken, and Theile.[28]

27 Ed. Carl Dahlhaus, Denkmäler norddeutscher Musik 1 (Cassel, 1965).
28 On the group portrait see Christoph Wolff, "Das Hamburger Buxtehude-Bild: Ein Beitrag zur

J. S. Bach had strong musical connections to at least two of these men: he had met both Buxtehude and Reinken, and had spent a good deal of time with the former. Bach's cousin Johann Gottfried Walther copied Theile's *Musicalisches Kunstbuch*, long considered an influence on Bach's *Art of Fugue*, and Bach is likely to have known it – and perhaps other Hamburg theoretical materials – through Walther.[29] If the 36-voice canon indeed passed through the hands of J. S. Bach attributed to Thomas Selle, it might further document his contact with both the theoretical and practical sides of the Hamburg school. There is also some evidence that the 36-voice canon was known in Dresden after Bach's time, and it is possible that he came to know it through Dresden connections.[30]

Wherever he may have encountered this piece, J. S. Bach's interest in canons needs hardly be stressed. We have a number of short canons in Bach's hand, of course, including several from autograph album entries. But canons figure prominently in larger works, too: in the *Goldberg Variations* (published *c.* 1741), both in the variations themselves and in the fourteen canons on the theme's bass Bach entered in his own copy of the printed edition; in the *Canonic Variations on "Vom Himmel hoch"* (published *c.* 1746–7); and a set of canons that form part of the *Musical Offering* (published 1747). The later revisions of the *Art of Fugue*, with their increased emphasis on canons, date from the late 1740s. Finally, there is the triple canon BWV 1076 Bach had printed in conjunction with his induction into Mizler's Corresponding Society of Musical Sciences and that appears in the famous Haussmann portrait, painted in 1746 and copied in 1748. (The inclusion of the canon in the portrait is important, because it is a clear link to the depiction of learned musicians of the previous centuries. In contrast, it is difficult to imagine the mature Handel or Scarlatti arranging for the inclusion of a canon in a portrait.)

These examples of canon in Bach's composition are linked, of course, by their origin in the 1740s, the last decade of his life. Bach's interest in counterpoint – especially abstract contrapuntal works – in this period has been recognized for some time. It may well be no accident, then, that the evidence of the 36-voice canon points to a family member's contact with it in the 1740s. And though the attribution to Thomas Selle is incorrect, the work and it supposed composer point to a part of the musical past that must particularly have interested the musicians of the Bach family.

musikalischen Ikonographie und zum Umkreis von Johann Adam Reinken," in *800 Jahre Musik in Lübeck*, ed. A. Graßmann and W. Neugebauer (Lübeck, 1982), 64–79. A portrait of Selle decorated with a canon is reproduced in his biographical article in *New Grove*.

29 See *Johann Gottfried Walther. Briefe*, ed. Klaus Beckmann and Hans-Joachim Schulze (Leipzig, 1987), *passim*.

30 See n. 5.

Chapter eight

Some questions of performance in J. S. Bach's *Trauerode*

JOSHUA RIFKIN

I

We know more about the history of Bach's *Trauerode* BWV 198 than about any other composition of his. We know who commissioned it, when, and why; we know who wrote the text; we know when Bach started work on the music and when he finished; we know just where and under what conditions the first – and, in Bach's lifetime, no doubt the only – performance took place; and we even have a description of the performance itself. With all this information, we might think ourselves uniquely well equipped to provide informed answers to the most basic practical questions that confront us in dealing with the piece today: the size and disposition of the performing forces, and the particulars of their deployment from one movement to the next. Yet the *Trauerode* may in fact pose more difficulties in this regard than any comparable work of Bach's.

The roots of this paradox lie both in the origins of the *Trauerode* and in the form in which the piece itself has come down to us. Let us start with the origins. The story – of which I need provide no more than a brief summary here – begins with the death of Christiane Eberhardine, Electress of Saxony and Queen of Poland, on September 5, 1727. The queen's Protestant subjects had venerated her because of her refusal to join her husband, August the Strong, in converting to Catholicism to gain the Polish crown.[1] On September 12, 1727, a

This paper grew out of preparatory research for a performance of the *Trauerode* by the Bach Ensemble at its first Academy for Early Music in Brixen/Bressanone, Italy, on August 8, 1992. I presented an initial version as part of a Round Table on Performance Issues held April 25, 1992 at the Joint Meeting of the American Bach Society and American Schütz Society in New York; my thanks to Robert Marshall for soliciting my participation in the Round Table and for his comments on an early draft. The final version has benefited considerably from criticisms and suggestions offered by David Schulenberg and Michael Marissen.

1   For a handy summary of the larger political and confessional background, see Wolfgang Horn, *Die*

student of noble origin named Hans Carl von Kirchbach approached the University of Leipzig with a request to hold a memorial ceremony in the so-called Paulinerkirche, the university's assembly hall and place of worship.[2] Given the delicate confessional situation – not to mention a general ban on musical performances during the official period of mourning – he did not immediately succeed; only the approval of August the Strong himself, granted at Dresden on October 3, assured that the project would go ahead.[3] By this time, it would appear, Kirchbach had already obtained the text of a funeral ode from the influential literary arbiter Johann Christoph Gottsched and engaged Bach to set it to music – a move that led the university music director, Johann Gottlieb Görner, to protest what he saw as an unwarranted intrusion on his prerogatives. On October 10, Kirchbach replied that he could no longer retract the commission as Bach had already received his fee for the piece and "had been at work on it for the last eight days."[4] After further wrangling, the parties reached an accommodation, and the ceremony took place as planned on October 17, two days after Bach marked the completion of his score with one of his rare dated inscriptions: "Fine SDG Lipsiae aō. 1727. d. 15 Oct: J S Bach." The foremost representatives of Leipzig society all attended, lending quasi-official status to the event. Kirchbach himself delivered the oration between the two halves of Bach's music. The university chronicler Christoph Ernst Sicul described the performance with the following words:

Following preludes on the organ, played until everyone took his place, and after the [text of the] mourning ode, written by Magister Johann Christoph Gottsched, member of the Collegium Marianum, was distributed among those present by the beadles, there was heard the mourning music, which Kapellmeister Johann Sebastian Bach had composed for the occasion in the Italian manner, with *Clave di Cembalo*, which Herr Bach himself played, organ, *Violes di Gamba*, lutes, violins, *Fleutes douces* and *Fleutes traverses*, etc., half being heard before and half after the oration of praise and mourning.[5]

Dresdner Hofkirchenmusik 1720–1745: Studien zu ihren Voraussetzungen und ihrem Repertoire (Stuttgart and Cassel, 1987), 15–26.

2 For the documents concerning the *Trauerode*, on which the following account relies, see *Dok* II/225–35. Whether Kirchbach conceived the memorial on his own remains unclear. Perhaps he merely served as the representative of a student syndicate; perhaps, as Werner Neumann has surmised (NBA I/38 KB, 126 n. 14), the poet Gottsched himself lay behind the plan – although in view of the apparent distance, not to say coolness, between them, it does not strike me as likely that Gottsched would have turned to Bach for the music; cf., in this connection, Armin Schneiderheinze, "Über Bachs Umgang mit Gottscheds Versen," *Bericht über die Wissenschaftliche Konferenz zum III. Internationalen Bach-Fest der DDR, Leipzig, 18./19. September 1975*, ed. Werner Felix, Winfried Hoffmann, and Armin Schneiderheinze (Leipzig, 1977), 91–8.

3 On the mourning period, which lasted from September 7, 1727 until January 6, 1728, see Philipp Spitta, *Johann Sebastian Bach*, 2 vols. (Leipzig, 1873–80), 2: 789, as well as n. 114, below.

4 *Dok* II/226: "habe seit 8. Tagen dran componiret."

5 *Dok* II/232; translation adapted from *BR*, 113.

Gottsched's ode, a poem in nine strophes of eight lines each, survives in several printed versions, including a copy of what looks like the leaflet distributed at the memorial ceremony.[6] Bach's music, on the other hand, survives in only one source: the autograph score, a working document marked by the hasty script and copious revisions characteristic of its type.[7] While the score obviously tells us more than a little about how Bach meant the *Trauerode* to sound, it leaves many details of his intentions only sketchily rendered. Bach, after all, tended to relegate such compositionally subordinate matters as the precise make-up of his continuo group or refinements of articulation and dynamics to the parts used in performance, and the *Trauerode* clearly formed no exception to this rule. But the parts to the *Trauerode* do not survive.

For many of Bach's works, such a loss, while depriving us of much we could not know otherwise, proves far from crippling. At each place and time in his career, Bach generally displays consistent enough patterns in his performance materials to allow reliable inferences about the type and number of parts contained in a set that no longer exists. Thanks largely to notational evidence, moreover, we can say how many singers or players would have read from each part.[8] In principle, therefore, we might not expect much difficulty reconstructing the forces of the *Trauerode*. In actuality, the attempt runs up against some formidable obstacles.

As even our abbreviated account of its history has made plain, the creation and performance of the *Trauerode* fell outside Bach's normal realm of activities; and as we shall soon discover, some fundamental aspects of its music have no real parallel elsewhere in his output. Accordingly, inferences from Bach's "usual practices" will not necessarily provide much help in filling the gaps left by the loss of the parts. Neither, unfortunately, does Sicul. Much as we may appreciate

6 For a conspectus of the textual sources, see NBA I/38 KB, 120–3; for facsimiles of the two most important items, see *Sämtliche von Johann Sebastian Bach vertonte Texte*, ed. Werner Neumann (Leipzig, 1974), 366–7 and 396–7.

7 For a description, see NBA I/38 KB, 98–119. Gustav Adolf Theill, *Die Markuspassion von Joh. Seb. Bach (BWV 247): Entstehung – Vergessen – Wiederentdeckung – Rekonstruktion*, 2nd edn. (Steinfeld, 1981), 95–134, reproduces the entire manuscript in greatly reduced form. For more legible reproductions of individual pages, see Alfred Dürr, *Johann Sebastian Bach: Seine Handschrift – Abbild seines Schaffens* (Wiesbaden, 1984), Plates 35–7; NBA I/38, x, and IX/2, 124–7; and the additional items cited in BC IV, 1562. I might take this occasion to indicate two small corrections to the score of the *Trauerode* in NBA I/38, 181–254: in No. 1, m. 2, Flute I should have a slur over the fifth and sixth notes (my thanks to Michael Willens for pointing this out); and in No. 8, m. 45, the text should read "Denkbild," not "Dreckbild" (cf. Schneiderheinze, "Über Bachs Umgang mit Gottscheds Versen," 95 and 98 n. 22).

8 For an overview of this evidence as it pertains to the vocal forces, see Joshua Rifkin, "Bach's chorus: a preliminary report," *The Musical Times* 123 (1982): 747–54, rev. German version as "Bachs Chor – ein vorläufiger Bericht," *Basler Jahrbuch für historische Musikpraxis* 9 (1985): 141–55. For some evidence concerning violin parts, see "The violins in Bach's St. John Passion," *Critica musica: essays in honor of Paul Brainard*, ed. John Knowles (forthcoming).

a touch like the picture of Bach at the harpsichord, we do not learn how many singers and instrumentalists joined him in the performance, nor which – if any – of the various musical organizations active in Leipzig they belonged to. In one detail, moreover, Sicul's description even seems to run into direct conflict with the autograph. So if we hope to reach any truly useful conclusions about the *Trauerode*, we shall have to dig more broadly – and more intensively.

II

In theory at least, Bach would have had a fair range of options for assembling his forces. The possibilities begin with the mix of schoolboys, students, and civic musicians who regularly sang and played his sacred music in Leipzig's two principal churches, St. Nicholas's and St. Thomas's.[9] As Reinhard Szeskus has recently discovered, Bach and his musicians took part in morning services at the Paulinerkirche every year on the feasts of Christmas, Easter, Pentecost, and Reformation, no doubt repeating the cantata they had just performed in St. Thomas's or St. Nicholas's.[10] It takes little effort, therefore, to see him bringing the same body of singers and players to the Paulinerkirche on this occasion as well – all the more so, perhaps, as the observance began with a procession from St. Nicholas's.[11]

On the other hand, common sense, while hardly a foolproof guide, suggests that an event instigated within the university would have drawn first and foremost on the considerable musical resources of the student community. Görner maintained a body of student musicians for academic ceremonies and for devotional services on a number of Sundays and feast days; these same musicians very likely formed the Collegium musicum that he led on the premises of the wine merchant Johann Schellhafer.[12] At first sight, admittedly,

---

9   For student involvement in Bach's church performances, see particularly Hans-Joachim Schulze, "Studenten als Bachs Helfer bei der Leipziger Kirchenmusik," *BJ* 70 (1984): 45–52.

10 See Reinhard Szeskus, "Bach und die Leipziger Universitätsmusik," *Alte Musik als ästhetische Gegenwart: Kongreßbericht Stuttgart 1985*, 2 vols., ed. Dietrich Berke and Dorothee Hanemann (Cassel 1987), 2: 405–12, as well as Werner Neumann's prescient remarks in NBA I/38 KB, 129.

11 See the descriptions in *Dok* II/233.

12 The only extended discussion of music at the university during Görner's period remains that of Arnold Schering, *Musikgeschichte Leipzigs*, vol. 3, *J. S. Bach und das Musikleben Leipzigs im 18. Jahrhundert* (Leipzig, 1941), 103–30; on Görner and sacred music, see also *Die Musikforschung* 21 (1968): 540, and Klaus Häfner, "Eine Kantatendichtung Picanders und ihr Komponist," *Die Musikforschung* 46 (1993): 176–80. According to Schering, *Musikgeschichte Leipzigs*, 3: 103, performances of cantatas under the university music director took place on feast days other than those covered by Bach and on Sundays during the New Year's, Easter, and Michaelmas fairs; this corresponds closely to the practice of the Neue Kirche as reconstructed by Andreas Glöckner, "Die Musikpflege an der Leipziger Neukirche zur Zeit Johann Sebastian Bachs," *Beiträge zur Bach-Forschung* 8 (1990): 70–2 and 131–2. On Görner's Collegium, see Schering, *Musikgeschichte Leipzigs*, 3: 131–9 (especially 136–9), and Werner Neumann,

we might think it unlikely for Görner to have turned over his ensemble to a rival invading his terrain; and Kirchbach, having bypassed Görner in commissioning the ode, could well have preferred either to recruit the performers himself or to make arrangements for Bach to bring singers and players of his own. Still, the contending parties did come to an accommodation. As both Alfred Dürr and Walter Emery have stressed, moreover, whatever rivalry existed between Bach and Görner would not appear to have extended to the personal level: Görner worked steadily under Bach as organist first at St. Nicholas's, then St. Thomas's; and after Bach's death, Anna Magdalena named him guardian of their under-aged children.[13]

Bach could also have had recourse to a different group of students, either an ad hoc assemblage or the Collegium musicum led by Georg Balthasar Schott and associated with the Neue Kirche and Zimmermann's Coffee House – the same Collegium whose secular activities Bach himself would take over some eighteen months later.[14] Student associations had, to all appearances, already enlisted Bach's services on previous occasions. The years 1725 and 1726, for example, saw the production of three cantatas – "Schwingt freudig euch empor" BWV 36c, "Zerreißet, zersprenget, zertrümmert die Gruft" BWV 205, and "Vereinigte Zwietracht der wechselnden Saiten" BWV 207 – honoring teachers at the university; and student enterprise lay behind the performance of the cantata "Entfernet euch, ihr heitern Sterne" BWV Anh. 9 for the birthday of the elector in May, 1727.[15] While we do not know for sure who actually sang and played these works, it seems obvious that we should look first to the

"Das 'Bachische Collegium Musicum,'" *BJ* 47 (1960): 13–22. While I have no proof for the identity of the musicians at Schellhafer's with those at the Paulinerkirche, the relationship between Leipzig's other Collegium musicum and the Neue Kirche (see n. 14, below) certainly points in this direction, as does the proximity between the date of Görner's appointment as university music director – April 3, 1723 (see *Dok* II/166) – and the first word of his Collegium, which we get from a Leipzig guidebook of the same year (see Spitta, *Bach*, 2: 33 and 768). See also the reference in Neumann, "Das 'Bachische Collegium Musicum,'" 13, to the performance of a clearly secular cantata in the university church.

13 Cf. the articles on Görner by Alfred Dürr and Walter Emery in, respectively, *MGG* and *New Grove*.

14 For general information on the Collegium, see the works of Schering and Neumann cited in n. 12; for what little we know specifically of its activities under Schott, see Arnold Schering, *Musikgeschichte Leipzigs*, vol. 2, *Von 1650 bis 1723* (Leipzig, 1926), 355, and *Musikgeschichte Leipzigs*, 3: 135 and 139. The newer Bach literature has tended to obscure the relationship, not to say the identity, of the Collegium and the concerted music at the Neue Kirche. But see Spitta, *Bach*, 2: 27–8 (with particular reference to the documents printed ibid., 854, 858, and 866–8); Schering, *Musikgeschichte Leipzigs*, 2: 118–20; Glöckner, "Die Musikpflege an der Leipziger Neukirche," 74; and, for particularly vivid testimony, Gottfried Heinrich Stölzel's recollections of Melchior Hoffmann in Johann Mattheson, *Grundlage einer Ehren-Pforte* (Hamburg, 1740), 117–18.

15 For BWV 205 and 207, see principally NBA I/38 KB, 37 and 75–6; on BWV 36c – whose connection to the university community admittedly rests essentially on inference – see NBA I/39 KB, 34 (Werner Neumann). On BWV Anh. 9, see particularly Hans-Joachim Schulze, "'Entfernet euch, ihr heitern Sterne', BWV Anh. 9. Notizen zum Textdruck und zum Textdichter," *BJ* 71 (1985): 166–8.

students themselves rather than the Thomasschule or the corps of civic musicians.[16] Hints at a specific tie to Schott's Collegium, moreover, come from a number of quarters.[17] Bach stood on sufficiently close terms with Schott to have the latter deputize for him when other obligations took him away from Leipzig – which surely encourages the suspicion of exchanges in the other direction as well.[18] The parts to the Ouverture BWV 1066, copied in the last months of 1724 or shortly afterwards, seem also to bridge their two domains: Carl Gotthelf Gerlach, who wrote most of the set but appears otherwise never to have copied for Bach, succeeded Schott as organist at the Neue Kirche in 1729, while the remaining three scribes – Christian Gottlob Meißner, Johann Christian Köpping, and the so-called Anonymous Ip – all worked for Gerlach after leaving Bach's employ.[19] As Werner Neumann has pointed out, moreover,

16 Even this assumption, though, cannot not go wholly unqualified. Civic musicians did take part in Bach's last two cantatas written to student commission, the *drama per musica* BWV 215 of 1734 and the lost *Abendmusik* BWV Anh. 18 of 1738: the composer's remuneration for BWV Anh. 18 included a special payment for the Stadtpfeifer, while the well-known tale of Gottfried Reiche's death testifies to the involvement of at least one municipal trumpeter in BWV 215; cf. *Dok* I/122 and II/353. In both instances, moreover, the identification of the remaining performers opens up tantalizing ambiguities. Neumann, "Das 'Bachische Collegium Musicum,'" 11 and 17–18, has shown that Bach's Collegium could not have taken part in the performance of BWV Anh. 18; and while Neumann proposes instead the participation of a university "Chorus musicus," Görner's forces at least would scarcely have needed the extra support implied by the payment to the *Stadtpfeifer* (see below). It would thus seem more likely that Bach assembled the requisite singers and players from a variety of sources – very possibly including pupils from the Thomasschule. Much the same might have occurred with BWV 215. Reiche points in the direction of Bach's church ensemble; so, too, does a student named Johann Christoph Hoffmann, who wrote in a letter of application that he had sung in BWV 215 and "assisted in Herr Capellmeister Bach's church music for four years now as a bass" (*Dok* II/356: "bey des HErrn Capell-Meister Bachens Kirchen Music nun mehro 4 jahr, als Bassiste, assistiret") but says nothing about Bach's Collegium Musicum. Perhaps, then, we should not take a reference in a Dresden newspaper to "the student Collegium Musicum" (*Dok* II/353: "das Collegium Musicum Studiosorum aber brachte . . . eine vortreffliche Abend-Music") too restrictively, especially as Bach had to assemble his forces for the performance on unusually short notice; on this last point, cf. NBA I/37 KB, 65–8 (Werner Neumann).

17 Glöckner, "Die Musikpflege an der Leipziger Neukirche," 84–5, has already raised some of the points that I make here, although from a slightly different perspective and not always in precise detail. Christoph Wolff, "Bach's Leipzig chamber music," in *Bach: essays on his life and music* (Cambridge, Mass., 1991), 226, finds "circumstantial evidence" for Bach's involvement with the Collegium before 1729 in "a notable emphasis on large-scale orchestral sinfonias to the cantatas between 1726 and 1729, which probably required the participation of the Collegium Musicum." Apart from the sinfonia BWV 174/1, however, none of the pieces to which Wolff refers used forces in excess of what Bach's cantatas typically require – and even BWV 174/1 exceeds the norm only in its large and unusual assortment of string parts; cf. Joshua Rifkin, "More (and less) on Bach's orchestra," *Performance Practice Review* 4 (1991): 11. The participation of the Collegium musicum in this particular cantata would seem questionable in any event. Bach performed BWV 174 on the second day of Pentecost; and assuming that he had not broken the traditional connection between the Collegium and the performance of figural music at the Neue Kirche, the student musicians would have had to sing and play for the service there. Cf. Glöckner, "Die Musikpflege an der Leipziger Neukirche," 70–2 and 131–2, and n. 14, above.

18 See *Dok* II/383 as well as Andreas Glöckner, "Bemerkungen zu den Leipziger Kantatenaufführungen vom 3. bis 6. Sonntag nach Trinitatis 1725," *BJ* (1992): 73–6; cf. also Kirsten Beißwenger, *Johann Sebastian Bachs Notenbibliothek* (Cassel, 1992), 76 n. 114.

19 For the scribes of BWV 1066, compare NBA VII/1 KB, 20–1 (Heinrich Besseler and Hans Grüß), with,

Bach and Gerlach plainly cut a deal over the leadership of the Collegium, which had traditionally gone to the organist of the Neue Kirche; prior collaborations with the Collegium would do much to explain Bach's interest in this arrangement.[20]

Each of these scenarios regarding the performers of the *Trauerode* has potential implications for our own approach to the piece. If, for example, we imagine Bach using his regular cast of church musicians, we have a fairly reliable guide to the constitution of the ensemble. All but invariably, the performance materials for his Leipzig sacred works included single copies of the voice and wind parts; two copies each of Violin I and Violin II; a single viola part; and three continuo parts in all – two without figures and a figured part transposed a tone lower to accommodate the high pitch of Leipzig's organs.[21]

most conveniently, Hans-Joachim Schulze, *Studien zur Bach-Überlieferung im 18.Jahrhundert* (Leipzig, 1984), 101–2 and 121–3; for Meißner, Köpping, and Anonymous Ip in materials from the Neue Kirche, see Glöckner, "Die Musikpflege an der Leipziger Neukirche," 95, 99, 102–3, 106, 118, and 122–3. On the basis of Köpping's script, Beißwenger, *Johann Sebastian Bachs Notenbibliothek*, 204–7, shows that the parts must have originated after June 4, 1724 but before a copy of a Telemann cantata that all but certainly predates May, 1725. Meißner's contribution enables us to narrow the period still further: the shapes of his natural signs, quarter rests, and upstemmed notes correspond most closely to those in cantata manuscripts written from October, 1724 to February, 1725.

20 On the transfer of the Collegium, see Neumann, "Das 'Bachische Collegium Musicum,'" 11–12, and *Dok* II/261.

21 See, among other sources, Alfred Dürr, *Zur Chronologie der Leipziger Vokalwerke J. S. Bachs,* 2nd edn. (Cassel, 1976), 9, or the handy overview of the original parts to Bach's vocal works in Laurence Dreyfus, *Bach's continuo group: players and practices in his vocal works* (Cambridge, Mass., 1987), 183–207. Without exception, sets that now lack duplicate violin and continuo parts would appear to have lost them through vagaries of transmission. In only two instances, the final versions of BWV 82 and BWV 245, do the materials include more than the usual number of upper strings; on these, see Rifkin, "More (and less)," 10–1. Only two sets as well, those of BWV 23 and for the G minor version of BWV 185, exceed the customary number of continuo parts, and in neither instance does this seem to indicate a larger section than usual. In the case of BWV 185, where the parts used for a performance in the 1740s include two labeled "Violoncello" and one labeled "Violone," the second cello part no doubt took its label from its model and could well have served for bassoon; cf. NBA I/17.1 KB (Yoshitake Kobayashi and Kirsten Beißwenger), 18–23, 34, and 38–9, as well as the following note. The materials from the first performance of BWV 23, in 1723, include three parts labeled "Violoncello" and one initially labeled "Baßon," which Bach subsequently figured and amplified with the inscription "è Cembalo"; see the descriptions in Christoph Wolff, "Bach's audition for the St. Thomas cantorate: the cantata 'Du wahrer Gott und Davids Sohn,'" *Essays*, 132, as well as the discussion in Dreyfus, *Bach's continuo group,* 38–40. Contrary to Wolff, 134, this set, too, remains well within normal tolerances. The second and third cello parts simply reproduce the nomenclature of Bach's autograph master copy; in performance, Bach presumably meant them for violone and bassoon, respectively. With the decision to transpose the entire cantata from C minor to B minor, the copy intended for the bassoon became useless, forcing Bach to have a new part copied for this instrument – this exemplar, too, the scribe first labeled "Violoncello" (cf. Wolff, 131–4, as well as Dreyfus, *Bach's continuo group,* 38 and 247 n. 27). We have no reason to think that the third cello part did not then go unused. On the addition of the harpsichord, see Joshua Rifkin, "The Bach Compendium," *Early Music* 17 (1989): 83. As the example of this cantata reminds us, a number of untransposed continuo parts from Bach's early Leipzig years contain figuring, sometimes as a later addition, but sometimes as part of the original copying process; cf. Dreyfus, *Bach's continuo group,* 32–58 and 209–18. Such figures, however, all but vanish by the time of the *Trauerode* and do not recur in any significant measure until Bach's final decade (the list in Dreyfus, 49, errs in

For the *Trauerode*, therefore, we could reckon with doubling of at least the violins, and a continuo group that included a violone reinforcing the bass line at the sixteen-foot register.[22] The number of singers, too, would presumably have reflected what the parts typically sustained, although we cannot exclude the possibility that Bach would have enlarged his choir with *ripieno* voices, as he sometimes – if by no means always – did when circumstances allowed.[23]

As soon as we step outside the principal churches, however, the picture becomes less clear. Of the dozen or so vocal works that we know Bach to have performed at other locations in or near Leipzig between his arrival there in 1723 and the time he took charge of the Collegium, parts survive for only two, BWV 194 and 207; and these would seem to give us liberty to imagine forces either greater or smaller than the norms just established.[24] The *drama per musica*

including BWV 36b, a secular work; nor does the dating of some figures in one of the cello parts for BWV 23 to the years 1728–31 have a solid basis). See also the discussion in Section V, below.

22   While the great majority of Bach's continuo parts carry only a generic label, instances of more specific nomenclature in such cantatas as BWV 42, 49, 62, 100, and 195 support the assumption that he would have assigned the two untransposed parts to cello and violone, respectively. On the pitch of the violone at Leipzig, see Dreyfus, *Bach's continuo group*, 158–64. Whether a bassoon might have played from one of the untransposed parts, amplifying or displacing the stringed instrument, represents a problem still not adequately resolved, despite the discussions in Konrad Brandt, "Fragen zur Fagottbesetzung in den kirchenmusikalischen Werken Johann Sebastian Bachs," *BJ* 54 (1968): 65–79, and Dreyfus, *Bach's continuo group*, 113–18. Seven works – BWV 18, 23, 110, 194, 215, 241, and 248[I] – have, or had, a separate bassoon part, either partially obbligato or simply doubling the bass line, in addition to two untransposed continuo parts (on BWV 194, see the literature referred to in n. 22, below; on the somewhat complicated reshuffling of parts necessary for the bassoon to play BWV 18 in the Leipzig, see Dreyfus, 248 n. 34; on the number of untransposed continuo parts in BWV 110, cf. NBA I/2 KB, 66–7 [Alfred Dürr]). But other pieces with bassoon show a more ambiguous picture. BWV 52 and – at least in the version of its earliest performances – BWV 42 both lack duplicates for the untransposed continuo (cf., for BWV 42, NBA I/11.1, vi and KB, 70 and 83 [Reinmar Emans]). In BWV 44 and 70, Johann Andreas Kuhnau relabeled one of the two untransposed parts "Bassono" (cf. NBA I/12 KB, 274 [Alfred Dürr], and I/27 KB, 106 [Alfred Dürr], which erroneously credits the new instrumental designation to Bach). Bach himself, finally, assigned one of the two untransposed continuo parts of BWV 97 to "Bassono e Violoncello"; added the words "et Bassono" to a violoncello part in Johann Ludwig Bach's cantata "Ich aber ging für dir über" JLB 16 (for the siglum, cf. Dürr, *Chronologie*, 5); and applied the designation "Violoncello e Bassono" to a part in Wilhelm Friedemann Bach's cantata "Lasset uns ablegen" Fk 80. (See Figure 12.1) Cf. NBA I/34 KB, 84 [Ryuchi Higuchi]; Dreyfus, *Bach's continuo group*, 115; Beißwenger, *Johann Sebastian Bachs Notenbibliothek*, 262; and Peter Wollny, "Studies in the music of Wilhelm Friedemann Bach: sources and style" (Ph.D. diss., Harvard University, 1993), 1:305–6 (Wollny errs, though, in writing that the label "'Violoncello e Bassono' . . . is quite commonly found among Johann Sebastian Bach's performing materials"). All other surviving bassoon parts of Bach's belong either to sets that survive in less than fully complete form or to works that Bach did not perform – or did not perform using bassoon – in Leipzig and thus have no real bearing on the present question; cf. Dreyfus, *Bach's continuo group*, 114–15. In any event, the use of the bassoon in the *Trauerode* would not seem very likely, both on account of the unusually full bass contingent established in at least some movements by the lutes and because of its absence from Sicul's list.

23   Cf. Rifkin, "Bach's chorus," especially 751.

24   Apart from BWV 194, BWV 207, and the *Trauerode*, my list includes BWV 36c (although see n. 15, above), 157, 193a, 204, 205, 216, 249b, Anh. 9, Anh. 20, Anh. 196, and possibly BWV 210a (see n. 86, below). I omit BWV 244a, for Cöthen; BWV 249a, the performance of which presumably took place in Weissenfels with the forces of the court chapel there; and BWV Anh. 15, for which the dating

BWV 207, performed towards the end of 1726, has a larger number of string parts – though not voice parts – than any known sacred composition: three each for the violins and two for the viola.[25] Conversely, "Höchsterwünschtes Freudenfest" BWV 194, as presented for the dedication of the organ at Störmthal in 1723, includes only single parts for the violins and continuo.[26] Extending the chronological net into the 1730s only reinforces the lack of unity. Admittedly, all of the larger secular cantatas for which we have complete or reasonably complete sets of parts – BWV 30a, 36c, 201, 206, 207a, 213, and 215 – conform in essence to the pattern visible in the churches: while the number of surviving bass parts varies, all have the usual four violins, and only BWV 201, with its ingenious eight-voice ensemble, has more than a single copy of any voice part.[27] But more lightly scored pieces like the Coffee Cantata BWV 211, or, in its original state, the solo cantata "O holder Tag, erwünschte Zeit" BWV 210 include only single violin parts and make no apparent provision for the violone.[28] Nor do the exceptions remain confined to secular music: as I have argued elsewhere, the *Missa* in B minor, written for Dresden, would appear to reckon with a lighter string and continuo group than any work performed in Leipzig.[29]

of 1724 suggested by Schering, *Musikgeschichte Leipzigs*, 3: 102 and 123, has no foundation. In her article "Zur Entstehung der Kantate 'Ihr Tore zu Zion' (BWV 193)," *BJ* 77 (1991): 184, and again in NBA I/32.1 KB, 122, Christine Fröde proposes that each of the four violin parts to the gratulatory cantata BWV 193 derived from a separate exemplar; if true, this would have obvious implications for the parts to the lost cantata BWV 193a. But neither the readings Fröde cites nor her supporting arguments strike me as persuasive; indeed, several of the readings – No. 1, mm. 28, 75, and 96; No. 3, mm. 21–3 – strongly indicate a common parent for both copies of each violin.

25 Cf. NBA I/38 KB, 59–69, as well as Rifkin, "More (and less)," 11. The set also contains an exceptional fourth continuo part, which, however, remained incomplete.

26 Cf. NBA I/31 KB, 123 (Frieder Rempp). It would seem fairly clear that the materials used at Störmthal did not have any further violin or continuo parts, as Bach prepared new duplicates for them when he reperformed the cantata at Leipzig in 1724 (cf. *ibid.*, 124); for parallel cases and their implications, see Rifkin, "More (and less)," 8. Given the proximity of Störmthal to Leipzig, we may suspect that Bach presented BWV 194 with members of his regular church ensemble; if so, this could further qualify the implications of that ensemble as usually constituted for the performance of the *Trauerode*.

27 BWV 201 has six voice parts – soprano, alto, two tenors, and two basses – representing the characters of the drama, plus an extra soprano and alto part for the opening and closing numbers; since the basses in these numbers proceed either in unison or in octaves, the resulting texture approximates the standard layout of Bach's orchestra, with its doubled outer parts and more thinly scored middle voices. See NBA I/40 KB, 123–4 (Werner Neumann); the score in NBA I/40, 119–92, obscures this arrangement, as do the incipits in BC IV, 1629–36.

28 On BWV 211, see Rifkin, "More (and less)," 8. We can infer the lack of a violone in the original version of BWV 210 from the fact that Bach added this part in his own hand to a set largely copied from earlier materials by Johann Friedrich Agricola; cf. Yoshitake Kobayashi, "Zur Chronologie der Spätwerke Johann Sebastian Bachs: Kompositions- und Aufführungstätigkeit von 1736 bis 1750," *BJ* 74 (1988): 42, as well as the notes to the recording of BWV 210 on Nonesuch D–79013.

29 See particularly my review of the facsimiles *Johann Sebastian Bach: Messe in h-Moll/Mass in B minor BWV 232* ed. Alfred Dürr, (Cassel, 1983), and *Johann Sebastian Bach: Missa h-Moll BWV 232¹*, ed. Hans-Joachim Schulze (Stuttgart, 1983), *Notes* 44 (1987–8): 796–7.

A glance sideways at Schott and Görner does not significantly clarify matters. We have no parts that we can definitely assign to Schott, either in concerts with the Collegium or for performances at the Neue Kirche.[30] Reports of performances under Schott's predecessor Melchior Hoffmann, who held his post from 1704 until his death in 1715, speak of forty, fifty, even sixty musicians; how literally we should take this remains an open question.[31] Certainly, the few materials surviving from Hoffmann's era – and, indeed, from that of Telemann before him – never go beyond the single voice parts typical of Bach's Leipzig church music; Hoffmann's works, however, sometimes contain duplicate violin parts and very possibly did so as a norm.[32] The more numerous materials from Gerlach's era at the Neue Kirche also hold to the pattern of single voices; but in contrast to Hoffmann's materials – and Bach's – they generally have single violins and never have more than one untransposed continuo part.[33] The preponderance of single voice parts fits neatly with evidence from both early in the century and from the 1730s and 1740s, all of which shows the regular *Singechor* of the church to have consisted of just four members.[34]

30 See Glöckner, "Die Musikpflege an der Leipziger Neukirche," 85.

31 For forty musicians, see Stölzel in Mattheson, *Grundlage einer Ehren-Pforte*, 118; for fifty or sixty, see the report quoted by Glöckner, "Die Musikpflege an der Leipziger Neukirche," 43. The number forty, at least, seems to have a special history of figurative usage; see Joshua Rifkin, "Bach's chorus: some red herrings," *Journal of Musicological Research* 14 (1994): 229 and 233–4.

32 Glöckner, "Die Musikpflege an der Leipziger Neukirche," 47, 53–4, and 56–8, catalogues six original, and two possibly original, sets of parts for works of Hoffmann; the three unquestionably original sets for works with four-voice scoring all have doubled violins. For Telemann's early Leipzig sacred pieces, see *ibid.*, 26–36; none include duplicate string parts.

33 Glöckner has identified and catalogued twenty-seven sets of parts traceable to Gerlach, two of them holdovers from Hoffmann's period, and all but one of them evidently complete or substantially so; see "Die Musikpflege an der Leipziger Neukirche," 97–106, 112–19, 122–5, 128–9, and 131. The untransposed continuo usually bears the label "Violoncello" or "Violone." Vocal *ripieno* parts or otherwise doubled voices appear in only three sets, one of them Telemann's Passion oratorio *Seliges Erwägen* (see *ibid.*, 97–8, 112, and 131); and only four sets – described on 103–4, 106, 112, and 113, respectively – have more than two violin parts in all (the materials to BWV Anh. 21, described on 112–13, do not contain true duplicates but consist of two separate sets). Glöckner thus overstates the case when he writes (*ibid.*, 134) that doublets for the first and second violin parts "are usually, if not always, present"; and since many pieces survive with both score and parts intact, we have no *prima facie* reason for thinking that a significant number of doublets would have got lost. Glöckner also creates a misleading impression in claiming that continuo figures "frequently" occur in both the transposed and untransposed parts of a set (*ibid.*) – a matter of no little interest in light of the discussion in Section V below. Only one untransposed continuo part among Hoffmann's manuscripts contains any figures (*ibid.*, 47); Gerlach's include another, carried over from an earlier generation (*ibid.*, 99–100), as well as two parts marked "Cembalo," one of which contains no figures (*ibid.*, 98–9 and 112).

34 For the *Singechor* earlier in the century, see Stölzel in Mattheson, *Grundlage einer Ehren-Pforte*, 117–18; for the later evidence, see Glöckner, "Die Musikpflege an der Leipziger Neukirche," 136–7 and 156–8. The precise function of the "two persons who help out partly in singing, partly with the music" referred to in 1741 (*ibid.*, 136: "2 Persohnen, die theils beym Singen oder auch bei der Music assistieren") remains unclear; the first section of Bach's *Entwurff einer wohlbestallten Kirchen Music* (Dok I/22) indicates that "Singen" refers to motets and chorales, and "Music" to the performance of concerted works.

We know even less about Görner's forces. Nothing appears to survive from any performance given under his direction. Schering wrote that he had only a handful of students, "among them two falsettists for the soprano and alto parts of the choruses."[35] We need not take this to mean, however, that Görner presented concerted music with a significantly smaller body of singers and players than Bach, Schott, or Gerlach. If, as the reference to the two falsettists suggests, he had four singers in all, this would correspond to the situation at the Neue Kirche – and even, I have argued elsewhere, to the effective practice in the principal churches.[36] Documents show, moreover, that the music heard both in Görner's Collegium and in university ceremonies under his direction included pieces with trumpets and drums, and he clearly used trumpets and drums as well in his dedicatory cantata for the church of Zwenkau, near Leipzig, in 1727.[37] Presumably, then, Görner could call on a performing apparatus more or less equivalent to those elsewhere in Leipzig.[38] Indeed, we get some indirect testimony to this effect from Gerlach. In a memorandum submitted to the town council on January 11, 1736, Gerlach wrote that he had to "look after . . . a music as strongly staffed as is the case in other churches."[39] The "other churches" obviously included the Paulinerkirche – not to mention St. Nicholas's and St. Thomas's.

Andreas Glöckner, "Leipziger Neukirchenmusik 1729–1761," *Beiträge zur Musikwissenschaft* 25 (1983): 109, takes the occasional appearance of vocal *ripieno* parts or eight-voice compositions like the cantata BWV 50 among Gerlach's repertory to mean that performances at the Neue Kirche regularly used more singers than the four attested by Stölzel and the later documents. But the logic does not hold. Obviously, Gerlach would have mustered the necessary forces for these pieces, just as he would have made sure to obtain trumpets and drums for any work that used them. But we can no more assume that singers engaged for particular works requiring more than four voices would have sung in works of more conventional scoring than we can assume that trumpets and drums played in every cantata.

35 Schering, *Musikgeschichte Leipzigs*, 3: 105.
36 See Rifkin, "Bach's chorus." The discrepancy in statutory size between the chorus at the principal churches – eight singers, which Bach hoped to enlarge to twelve – and those of the Neue Kirche and, it would appear, the Paulinerkirche had to do less with the performance of concerted music than with the existence or absence of other duties. Bach's singers had to cover not only four-voice cantatas but also eight-voice motets; the Singechor of the Neue Kirche, by contrast, had no obligations beyond concerted music, as the motets lay in the hands of pupils from the Thomasschule. See the sixth and seventh paragraphs of Bach's *Entwurff* (*Dok* I/22), and the commentary in "Bach's chorus," 750 (more fully in "Bachs Chor," 148–50).
37 For trumpets and drums at Görner's Collegium, see Neumann, "Das 'Bachische Collegium Musicum,'" 16 and 18–19; for the university, see Schering, *Musikgeschichte Leipzigs*, 3: 125–8. On the performance at Zwenkau, for which locals procured the timpani and arranged lodging for the musicians – presumably Görner's own – see Häfner, "Eine Kantatendichtung Picanders," 178–9.
38 Schering's dismissive treatment of Görner's forces may in part reflect an unconscious tendency to downgrade Görner as a supposed rival of Bach; cf. Szeskus, "Bach und die Leipziger Universitätsmusik," 405.
39 Glöckner, "Die Musikpflege an der Leipziger Neukirche," 136 and 155: "ich aber sowohl vor die Orgel, als auch vor eine eben so starke Music, als wie in anderen Kirche geschiehet zu sorgen habe . . ."

Disorienting as all these variations from one situation to another may at first appear, Gerlach's observation reminds us that they in fact move within very narrow parameters. With only a single exception, the number of parts per violin line in Leipzig during the period under discussion amounted to one or two, and the same goes for continuo parts other than the organ. All other instrumental parts come singly, and so, overwhelmingly, do the voices. In other words, even with the most audacious stretch of the imagination we can hardly envisage Bach's forces for the *Trauerode* as either very much larger or very much smaller than those with which he presented his normal run of church cantatas. Still, as those with practical experience will know, even a minimal difference in the number of instruments or voices can have a considerable impact on the character of a performance. So the inability of the musical sources to deliver reliably consistent answers remains frustrating.

III

If the musical sources and documentary evidence fail to provide unambiguous answers, we might well think to seek a solution in the music itself. Yet here, too, we encounter anything but a clear-cut situation.

As I have already intimated, the *Trauerode* owes its singular position in Bach's output not merely to the circumstances of its creation but to musical characteristics as well. No description of the piece gets very far without calling attention to the lutes and gambas – two of each – that lend such a distinctive tone to its instrumentation. In no other work does Bach employ two lutes. Indeed, apart from the *Trauerode* and his solo music for the instrument, he seems never to have used the lute at all beyond three obbligato numbers in the earliest versions of his two extant Passions – the arioso "Betrachte, meine Seel" in the *St. John*, the recitative "Ja, freilich will in uns das Fleisch und Blut" and the aria "Komm, süßes Kreuz" in the *St. Matthew*. The gamba, too, appears rarely, and almost exclusively as an obbligato instrument in solo numbers.[40] Two gambas play only in the Sixth Brandenburg Concerto and the early funeral cantata *Actus tragicus* BWV 106; in this last work, moreover, they function as part of a "soft" ensemble made up solely of themselves and two recorders, whereas the *Trauerode* sets them among Bach's usual Leipzig band of flutes, oboes, and the full range of strings.

No one, to the best of my knowledge, has ever really explained why Bach

40   On Bach and the gamba in the context of ensembles, see most recently Dreyfus, *Bach's continuo group*, 166–9, but as modified in Rifkin, "The violins in Bach's St. John Passion," n. 7, and n. 46, below.

has the lutes and gambas in the *Trauerode*. The oft-mentioned topoi of royalty and death probably have something to do with it, and so might the gender of the deceased; we might also ask if the lutes at least do not in some way represent the student community as well.[41] At the same time, the lutes could perhaps document the survival of an older Leipzig performance custom. Earlier in the century, Kuhnau appears regularly to have employed a pair of *colochons* – "lutes of a sort, but which penetrate and are necessary in all present-day ensembles" – in his sacred works; he refers to them in memorandums of 1704, 1709, and 1717.[42] In the principal churches at least, the use of the *colochons* seems to have died out by the time Bach got to Leipzig.[43] But conceivably it lived on in the form of two lutes at the University Church. If so, of course, this would strengthen the possibility that Bach used Görner's musicians for the *Trauerode*.

A more important question about the lutes and gambas, however, concerns their musical function. Should we think of them as part of an idiosyncratically expanded ensemble or as a more or less self-contained adjunct to Bach's customary instrumental group? Under the first assumption, the soft tone of the gambas in particular might encourage us to conceive of the overall forces in

41   The rich tradition of lute-playing in Leipzig appears to have had a special point of focus in the university; cf. the chapter on lute music in Arnold Schering, *Musikgeschichte Leipzigs*, 2:413–23, as well as Hans-Joachim Schulze, "Wer intavolierte Johann Sebastian Bachs Lautenkompositionen?" *Die Musikforschung* 19 (1966): 36–9, and *Dok* I/67. Schulze, "Bachs Lautenkompositionen," 38, writes that Johann Christian Weyrauch, a former university student who intabulated the lute works BWV 997 and 1000 (*ibid.*, 36), would "surely" have played one of the parts in the *Trauerode*; for more on this question, see n. 57, below. Konrad Junghänel, "Bach und die zeitgenössische Lautenpraxis," *Johann Sebastian Bachs Spätwerk und dessen Umfeld: Perspektiven und Probleme. Bericht über das Wissenschaftliche Symposium anläßlich des 61. Bachfestes der Neuen Bachgesellschaft Duisburg, 28.–30. Mai 1986*, ed. Christoph Wolff (Cassel, 1988), 97, suggests that Johann Ludwig Krebs might have served as Weyrauch's partner; but while Krebs later enjoyed something of a reputation for his lute-playing, at the time of the performance he had barely passed his fourteenth birthday (cf. *Dok* I/71). We might better think of Jacob Schuster, the apparent dedicatee of the suite BWV 995; see the discussion of Schuster in Section IV and particularly n. 57, below.

42   For the quoted passage, from 1704, see Spitta, *Bach*, 2: 854: "die so genannten Colochonen (eine Art von Lauten, die aber penetriren, und bey allen itzigen Musiquen nötig sind)"; a slightly different translation appears in Dreyfus, *Bach's continuo group*, 170. In 1709, Kuhnau spoke of needing "at least one good *colochon* both for use in the school and, particularly, for the church music, in which there are usually at least two of them" (Spitta, 2: 856: "Doch wäre . . . zum wenigsten ein guter Colocion so wohl zum Gebrauche in der Schule, alß sonderlich bei der Kirchen Music, dabey auffs wenigste ihrer zwey zu seyn pflegen, von nöthen"; for a further reference in the same document, see *ibid.*, 2: 859). On the colochon itself – and its difference from the *colascione* – see Donald Gill, "Mandores and Colachons," *The Galpin Society Journal* 34 (1981): 130–41; *idem*, "Colascione," *New Grove*; Rudolf Lück, "Zur Geschichte der Baßlauten-Instrumente Colascione und Calichon," *Deutsches Jahrbuch der Musikwissenschaft* 1960, 69–75; and Dreyfus, *Bach's continuo group*, 170–1 and 256–7.

43   See Dreyfus, *Bach's continuo group*, 170–2. Not only Bach's performing materials, but those of Christoph Graupner's test pieces for the St. Thomas cantorate show no trace of the *colochon*; cf. Wolff, "Bach's audition," 133.

more intimate terms, specifically with single strings and without *ripieno* voices. This interpretation would seem especially suited to several places in the opening chorus – mm. 11, 16, 21, 43, 48, and 53 – where Bach tosses a single figure from flutes to oboes to strings to gambas or back again while the singers declaim the words "Laß, Fürstin" or "und sieh." Given, moreover, the amplification of the bass line by the lutes, we may wonder if Bach might not have dispensed with the violone – a question raised as well by the beginning of the last movement in Part I, whose rushing eighth-notes under the upper voices in mm. 4–9 have no counterpart in the fugal exposition of any Leipzig chorus but recall the *senza violone* opening to the last movement of the Fourth Brandenburg Concerto.[44]

As everyone knows, however, the relationship between musical structure and performing forces in Bach never follows simple and predictable lines; and we could make a case for reading the role of the lutes and gambas differently. We might note, first, that the two pairs of instruments always appear together: no movement has gambas without lutes, or lutes without gambas. We might also note that the gambas in particular assume an obbligato function mostly in places of reduced scoring, as with the aria that begins Part II or in two passages – mm. 37–42 of the opening chorus and mm. 29–46 of the last chorus in Part I – that briefly resurrect the flute-and-gamba combination of *Actus tragicus*. If we consider, too, how Bach reserves the crucial aria "Wie starb die Heldin so vergnügt" for gambas and lutes alone, we may surmise that he viewed these instruments as an essentially autonomous entity, whatever his occasional moves at integrating them into the larger context.[45] But if, as this interpretation suggests, the gambas and lutes function more outside the ensemble than within it, then they no longer have any implications for the constitution of that ensemble. In other words, the music does not ultimately pose any obstacle to our imagining forces more akin to Bach's Leipzig ecclesiastical norm – should we wish to do so.

---

44   For a point of contrast, readers may turn to the first chorus of "Sehet, welch eine Liebe hat uns der Vater erzeiget" BWV 64; although extensive passages of running eighth-notes occur in this movement as well, they all appear after the exposition and in unison with the lowest voice. The example of the Fourth Brandenburg Concerto could appear to suggest a slightly different approach to the chorus in the *Trauerode*: not dispensing with the violone entirely but keeping it silent until the entry of the bass voice in m. 13. Leipzig continuo parts, however, offer little evidence for this sort of differentiation.

45   On the scoring of "Wie starb die Heldin so vergnügt," see Sections IV and V below. Bach, of course, not infrequently placed single movements of "special" instrumentation in works otherwise written for more conventional forces; to remain within an academic setting, I might cite as an example the aria "Frische Schatten, meine Freude" in the gratulatory cantata BWV 205. See also the discussion of the cantatas BWV 27 and 154 in Section V below.

IV

Beyond the issue of their significance in the larger scheme of the *Trauerode*, the gambas and, particularly, the lutes pose some more narrowly focused questions as well. These begin with the simplest question of all: in just what movements do they play? Bach explicitly calls for lutes and viols in Nos. 1, 4, 5, 7, 8, and 10 – the opening and closing choruses, the chorus that ends Part I, and three solo numbers. But might they not also have joined the continuo line in the remainder? Without the parts, of course, we cannot know for sure. Nevertheless, I suspect that they remain silent elsewhere. The few gamba parts in Bach's Leipzig performance materials rarely include even minimal continuo participation beyond the obbligato numbers they contain; and while we have no original lute parts whatever, the autograph score of the *Trauerode* proves highly suggestive.[46] Even though the lutes double the continuo note-for-note in the opening and closing choruses, Bach gives them a fully written-out system of their own in both movements. Given this almost supererogatory exactitude, we may surely take him at his word and not use the lutes – and the gambas – where he does not specifically ask for them.

The gambas pose no further problems. Not so, however, the lutes; for even after we identify the numbers in which they played, we face more than a little uncertainty about what they actually did. The uncertainty, in fact, begins with the nature of the instruments themselves. BWV 198 would seem to call for a lute that did not exist. The lute of Bach's day typically had six main courses tuned in a descending D minor triad, f'–d'–a–f–d–A, plus a number of further courses – usually five or seven – proceeding in a scale down from G.[47] Lutenists appear to have avoided stopping more than the first of these lower courses with any frequency, as this entailed awkward stretches of the left hand; indeed, on a thirteen-course lute, the lowest two courses would seem not even to have allowed the possibility of stopping, as they did not lie on the fingerboard. The tuning of the bass courses, therefore, would often vary with the tonality of the music played. As the lute parts of the *Trauerode* extend down to BB – a note reached in m. 62 of No. 5 – we might imagine them performed on a

---

46   For Bach's gamba parts, see Dreyfus, *Bach's continuo group*, 166–9; to the examples described there, readers should add the gamba part for Chorus I in the *St. Matthew Passion*, which contains only the recitative "Ja, freilich will in uns das Fleisch und Blut" and the aria "Komm, süßes Kreuz" but no continuo movements at all (see the facsimile in NBA II/5, xiii, and the description *ibid.*, KB 52 [Alfred Dürr]). On the question of whether lutes might have played from parts labeled merely "Continuo," see chiefly Dreyfus, 171–2, and also n. 124, below.

47   This and the following rely in large measure on the information provided by Thomas Kohlhase in NBA V/10 KB, 93–6; I leave aside here questions concerning details of stringing – single courses, double courses, unisons, and octaves – which have little immediate bearing on the particular issue at hand.

thirteen-course instrument with the lowest courses tuned G–F♯–E–D–
C♯–BB–AA.[48] Such an arrangement would in fact work well in No. 8, the
aria "Der Ewigkeit saphirnes Haus," and in the final chorus: in each, the
players would have had to stop one of the "extra-territorial" courses no more
than a single time.[49] These demands remain comfortably within the boundaries
of Bach's other lute music, as well as that of Silvius Leopold Weiss.[50] But in
both the opening chorus and No. 5, the aria "Wie starb die Heldin so vergnügt," the more chromatic bass lines necessitate unusually extensive stopping
of the ninth and tenth courses.[51] The aria, moreover, calls for C-natural as well
as C♯. In the tuning just suggested, this would mean stopping the twelfth
course – something for which we have no evidence whatever and which, as
already intimated, would have lain beyond the realm of physical possibility on
any lute known to us. Nor can we fix the problem by tuning the lower courses
in the "normal" fashion G–F–E–D–C–BB–AA, or even by retaining F♯ but
replacing C♯ with C: this would increase the awkward stopping to the point of
utter impracticability.

Perhaps, though, Bach's lutenists did have an instrument on which they
could stop the twelfth course. Like the *Trauerode*, the Suite in G minor BWV
995 – the "Pièces pour la Luth à Monsieur Schouster" – requires a lute that no
one today has ever seen: in this case, an instrument with fourteen courses
extending down to GG.[53] While some earlier writers dismissed this as a
chimera, Thomas Kohlhase has pointed out that the theorist Jacob Adlung

48 On the BB in No. 5, see also Sections IV and V below.
49 No. 8, m. 57, requires stopping the tenth course, No. 10, m. 39, the ninth; here, as in the remainder
    of this discussion, the stopping extends only to the first fret.
50 See NBA V/10 KB, 94 (although as modified in the following discussion), as well as André Burguéte,
    "Die Lautenkompositionen Johann Sebastian Bachs. Ein Beitrag zur kritischen Wertung aus
    spielpraktischer Sicht," *BJ* 63 (1977): 28–9. Whatever the other problems of his lute writing, Bach
    normally pays due notice to practicality in regard to stopping the lowest courses. The lute version of
    "Komm, süßes Kreuz" (transcribed NBA II/5, 304–10; facsimile in NBA II/5a, fols. 22v–24r; I assume
    a D minor scale for the bass courses) requires stopping the tenth course for one note each in mm. 29
    and 30; "Betrachte, meine Seel" (NBA II/4, 66–7) has the ninth course – doubtless tuned to E♭ –
    stopped in mm. 3 and 8, the eighth course in m. 9. Among the solo lute works – I restrict myself to
    those expressly assigned to lute in at least one source – BWV 997 (leaving aside the Double; see NBA
    V/10 KB, 144–6) requires no stopping of the bass courses (for the tuning, see *ibid.*, 146), BWV 1000
    none of any course below the seventh (but see below, n. 57; for the tuning, see NBA V/10 KB, 160);
    BWV 999 has the eighth course stopped in mm. 11 and 12, possibly not even this (for the tuning, see
    ibid., 156, but also Burguéte, "Die Lautenkompositionen," 42 and 53), and BWV 998 calls for
    stopping the eleventh course in Movement 3, m. 47 (tuning NBA V/10 KB, 154). For BWV 995, see
    the discussion immediately following; for Weiss, see the comments in NBA V/10 KB, 94.
51 See No. 1, mm. 10, 21, 24, 26, 33, 34, 45, 52, 55, and 68; and No. 5, mm. 5, 21, 22, 24, 30, 32,
    49, 51, 69, and 77.
52 C occurs, with an explicit natural sign, in m. 22; at a recurrence of essentially the same music in m.
    30, Bach neglected to mark the accidental.
53 See NBA V/10 KB, 109–10.

testified to the stringing of lutes with as many as fourteen courses; and in any event, as Kohlhase adds, even the less than perfect understanding of the lute and its technique that Bach evidently had could scarcely have led him to write the suite in total ignorance of something so basic as its range.[54] The autograph of BWV 995 employs a paper-type that Bach used for the first time in the score of the *Trauerode* and then in further manuscripts until April, 1732.[55] We thus have good reason to assume the existence of at least one fourteen-course lute at Leipzig in the late 1720s – very likely in the possession of "Monsieur Schouster" himself, whom Hans-Joachim Schulze has persuasively identified as the Leipzig bookdealer and publisher Jacob Schuster.[56] With due caution, we may then ask if such an instrument could not have had its eleventh and twelfth courses lying on the fingerboard rather than beyond it.[57] Certainly, it would

54 See *ibid.*, 109–11; as Kohlhase also recognizes, the fact that a contemporary intabulation of BWV 995 transfers all the GGs up an octave reminds us only that the normal lute of the period had no more than thirteen courses but says nothing about the specific instrument for which Bach intended the piece. For a facsimile of the tablature, together with intabulations by Johann Christoph Weyrauch of BWV 997 and 1000, see *Johann Sebastian Bach: Drei Lautenkompositionen in zeitgenössischer Tabulatur (BWV 995, 997, 1000)*, ed. Hans-Joachim Schulze (Leipzig, 1975); for BWV 995 alone (without, however, its title page) see also NBA V/10 KB, 174–87. Although I cannot follow Kohlhase (*ibid.*, 127 and 157) in identifying the scribe of this tablature with the hand responsible for entering Breitkopf house signatures on both its title page and those of BWV 997 and 1000, the manuscript clearly originated in Leipzig, as it shares its paper-type with Weyrauch's tablature of BWV 997 (cf. *ibid.*, 106 and 127).

55 See *ibid.*, 103 and 107, as well as Kobayashi, "Chronologie," 20. For a facsimile of the autograph, see *Johann Sebastian Bach: Luitsuite in sol klein/Suite pour luth en sol mineur BWV 995*, ed. Godelieve Spiessens (Brussels, 1981).

56 See Hans-Joachim Schulze, "'Monsieur Schouster' – ein vergessener Zeitgenosse Johann Sebastian Bachs," *Bachiana et alia musicologica: Festschrift Alfred Dürr zum 65. Geburtstag am 3. März 1983*, ed. Wolfgang Rehm (Cassel, 1983), 243–50. Kohlhase (NBA V/10 KB, 110) cautions against assuming that Schuster owned the lute for which Bach wrote BWV 995, as the composer might not have added the dedicatory title until some time after he finished the body of the manuscript. But as the discussion immediately preceding makes clear (*ibid.*, 109), the proposed gap between the creation of the suite and its dedication represents an attempt to reconcile the date indicated by the paper of the manuscript with the long-held supposition that "Monsieur Schouster" referred to the Dresden court singer Joseph Schuster, whose documented career began, at the age of nineteen or twenty, in 1741; on this Schuster, see particularly Hans-Joachim Schulze, "Ein unbekannter Brief von Silvius Leopold Weiß," *Die Musikforschung* 21 (1968), 204, as well as idem, "Monsieur Schouster," 244–5. The script of the title-page differs in no appreciable fashion from the remainder of the manuscript; hence with Schulze's new biographical findings, there seems no reason any longer to doubt that Bach did indeed create BWV 995 with "Monsieur Schouster" in mind. Admittedly, as Schulze reminds us, we have no evidence that Jacob Schuster actually played the lute – "perhaps he only planned the printing of a collection in which Bach's suite was to be included" ("Monsieur Schouster," 250). But Schuster's attempts at music publishing – all apparently abortive – seem to have confined themselves to projects initiated and assembled by others; and his documented connections to Silvius Leopold Weiss, Adam Falckenhagen, and the lutenistic aspirations of Luise Adelgunde Victoria Gottsched imply an intimate acquaintance with the world of the lute. Cf. Schulze, "Ein unbekannter Brief," 203, and "Monsieur Schouster," 244–5 and 248–9. Under these circumstances, we may surely take the inscription of BWV 995 at face value: as a dedication to a lutenist.

57 These speculations obviously make Schuster a strong candidate for one of the lutenists' roles in the *Trauerode*. In this connection, his association with Adam Falckenhagen proves suggestive, as Schulze has shown that Falckenhagen must have had close childhood ties with Johann Christian Weyrauch

seem to have facilitated the stopping of other bass courses to a degree not otherwise encountered in Bach's lute works: as notated in the autograph, BWV 995 has the eighth or ninth course stopped at no fewer than nine different places; in no other solo composition, too, does Bach require the player to stop a lower and an upper course simultaneously.[58]

Even if, however, Bach's lutenists had a means of playing all the bass notes that he wrote, we cannot say with assurance just what else they did. Dreyfus assumes that they would have helped realize the continuo in Nos. 1, 5, 7, 8, and 10: "Although Bach nowhere else treats the lute as a continuo instrument, it is inconceivable, given the traditions of the instrument, that a lutenist would not have realized chords when confronted with a bass line."[59] But obvious as this may seem at first, a closer inspection raises doubts.

As its absence from Dreyfus' tally of continuo movements indicates, No. 4, the recitative "Der Glocken bebendes Getön," treats the lutes as single-line

(see "Bachs Lautenkompositionen," 36–7) – might Schuster indeed have come to know Falckenhagen, who had not lived in Leipzig since the early 1720s, through common acquaintance with Weyrauch? In view of Weyrauch's proposed involvement in the performance of BWV 198 (see above, n. 41), it would seem further worth asking if his two tablatures shed any relevant light on his instrument and playing practice (see the facsimile referred to in n. 54, above; a reproduction of BWV 997 appears as well in NBA V/10 KB, 188–93). At least at the time he wrote them – both evidently share a common date, even if the date itself appears less than certain (see Schulze, "Bachs Lautenmusik," 36, but in the light of NBA V/10 KB, 127 n. 71, and 159 n. 124) – Weyrauch clearly did not have a fourteen-course lute, as we see from the treatment of the bass line in BWV 1000, mm. 90–3, and BWV 997, Prelude, mm. 14–5. The tablatures also take a decidedly conservative stance on stopping the lowest courses. In BWV 1000, for which we have no other source, Weyrauch plainly avoids F♯ and E – which in the tuning called for here would have meant stopping the eighth and ninth courses – in mm. 76–7, and may have done so in m. 31 as well. In BWV 997, he introduces a stopped note on the eighth course at m. 22 of the Sarabande by transferring the original down an octave; but even in this work, he goes out of his way to avoid stopping the ninth course: see Prelude, mm. 15–6, and Gigue, mm. 9 and 33.

58 With the lowest courses tuned to a G minor scale, BWV 995 requires stopping both the eighth and ninth courses in m. 201 of the Prelude; the eighth course at six places (Sarabande, mm. 2 and 18; Gavotte II, mm. 1, 9, and 13; Gigue, m. 54); and the ninth course at two (Allemande, m. 29; Sarabande, m. 17). The stopped note at the beginning of Gavotte II clearly represents a considered decision on Bach's part, as he initially entered its accidental an octave higher; cf. NBA V/10 KB, 104. In the Allemande, the Gigue, and at m. 13 of Gavotte II, the player must stop an upper and lower course at the same time, although Bach equally goes out of his way to avoid this in mm. 69 and 190 of the Prelude. For the statistics on Bach's other lute music, see above, n. 50; double-stopping involving a lower course occurs otherwise only in "Betrachte, meine Seel," mm. 3 and 8. The tablature of BWV 995 retains the stopping of the eighth course at the start of the slow-moving Sarabande and even adds one extra note stopped on the eighth course at m. 14 of the Courante; otherwise, however, it transfers all stopped notes of the autograph version up an octave, and even rewrites a transposed bass line at mm. 169–70 of the Prelude to avoid stopping. For more on the relationship between the autograph and the intabulation of BWV 995, see Hans Radke, "War Johann Sebastian Bach Lautenspieler?" Festschrift Hans Engel zum siebzigsten Geburtstag, ed. Horst Heussner (Cassel, 1964), 284–9; and Robert Grossman, "Der Intavolator als Interpret: Johann Sebastian Bachs Lautensuite g-moll, BWV 995, im Autograph und in zeitgenössischer Tabulatur," Basler Jahrbuch für historische Musikpraxis 10 (1986), 223–44.

59 Dreyfus, Bach's continuo group, 230 n. 61, with direct reference to p. 31 and indirect reference to p. 170.

obbligato instruments. We may wonder if Bach did not intend something similar in No. 8, "Der Ewigkeit saphirnes Haus." Here, the lutes join the gambas in a fairly animated part written largely in the alto clef; while the line often parallels the continuo in elaborated form an octave above, it rarely proceeds in actual unison with it.[60] As such, it recalls a number of parts for members of the lute family in Italian ensemble music of the seventeenth century to which Lorenz Welker has recently devoted an illuminating study.[61] These parts, as Welker shows, typically did not entail more than a minimum of chordal realization, if any, even when moving in the bass register. Nor, according to Tharald Borgir, do they represent an isolated phenomenon; Borgir, indeed, argues that lutes regularly served as a purely melodic bass in the early Baroque period.[62]

Whether Bach knew these older traditions, of course, represents a more or less unanswerable question. Nevertheless, obbligato bass parts for members of the lute family continued to appear in print until at least 1700.[63] It seems worth noting, too, that one of Kuhnau's remarks about the *colochon* places it in a context more suggestive of doubling bass lines than realizing them. The memorandum of 1717 cited earlier amplifies a reference to "basses" with the explanatory phrase "that is, violones, cellos, calichons, bassoons"; the formulation unmistakably evokes those seventeenth-century title pages that equate a lute of some variety with the cello, "fagotto," or trombone.[64] Unfortunately, the few original parts that remain from Kuhnau's performances do not include any for colochon.[65] We can, however, gain some perspective – if an admittedly limited

60   The edition of the *Trauerode* in BG XIII/3, 3–72, mistakenly assigns the lutes to the bass line (55); cf. NBA I/38 KB, 139, and Dürr, *Bach: Seine Handschrift*, Plate 37.
61   See Lorenz Welker, "'. . . per un Chitarone, Fagotto, Ouero altro Istromento simile, pronto alla velocità': Chitarrone, Theorbe und Arciliuto in der italienischen Ensemblemusik des 17. Jahrhunderts," *Basler Jahrbuch für historische Musikpraxis* 12 (1988), 27–51.
62   See Tharald Borgir, *The performance of the basso continuo in Italian baroque music* (Ann Arbor, 1987), 101–7. While I do not find all of Borgir's arguments persuasive, their overall thrust would definitely seem corroborated by the more detailed investigations of Welker. I should perhaps note that some confusion could arise from the fact that both Welker and Borgir concern themselves exclusively with "extended" members of the lute family – the chitarrone, or theorbo, and the archlute. By Bach's time, however, any essential distinction between extended and normal lute had vanished; the only differences between lute, archlute, and theorbo concerned details of tuning and construction not immediately relevant to our discussion.
63   See the survey in Welker, "Chitarrone, Theorbe und Arciliuto," 52–7. I must note, though, that the few publications in Welker's list that I have seen first-hand – Corelli, Op. 1 and 3; Torelli, Op. 1; and Gregori, Op. 2 – treat the lute for the most part as a figured continuo instrument and contain very little obbligato material.
64   See Spitta, *Bach*, 2: 862 ("Bässen, als Violonen, Violoncellen, Calichonen, Bassonen"; for a differing interpretation, see Dreyfus, *Bach's continuo group*, 170–1), and Welker, "Chitarrone, Theorbe und Arciliuto," 27 in particular; on the meaning of "fagotto" in this context, cf. Ulrich Prinz, "Zur Bezeichnung 'Bassono' und 'Fagotto' bei J. S. Bach," *BJ* 67 (1981): 110–12.
65   I know of only six works for which we can trace parts to Leipzig's principal churches in the era of

one – on its use at Leipzig through a handful of sources from the Neue Kirche. Materials for two early works by Telemann and one piece by Melchior Hoffmann include bass parts for a "*calcedon*," surely the same instrument; in no instance do they show figures, even when these appear in other bass parts.[66] Telemann, moreover, went on to use the *calcedon* in many of his later vocal works, as well as in at least three instrumental concertos.[67] What little specific information I have managed to gather on the vocal music shows the same picture as at the Neue Kirche: figures in the keyboard continuo, none in the *calcedon*.[68]

Kuhnau or immediately afterwards: Kuhnau's cantatas "Nicht nur allein am frühen Morgen" and "Welt, adieu, ich bin dein Müde"; his motet "Gott hat uns nicht gesetzt zum Zorn"; a cantata by Georg Friedrich Kauffmann, "Unverzagt, beklemmtes Herz"; an anonymous set of Christmas interpolations for the Magnificat; and a complete Magnificat, also anonymous. None of these includes a part for *colochon*. For the sources, see Friedhelm Krummacher, *Die Überlieferung der Choralbearbeitungen in der frühen evangelischen Kantate: Untersuchungen zum Handschriftenrepertoire evangelischer Figuralmusik im späten 17. und beginnenden 18. Jahrhundert* (Berlin, 1965), 532; Yoshitake Kobayashi, "Neuerkenntnisse zu einigen Bach-Quellen an Hand schriftkundlicher Untersuchungen," *BJ* 64 (1978): 60; Schulze, *Studien*, 122–3; Robert M. Cammarota, "The sources of the Christmas interpolations in J. S. Bach's Magnificat in E-flat major (BWV 243a)," *Current Musicology* 36 (1983): 82–9, and especially 84; Glöckner, "Die Musikpflege an der Leipziger Neukirche," 69, 99–100, and 114; and Joshua Rifkin, "Kauffmann, Georg Friedrich," *New Grove.*

66 A *Missa brevis* in B minor by Telemann (TVWV 9:14) includes a single part labeled "Calcedono," a "Sanctus" in F major (TVWV deest), two; Hoffmann's cantata "Singet dem Herrn ein neues Lied," dated 1708, has a part for "Calcedon." While the organ part for Telemann's Mass has no figures, and that of the Sanctus does not survive, the Hoffmann cantata has partially figured parts for both "Continuo" and "Organo transposto." For details on the sources, see Glöckner, "Die Musikpflege an der Leipziger Neukirche," 30–1, 33, and 47, and the edition of TVWV 9:14 by Klaus Hofmann (Stuttgart, 1994). Despite the obvious phonetic difference between *colochon* and *calcedon*, the coincidence of musical characteristics, time, and place would seem to argue for equating the instrument employed by Telemann and Hoffmann with that referred to by Kuhnau.

67 References to Telemann's use of the *calcedon* include Caroline Valentin, *Geschichte der Musik in Frankfurt am Main vom Anfange des XIV. bis zum Anfange des XVIII. Jahrhunderts* (Frankfurt, 1906), 229; Werner Menke, *Das Vokalwerk Georg Philipp Telemann's: Überlieferung und Zeitfolge* (Cassel, 1942), 56; Siegfried Kross, *Das Instrumentalkonzert bei Georg Philipp Telemann* (Tutzing, 1969), 33–4 and 105; Gill, "Mandores and Colachons," 138; and idem, "Colascione," 435–6. For details on the vocal works, including precise itemization of their parts, readers may consult Werner Menke, TVWV, or Joachim Schlichte, *Thematischer Katalog der kirchlichen Musikhandschriften des 17. und 18. Jahrhunderts in der Stadt- und Universitätsbibliothek Frankfurt am Main (Signaturengruppe Ms.Fr.mus)* (Frankfurt, 1979), 187–381; see also the following note. For details on the concertos, see n. 70, below.

68 I rely here on the information – sometimes gratifyingly explicit, sometimes less so – provided in the following editions: "Danket dem Herrn" TVWV 1:163, ed. Felix Schroeder, Leuckartiana, No. 45 (Munich, 1978); "Gott sei mir gnädig" TVWV 1:681, ed. Traugott Fedtke, Edition Peters 8607 (Frankfurt, 1987); "Ich danke dem Herrn von ganzem Herzen" TVWV 7:14, ed. Klaus Hofmann, Hänssler-Edition 39.107/01 (Neuhausen-Stuttgart, 1977); "Machet die Tore weit" TVWV 1:1074, ed. Traugott Fedtke and Klaus Hofmann, Hännsler-Edition 39.105/01 (Neuhausen-Stuttgart, 1975); and "Siehe, das ist Gottes Lamm" TVWV 1:1316, ed. Reinhold Kubik, Hännsler-Edition 39.128/01 (Neuhausen-Stuttgart, 1982). Unfortunately, none of the literature cited in the preceding note – not even the catalogues of Menke and Schlichte – provides any really pertinent information; at best, we may regard Valentin's description of the *calcedon* as "an instrument notated in the bass clef" as more consistent with the absence of figures than with their presence. *Calcedon* parts also appear frequently in the cantatas of Telemann's Frankfurt successors Johann Christoph Bodinus and Johann Balthasar König; see Schlichte, *Katalog der kirchlichen Musikhandschriften*, 50–4 and 105–14.

Indeed, the *calcedon* seems principally intended as a reinforcement to the cello: where the cello and keyboard parts differ from one another, the *calcedon* goes with the bowed instrument.[69] In the concertos – which treat the *calcedon* as an obbligato bass to a pair of flutes – the absence of authentic parts makes it hard to determine what might actually have happened in performance.[70] Telemann's autographs, in any event, appear to leave the *calcedon* line unfigured but for a single unusual passage in one concerto; and one of the other concertos indicates the possibility of replacing the *calcedon* with bassoon.[71]

All in all, then, any consideration of the lutes in the *Trauerode* would do well to keep the possibility of obbligato treatment in mind. This possibility, in fact, would seem to extend beyond No. 8 alone. In the chorus directly before it, "An dir, du Fürbild großer Frauen," the lutes do not join the continuo in accompanying the first fugal exposition but remain silent until the entry of the vocal bass; both at this point and in the second exposition, moreover, they double the voice literally rather than sharing the simplified form of its head-motive found in the continuo. Although they seem ultimately to shift allegiance, joining with the continuo in an elaborated version of the voice line shortly before the two main cadences, their prevailing behavior could well imply that Bach regarded them here more as melodic instruments than as members of the continuo group.[72] In this connection, a detail of the autograph may take on

69   The editions of TVWV 1:681 and 7:14 indicate that the scribe of the *calcedon* part copied it directly from the cello; I might also note that the cantata "Was Jesus nur mit mir wird fügen" TVWV 1:1523 has a part marked "Violoncello è Calcedono."

70   The three concertos – listed by Kross as 2 Fl. e, Conc. gr. D, and Conc. gr. h – survive in autograph scores that clearly predate Telemann's Dresden visit of 1719 and in parts copied at Darmstadt in the 1720s; the Darmstadt copies either replace the *calcedon* with bassoon or leave its part undesignated. For details, see Kross, *Das Instrumentalkonzert bei Georg Philipp Telemann*, 147, 168, and 171; Ortrun Landmann, *Die Telemann-Quellen der Sächsischen Landesbibliothek: Handschriften und zeitgenössische Druckausgaben seiner Werke* (Dresden, 1983), 121 and 127; and Manfred Fechner, "Notwendige Bemerkungen zu einigen Dresdner Telemann-Quellen und deren Schreiber," *Georg Philipp Telemann – Werküberlieferung, Editions- und Interpretationsfragen: Bericht über die Internationale Wissenschaftliche Konferenz anläßlich der 9. Telemann-Festtage der DDR Magdeburg, 12. bis 14. März 1987*, ed. Wolf Hobohm and Carsten Lange (Cologne, 1991), 82–3. The dating of the Darmstadt manuscripts comes from a study of their papers carried out by Brian Stewart and communicated in the "Penn State Telemann-Nachrichten" of October 18, 1988; my thanks to Dr. Stewart for sharing this information.

71   The autograph of Conc. gr. h has figures in the *calcedon* at mm. 109–17 of the second movement; see the facsimile in *Georg Philipp Telemann: Musikalische Werke*, 26 (Cassel, 1989), xiii, as well as the critical notes, xi. In Conc. gr. D, Telemann amplified the designation "Calchedon" with the words "o Violoncello," then replaced this with "ou Basson"; for a facsimile, see *ibid.*, xii. On Conc. gr. D, see also Gill, "Mandores and Colachons," 138 and 141 n. 28. Obviously, we cannot read too much into the absence of figures from the autographs, as Telemann leaves the harpsichord line unfigured as well. The Darmstadt parts preserve some of the figuring in Conc. gr. h but otherwise have no figures in either the obbligato line or the harpsichord.

72   The two entries occur at mm. 13 and 57, respectively, the shift to the elaborated line at mm. 23 and 71; we could, of course, take the identity of lutes and continuo at this point to mean that the continuo has joined the lutes rather than the other way around.

more than incidental significance: in all three choruses of the *Trauerode*, Bach places the lute system above the voices rather than in direct proximity to the continuo.[73] Obviously, this layout does not in itself preclude the possibility of at least some chordal realization.[74] But it surely reinforces the suspicions already gleaned from the music itself.

Technical considerations reinforce these suspicions as well. As already indicated, the single notated line shared by the lutes and the gambas in No. 8 falls comfortably on the Baroque lute; but the addition of any chordal amplification beyond the occasional upper third leads to more than a few awkward situations.[75] With No. 7, the problems become more severe. In such fast-moving passages as mm. 23–6 and 67–71, even a realization notably sketchier than what we might infer from Bach's practice in figuring keyboard parts would lie at the outer limits of playability – and at precisely such passages, I might add, even those seventeenth-century obbligato parts that include figures in more sustained music drop their figuring.[76] At best, we might conclude, Bach expected no more than minimal chordal participation from the lutes in these two numbers.

Just what he expected – and got – in the remaining movements with lute, Nos. 1, 5, and 10, seems harder to say. Whether or not Kuhnau used the *colochon* as a chordal instrument, the practice of lute continuos had scarcely vanished from the scene. At Dresden, to take just one conspicuous example, a theorbo regularly formed part of the ensemble in larger concerted music; in performance materials to Zelenka's works it receives a part identical in all essentials – including the figuring – to that for the keyboard instrument.[77] The

---

73 The score in NBA I/38 faithfully reflects this arrangement; BG XIII/3, 42, while also preserving the layout of the autograph, editorially calls for Lute I to double the continuo until the entry of the bass voice in m. 13. Bach's treatment of the lutes in the autograph recalls the "choral bass" characteristic of his cantatas from Mühlhausen and Weimar; on this subject, see the enlightening discussion in Beißwenger, *Johann Sebastian Bachs Notenbibliothek*, 146–55. See also n. 85, below.

74 Johann David Heinichen's cantata "La bella fiamma, o Tirsi," for example, has an obbligato theorbo part placed above the vocal system in both of its two arias; so far as the examples provided in Richard Lorber's recent dissertation allow us to judge, Heinichen figured those portions of the final aria – although not those of the first – where the theorbo does not play independently of the bass. See Richard Lorber, *Die italienischen Kantaten von Johann David Heinichen (1683–1729): Ein Beitrag zur Geschichte der Musik am Dresdner Hof in der ersten Hälfte des 18. Jahrhunderts* (Regensburg, 1991), 98, 148–9, and 355–7.

75 In mm. 1 and 3, for example, the hand position required for a full triad on the downbeat would eliminate any realistic possibility of playing the lower-octave afterbeats.

76 See, for instance, Welker, "Chitarrone, Theorbe und Arciliuto," Examples 2 and 7 (pp. 40–2, 48). The assumption that Bach would have figured lute parts, if at all, as fully as he did his keyboard parts receives support from Zelenka's practice as described in the following note.

77 For a general overview of continuo practice – including the role of the theorbo – in church music at Dresden, see Horn, *Die Dresdner Hofkirchenmusik*, 194–8, and Thomas Kohlhase, "Anmerkungen zur Generalbaßpraxis der Dresdner Hofkirchenmusik der 1720er bis 1740er Jahre," *Zelenka-Studien* I, ed.

outer choruses of the *Trauerode* would presumably have allowed the lutes to realize chords, should Bach have wanted this: neither the bass line nor the harmonies move too quickly, and the stoppings of the ninth and tenth courses in the first movement do not seem to force insuperable stretches of the hand.[78] In No. 5, too, we can well imagine a chordal elaboration, if hardly a very full one.[79] Nevertheless, experience sounds a qualifying note: I have yet to encounter any players, no matter how skilled, who have found it possible to realize these three movements without sacrificing a considerable amount of harmonic detail. The aria has proved especially recalcitrant; so a particular question mark must hang over it.[80]

This question mark may have implications that go beyond the lutes themselves. In the autograph, "Wie starb die Heldin" bears the legend "Aria 2 Viole da Gamb e 2 Liuti" to the left of the first brace, which contains three staves: two for the gambas and one for the bass line. If we follow the conventional understanding of Bach's performance practice, we would interpret this lowest staff as a continuo part with lute amplification. Indeed, the editors of

Thomas Kohlhase and Hubert Unverricht (Cassel, 1993), 233–40. The Dresden connection explains why Bach's score copy of Johann Christoph Schmidt's "Auf Gott hoffe ich" labels the figured continuo line "Organo ô Tiorba"; cf. Dreyfus, *Bach's continuo group*, 120–1, 123, and 256 n. 64, as well as Beißwenger, *Johann Sebastian Bachs Notenbibliothek*, 136. Zelenka's relatively few surviving performance materials present the following picture: the trio sonatas ZWV 181/4 and 181/5 both include a single figured part labeled "Violone ô Tiorba"; figured parts for both organ and theorbo appear in the "Kyrie" in A minor ZWV 27, the *Requiem* in D major ZWV 46, and the motet "Angelus Domini descendit" ZWV 161; and the oratorio *Gesù al Calvario* ZWV 62 has parts for theorbo and harpsichord. Of the remaining materials, the "Sanctus" ZWV 35, the "Miserere" ZWV 57 (many of the parts for which survive only in much later copies), and the motet "O magnum mysterium" ZWV 171 have parts for organ alone; the Sonata ZWV 181/2 has an unfigured part for violone; and the "Ave maris stella" ZWV 110 and the Capricci ZWV 182 and 185 include no continuo parts at all. For the sources of all these works, see Wolfgang Reich, *Jan Dismas Zelenka: Thematisch-systematisches Verzeichnis seiner musikalischen Werke ZWV* (Dresden, 1985), or Wolgang Horn and Thomas Kohlhase, *Zelenka-Dokumentation: Quellen und Materialien* (Wiesbaden, 1989), 2: 279–312.

78 The most difficult spot comes at the middle of m. 21, where the harmony would require stopping the ninth course simultaneously with two upper courses; all the other notes stopped on the lower courses (cf. n. 51, above) either occupy metric positions not demanding chords or necessitate stopping only a single upper course.

79 Significantly, most of the notes evidently stopped on the lower courses (cf. n. 51, above) fall between strong beats. Of the stopped notes that do occur in positions more obviously implying realization, only the diminished sonority in m. 49 would have forced the player to stop an upper course. See also the example of a written-out lute accompaniment by Weiss in Jesper Bøje Christensen, "Zur Generalbaß-Praxis bei Händel und Bach," *Basler Jahrbuch für historische Musikpraxis* 9 (1985): 53.

80 Gwendolyn Toth, who directed a performance of the *Trauerode* in conjunction with the meeting where I first presented this paper, has proposed that the lutes could have realized the continuo by having one play only the bass line while the other played chords above it. This could provide an alternative explanation for the use of two lutes written in unison; for even the player realizing harmonies would have needed the bass line, presumably augmented with figures, to do so. But so far as I know, no record of such a practice exists. For counsel on this and other lutenistic matters, I must record my thanks to Angelika Oertel and Joachim Held, the lutenists at the performance of the *Trauerode* referred to at the start of this paper.

both the Bach-Gesellschaft edition and the Neue Bach-Ausgabe read it in just this fashion.[81] More recently, however, Laurence Dreyfus has proposed that the lutes would have supported the upper parts on their own, without cello, violone, or a keyboard instrument.[82] The editors of the *Bach Compendium* echo this suggestion, although with some hesitation.[83] I should like to second it more forcefully.[84] Admittedly, Bach almost never actually labels the continuo line in his scores, especially in composing manuscripts, and the *Trauerode* presents no exception in this regard. Yet his separation of lutes and continuo in the outer choruses warns us against assuming too easily that he meant to collapse both into a single bass line for the aria, and a look at the music itself argues for further caution.[85] For all the serene elegance of the upper parts, the bass abounds in extreme registral disjunctions unparalleled in any Bach continuo part I know that presupposes the involvement of a bowed string instrument.[86] But the lute could handle the numerous leaps with ease – just as it could also play the low BB called for in measure 62, a note obviously not available on the cello and, so far as I know, never found in the continuo parts of Bach's Leipzig compositions for larger ensembles.[87] The unmediated shifts of

---

81   See BG XIII/3, 35, and NBA I/38, 214.

82   See Dreyfus, *Bach's continuo group*, 170 and, by implication, 31.

83   See BC IV, 1565.

84   See, however, the discussion in Section V below.

85   In contrast to his treatment of the lutes in the choral movements, Bach places their system here below the voice. This does not necessarily imply the presence of a further continuo, however: Bach almost always notates the lowest sounding part beneath the voice line, even when the instrument or instruments in question would normally lie above it in a score. For example, of the eight *bassetto* movements listed by Hans-Werner Boresch, *Besetzung und Instrumentation: Studien zur kompositorischen Praxis Johann Sebastian Bachs* (Cassel, 1993), 53, all but one, BWV 46/5, survive in autograph score; and of the remaining seven, only two – both in the *St. Matthew Passion* – assign the voice to the lowest system. See also Beißwenger, *Johann Sebastian Bachs Notenbibliothek*, 152 n. 179.

86   For comparison, I might point to two roughly contemporaneous arias, the thematically similar "Ruhet hie, matte Sinne" from "O angenehme Melodei" BWV 210a (on the date of this work, see Kobayashi, "Chronologie," 42–3), and "Phoebus, deine Melodei," from "Geschwinde, ihr wirbelnden Winde" BWV 201. The bass line of "Ruhet hie" – which, admittedly, we know only from the voice-harpsichord *particell* of the later cantata BWV 210 – includes no unmediated leaps of more than an octave, while that of "Phoebus, deine Melodei" has only a single jump greater than a tenth. By contrast, the bass in BWV 198/5 often vaults an octave and a seventh, and twice (mm. 27 and 28) traverses two octaves with only a single note in between.

87   Cf. BG XIII/3, viii. I do not, of course, have in mind here the transposed organ parts, which occasionally include notes lower than C through inadvertence (I include among these parts the "Violone. et Organo" of BWV 63; cf. NBA I/2 KB, 13–4). While BB♭ appears in the two untransposed parts used for the performance of the cantata "Ich hatte viel Bekümmernis" BWV 21 in 1723, both parts originated in Weimar – although even in that context, the low note presents something of a mystery; cf. NBA I/16 KB, 128 (Robert Moreen, George S. Bozarth, and Paul Brainard). Among works of smaller scoring, the continuo line of the flute sonata BWV 1034 goes down to BB, that of the trio sonata BWV 1039 to BB and AA. In neither instance, however, do we have to assume the presence of a cello: the part bears the label "Cembalo" in at least one source. See the facsimile in NBA, VI/3, x, as well as *ibid.*, KB (Hans-Peter Schmitz), 22 and 48–9.

register, moreover, seem to hint at the kind of hidden polyphony specially associated with the lute; for examples, we need look no further than the sigh motifs of mm. 2–4 or the broken tenths in mm. 6–7. In light of all this, we must surely imagine the aria without the lower string sonority otherwise all but omnipresent in Bach's Leipzig vocal works; and unlike the only comparable instance that comes to mind – the aria "Erleucht auch meine finstre Sinnen" in Part V of the *Christmas Oratorio* BWV 248 – we must surely imagine it without the organ as well.[88] In this remarkable movement, then, all three members of Bach's "regular" bass contingent plainly kept silent. Hence if the lutes did not play a fully realized continuo, a new question confronts us: who – if anyone – did? Rather than address it directly, however, I should like first to consider a somewhat different set of issues.

V

Let us go back to Sicul. As I indicated earlier, one of the details in his account of the *Trauerode* must seem odd to anyone who knows the piece. While Sicul writes that the orchestra included both recorders and transverse flutes – "Fleutes douces" and "Fleutes traverses" – Bach's autograph calls for transverse flutes alone. Commentators have tended to dodge the issue with appeals to the missing parts. But this will not really do; for even with the imagination stretched to the utmost, it seems all but impossible to find a plausible role for the recorders. Considerations of key and range eliminate any real likelihood that they would have played any of the existing wind lines.[89] Recently, Hans-Werner Boresch has proposed that they could have doubled the two gambas in No. 5 at the upper octave.[90] Yet this suggestion, too, founders on questions of instrumental capability: not only does D major lie uncomfortably for the recorder, but the second gamba part would have needed extensive rewriting even to fit within its compass.[91] Should Bach in fact have wanted to double the

88 For "Erleucht auch meine finstre Sinnen," see NBA II/6, 223, and *ibid.*, KB, 301–2 (Walter Blankenburg and Alfred Dürr). While at least one early Bach continuo part no doubt meant for organ alone, that of the duet "Meine Seele wartet" in "Aus der Tiefen rufe ich, Herr, zu dir" BWV 131 (cf. Dreyfus, *Bach's continuo group*, 133), matches "Wie starb die Heldin so vergnügt" in its registral disjunctiveness, it does not include any notes physically unavailable on the instrument; in BWV 198/5, on the other hand, the transposition required by the Leipzig organs would have rendered not only the BB, but also the Cs, C♯s, and even, in all probability, the D♯ of m. 51 unplayable.

89 Cf. particularly Neumann's discussion in NBA I/38 KB, 127–8.

90 See Boresch, *Besetzung und Instrumentation*, 105–7.

91 This last point vitiates a supposed parallel introduced by Boresch (*ibid.*, 106) in support of his hypothesis: when Bach enriched the scoring of the cantata "Gleichwie der Regen und Schnee vom Himmel fällt" BWV 18 with two recorders doubling viola parts at the upper octave, he had to make only minor adjustments to the original lines.

gambas in this movement, the transverse flutes – whose association with the gambas elsewhere in the *Trauerode* we have already remarked on – would surely have done better; and in any event, given the extreme delicacy of the bass scoring, the entire prospect of octave doubling looks implausibly top-heavy.

What, then, did Sicul have in mind? Alfred Dürr has wondered if he might not simply have conjured up the recorders more or less unconsciously out of an urge to make the commemoration appear as impressive as possible.[92] But I think the key to the problem lies elsewhere. Assuming Sicul followed the long established practice of using the word "violins" to refer to "strings" in general, then his list of instruments – as readers can see from Table 8.1 – tallies remarkably well with the forces specified in the autograph of the *Trauerode*.[93] Indeed, it tallies perfectly but for the inclusion of the recorders and for an equally curious omission: the two parts described in the score as "Hautbois" and clearly intended for that particular variety of oboe that Bach and other contemporary musicians tended to call by its French name, "Hautbois d'Amour."[94] Perhaps we may see a connection here. No one, I think, can fail to catch the associative resonance between the modifiers "douces" and "d'amour" – a resonance all the stronger in German, where "doux" commonly translates as "lieblich." The very order in which Sicul enumerates the orchestra also proves suggestive. Starting with the continuo group, the list goes from the bottom of the score to the top: after the harpsichord and organ come the viols and lutes, then the strings, and finally the winds.[95] If we follow this progression, the recorders fall precisely in the slot where we would expect the oboes. We might thus hazard a guess that Sicul simply got Bach's second pair of wind instruments mixed up.[96]

---

92   Alfred Dürr, "Bachs Trauer-Ode und Markus-Passion," in *Im Mittelpunkt Bach: ausgewählte Aufsätze und Vorträge* (Cassel, 1988), 120.

93   The synechdoche of "violins" for "strings" went back at least as far as the *24 Violons du Roi* in seventeenth-century France. In a related vein, Bach's *Entwurff einer wohlbestallten Kirchen Music* of 1730 uses the term "violist" to cover any string player – violinists and "those who play the violas, the violoncellos, and the violons"; see *Dok* I/22 (*BR*, 121).

94   Bach's earliest autograph parts for oboe d'amore, those to the cantata "Du wahrer Gott und Davids Sohn" BWV 23, call it "Hautbois d'Amour"; and while he subsequently makes occasional use of Italian or mixed nomenclature for the instrument, the French version appears to predominate, both in autograph manuscripts and in those of Bach's copyists. Johann Gottfried Walther refers to the oboe d'amore by its French title exclusively; see *Musicalisches Lexicon* (Leipzig, 1732), 304.

95   Admittedly, the order does not exactly match that of Bach's autograph – Sicul switches the lutes and viols; but he hardly needed to use an actual score to come up with his sequence.

96   At the presentation of this paper in New York, Gwendolyn Toth suggested that Sicul might have identified the winds by their players rather than the instruments themselves. This would presuppose, however, that a player identified chiefly with the recorder would have "doubled" oboe d'amore; if anything, surely, we might better assume the opposite.

Table 8.1. *Instruments in the* Trauerode

Bach	Sicul
2 flutes	*fleutes traverses*
–	*fleutes douces*
2 oboes (d'amore)	–
strings	"violins"
2 lutes	lutes
2 violas da gamba	*violes di Gamba*

With this, however, a new difficulty arises. For if Sicul, whatever his prevailing reliability, failed to get a fairly basic piece of instrumental terminology straight, how much can we trust him on other details? We commonly think of Sicul's report as an eyewitness account. Yet by every indication, Bach and his musicians would have played and sung from the organ loft on the west wall of the Paulinerkirche, behind the congregation.[97] Despite the relatively low height and open design of the loft, therefore, the ensemble must have remained invisible to most of those present, at least during the performance; unless he sat facing the congregation, Sicul would have had to crane his head backwards or creep up to the loft to observe such things as "Herr Bach himself" at the harpsichord. There would seem a good chance, then, that he relied at least in some measure on the word of an informant, an insider who knew exactly who played the "Clave di Cembalo." But if he did, we now do not know where the informant stops and Sicul begins – just who, for instance, first said "Fleutes douces" when he meant "Hautbois d'amour"? And with this, we have to wonder if other errors may not have crept into the account.

Such misgivings assume particular relevance in connection with the most famously vexing problem in Sicul's list of instruments – the presence of both organ and harpsichord.[98] Recently, Laurence Dreyfus and Hans-Joachim Schulze have in effect told us that no problem exists: organ and harpsichord, they maintain, would simply have provided simultaneous continuo support

---

97 See Schering, *Musikgeschichte Leipzigs,* 2: 316–17. For a picture of the loft, see Charles Sanford Terry, *Bach: A Biography,* 2nd edn. (London, 1933), Illustration 72; for a view facing the altar, see Martin Petzoldt and Joachim Petri, *Johann Sebastian Bach: Ehre sei dir Gott gesungen; Bilder und Texte zu Bachs Leben als Christ und seinem Wirken für die Kirche* (Göttingen, 1986), 56. I wish to thank Christoph Wolff for valuable first-hand information on the church and its loft.

98 Among earlier attempts to wrestle with this, see particularly Spitta, *Bach,* 1: 829, and 2: 447–8; Arnold Schering, *Musikgeschichte Leipzigs,* 3: 119–20; and Dürr, "Bachs Trauer-Ode und Markus-Passion," 120.

throughout the entire length of the composition, a practice allegedly common in Bach's Leipzig church music.[99] Indeed, Dreyfus invokes the *Trauerode* as a principal witness to this practice.[100] Yet I remain uneasy. Not that I wish to doubt Bach's place at the harpsichord: whether or not this comes to us firsthand, we may surely believe it. Nor do I mean to open an inquiry into the theory of dual accompaniment itself.[101] But as we have already seen in other connections, the singularity of the *Trauerode*, both musically and otherwise, ought to make us think twice before subsuming any aspect of its performance under a supposed norm; and without the original parts to tell us with certainty just what the organ and harpsichord did or did not do, we obviously cannot use it as evidence for such a norm either.

In any event, the *Trauerode* does not really fit the theory of dual accompaniment all that snugly. If Bach accompanied, and presumably led, the performance at the harpsichord, he most likely did so from score. Admittedly, he would seem to have played his harpsichord concertos from a separate solo part.[102] More than a few of his contemporaries and predecessors, moreover – Kuhnau, perhaps, among them – directed large-scale vocal works from continuo parts specially written for this purpose; and Bach himself appears to have prepared

---

99 See in particular Dreyfus, *Bach's continuo group*, 10–71, and especially 30–1; Hans-Joachim Schulze, "Zur Frage des Doppelaccompagnements (Orgel und Cembalo) in Kirchenmusikaufführungen der Bach-Zeit," *BJ* 73 (1987): 173–4; and idem, "Wunschdenken und Wirklichkeit. Nochmals zur Frage des Doppelaccompagnements in Kirchenmusikaufführungen der Bach-Zeit," *BJ* 75 (1989): 231–3.

100 See Dreyfus, *Bach's continuo group*, 30–1.

101 I should, however, clear away one misconception especially relevant to the *Trauerode*. Proceeding from his supposition that "the lutes played a simultaneous – that is, additive – continuo part" in BWV 198, Dreyfus, *Bach's continuo group*, 31, writes, "To retain any scruples regarding the combination of organ and harpsichord in light of an already redundant continuo realization begins to seem a little foolish." Schulze, "Wunschdenken und Wirklichkeit," 233, treats Kuhnau's use of the *colochon* in a similar vein. Leaving aside the questions already raised about the role of the lutes or *colochons* in these particular examples, simple logic tells us that a continuo of lute and organ, or lute and harpsichord – combinations documented as far back as Monteverdi's *L'Orfeo* of 1607 – does not necessarily imply a continuo of organ and harpsichord, for which we hardly have such rich substantiation. As we have seen, Zelenka used the theorbo to realize basses simultaneously with organ or harpsichord (cf. n. 77, above); but in no instance did he use the two keyboard instruments together. Indeed, Thomas Kohlhase emphasizes that organ and harpsichord never appear simultaneously at Dresden: the harpsichord played only during Passion week, when the organ fell silent; see Kohlhase, "Anmerkungen zur Generalbaßpraxis der Dresdner Hofkirchenmusik," 240 n. 17.

102 Autograph solo parts survive for the Fifth Brandenburg Concerto as well as the Leipzig concertos BWV 1055 and 1057. While Bach conceivably entrusted the later works to other players – see, for example, the speculation in Georg von Dadelsen, "Bemerkungen zu Bachs Cembalokonzerten," *Bericht über die Wissenschaftliche Konferenz zum V. Internationalen Bachfest der DDR in Verbindung mit dem 60. Bachfest der Neuen Bachgesellschaft, Leipzig, 25. bis 27. März 1985*, ed. Winfried Hoffmann and Armin Schneiderheinze (Leipzig, 1988), 239 – surely no one but him played the solo in the Fifth Brandenburg. We could, of course, also imagine Bach playing from the two harpsichord parts for BWV 154 and 27 considered in Section V, below; but these parts, as we shall see, stand at even further remove from the theory of dual accompaniment.

the figured continuo of the *Missa* in B minor with such use in mind.[103] But these examples do not really have much bearing on the *Trauerode*. The concertos would hardly have required the same measure of directorial intervention as a piece of its size – the sort of intervention so famously evoked in Johann Matthias Gesner's depiction of Bach among his corps of musicians.[104] Nor do we have any reason to think that Bach meant the bass part of the *Missa* for a performance of his own – quite the contrary.[105] Certainly, nothing comparable survives in any of his other materials.[106]

A group of sources roughly contemporary with the *Trauerode*, moreover, illuminates Bach's practices more directly. In 1726 and the years immediately following, Bach composed a handful of cantatas that used the organ in a solo capacity.[107] The autograph scores of these works typically notate the obbligato numbers in the transposed form that a player would have required; usually, these movements lack a bass line separate from the lower staff of the organ part.[108] In two cantatas from the second half of 1726 – "Geist und Seele wird

---

103 For examples of organist-director's parts from Salzburg, see Manfred Hermann Schmid, "Zur Mitwirkung des Solisten am Orchester-Tutti bei Mozarts Konzerten," *"Basler Jahrbuch für historische Musikpraxis* 17 (1993): 98–101; Friedrich Wilhelm Riedel, *Kirchenmusik am Hofe Karls VI. (1711–1740): Untersuchungen zum Verhältnis von Zeremoniell und musikalischem Stil im Barockzeitalter* (Munich, 1977), 21, documents the use of similar parts in Vienna. For Kuhnau, see Spitta, *Bach*, 2: 160, but as qualified by the source information in Schering, *Musikgeschichte Leipzigs*, 2: 25; and Friedhelm Krummacher, *Die Choralbearbeitung in der protestantischen Figuralmusik zwischen Praetorius und Bach* (Cassel, 1978), 348. On the continuo part to the *Missa*, see my review in *Notes* 44 (1987–8): 792.

104 For the original Latin text and translations, see, variously, *Dok* II/432; Spitta, *Bach*, 2: 90; and *BR*, 131. Dreyfus, *Bach's continuo group*, 29–30, reads Gesner to show Bach directing from the harpsichord. The interpretation, however, rests on a questionable translation. *BR*, on which Dreyfus relies, renders Gesner's "cum difficillimis omnium partibus fungatur" as "although he is executing the most difficult parts himself" – for Dreyfus, a reference to harpsichord playing. But Spitta, with his background in classical philology, recognized that Gesner more likely used the plural of *pars* in its common sense of "office," "function," or "duty," and thus translated the phrase as "obgleich er von allen die schwierigste Aufgabe hat" – "although he has the most difficult job of all." This leaves the matter considerably more open; "the most difficult job" can simply mean conducting, whether or not the conductor simultaneously plays an instrument. Hence while Spitta himself saw Bach at the harpsichord (*Bach*, 2: 159), Dürr writes, "The famous passage in Gesner's Quintilian commentary . . . says nothing of an instrument under Bach's hands"; see Alfred Dürr, "Die Bach-Kantate aus heutiger Sicht," *Im Mittelpunkt Bach*, 255. Apart from Gesner and Sicul, we lack even putative testimony to Bach's directing a vocal performance from the harpsichord.

105 See Rifkin, *Notes* 44 (1987–88), 792.

106 Although the early cantata "Gott ist mein König" BWV 71 includes a combined violin-bass part that superficially resembles the Salzburg director's parts mentioned in n. 103, above, Bach presumably intended it only for the leader of the string choir, as it omits those numbers that do not involve the violins, viola, and violone; cf. NBA I/32.1 KB, 27 (Christine Fröde).

107 Readers can get the most convenient overview of the pieces and their sources by comparing the tables in Dreyfus, *Bach's continuo group*, 63, and Philip Swanton, "Der Generalbaß in J. S. Bachs Kantaten mit obligater Orgel," *Basler Jahrbuch für historische Musikpraxis* 9 (1985): 103–4.

108 Admittedly, three arias that call in one form or another for organ – BWV 47/2, 128/4, and 170/5 – show untransposed notation. Bach, however, evidently began to notate BWV 47/2 in transposed form (cf. NBA I/23 KB, 170 [Helmuth Osthoff and Rufus Hallmark]; I hope to go into the reasons for the

verwirret" BWV 35 and "Ich geh und suche mit Verlangen" BWV 49 – Bach went still further: here he wrote out the entire bass line in transposition, even for movements without obbligato organ.[109] Considering the extra trouble to which this put not only him but also the scribes of the untransposed continuo parts, we can only assume that he intended the organist in these two works – neither of which includes an organ part among its otherwise complete performing materials – to play directly from the score; and given the state of the autographs in question, with their hasty script and extensive corrections, we can hardly imagine anyone other than Bach himself taking on this job.[110] While the placement of the organ would have kept him from physically directing the performance, the modest forces of both works – one or two voices, one or three oboes, and strings – probably meant that he did not need to.[111] But in two slightly later cantatas with obbligato organ, the situation changes. "Wir danken dir, Gott, wir danken dir" BWV 29 and "Herr Gott, Beherrscher aller Dinge" BWV 120a both involve considerably larger forces: four voices – which BWV 29 even augments with ripieno parts – and an instrumental ensemble including trumpets and drums. These works no doubt required Bach's active involvement as director. In both, significantly, the organ receives a separate part, obviously to leave Bach free to lead the combined singers and players – from score.

From every indication, then, reading Sicul in terms of dual accompaniment does indeed compel us to imagine Bach directing and playing the harpsichord with a score of the *Trauerode* before him. Yet the theory of dual accompaniment depends in its very essence on parts: parts supposedly intended for harpsichord – but not, by all indications, for Bach himself.[112] What little documentary

change elsewhere), and he may never have used obbligato organ in this piece at all (cf. *ibid.*, 182–4, as well as Swanton, "Generalbaß," 93 n. 9). Similarly, it would appear that he did not actually compose BWV 170/5 for organ (*ibid.*, and NBA I/17.2, vi, and KB, 105–6 [Reinmar Emans]). As for BWV 128, an examination of the autograph – graciously facilitated by Stephen Roe of Sotheby's, London – revealed that the inscription "Organo" comes not from Bach's hand but that of his son Wilhelm Friedemann (see the facsimile in NBA I/12, x; my thanks to Peter Wollny for confirming the identification).

109 Cf. the facsimiles from BWV 49 in Dreyfus, *Bach's continuo group*, 65–6.

110 For a slightly different formulation of this argument, see Dreyfus, *Bach's continuo group*, 64; see also Swanton, "Generalbaß," 103–4. The qualifications advanced by Hans-Joachim Schulze in *BJ* 84 (1988): 242–3 overlook the notation of the bass in BWV 35 and 49.

111 On the problem of directing from the organ, cf. Dreyfus, *Bach's continuo group*, 31; on the position of the organ in St. Thomas's, see Armin Schneiderheinze, "Bachs Figuralchor und die Chorempore in der Thomaskirche," *Beiträge zur Bachforschung* 1 (1982): 40. As Dreyfus has observed (*Bach's continuo group*, 231 n. 69), Bach would seem to have had the organ continuo to a number of his Weimar cantatas played from score. While Dreyfus does not identify Bach himself as the player in these instances, the personnel structure of the Weimar chapel makes it highly unlikely that anyone else would have done the job; cf. *Dok* II/60, 69, and 80. The Weimar cantatas, of course, routinely use forces substantially smaller than those customary at Leipzig; cf. Rifkin, "More (and less)," 8.

112 See Dreyfus, *Bach's continuo group*, as in n. 99, above. In the dissertation from which his book derives, Dreyfus described the parts as the "crux of the argument" for dual accompaniment; see Laurence

evidence we have for the use of harpsichord at St. Thomas's and St. Nicholas's has the instrument played by others – although Bach did notoriously intervene on occasion.[113] Hence even if he should have served as harpsichordist-conductor in the performance of the *Trauerode*, this does not add up to quite the same thing as the practice envisaged by Dreyfus.

To some, of course, the question of who actually played the harpsichord may seem like hair-splitting. But we have still other grounds for resisting too easy an assimilation of the *Trauerode* to the theory of dual accompaniment. The first of these concerns not the harpsichord but the organ. Did Sicul, who may not have known an oboe d'amore when he heard one, actually detect the organ in the midst of the *Trauerode*? Or did he simply infer its participation, especially as it had played while the congregation took its seats before the piece began, or include it in his list for reasons similar to those proposed by Alfred Dürr in connection with the recorders? Although it would again take us too far afield to document the point, we have good reason to believe that Bach often used the harpsichord as a substitute for rather than a supplement to the organ. Sicul alone does not provide a very safe basis for thinking that he could not have done so here as well.[114]

Yet even assuming that Sicul got it right about the organ, we have no real warrant for inferring full-fledged double accompaniment in the *Trauerode*. Among Bach's vocal compositions of the 1720s, the most explicit evidence for the participation of harpsichord and organ in the same performance of the same work comes from two cantatas not discussed by Dreyfus: "Mein liebster Jesu ist verloren" BWV 154 and "Wer weiß, wie nahe mir mein Ende" BWV 27. Both cantatas restrict the harpsichord to only a single movement. BWV 154 has the usual transposed continuo for organ plus another part with a harpsichord continuo for the aria "Jesu, laß dich finden" – in which the organ does not play. But it shows no sign of ever having included a fuller harpsichord part.[115] Similarly, the performance materials to BWV 27 include both a

Dreyfus, "Basso continuo practice in the vocal works of J. S. Bach: a study of the original performance parts" (Ph.D. diss., Columbia University, 1980), 110. The revisionist methodology proclaimed in *Bach's continuo group*, 231 n. 68, does not accurately reflect a changed situation.

113 See *ibid.*, 27–8.

114 The general mourning in force at the time of the *Trauerode* included a prohibition against the organ; see Spitta, *Bach*, 2: 789, and also Janice B. Stockigt, "Die 'Annuae Literae' der Leipziger Jesuiten 1719–1740: Ein Bach-Dokument?" *BJ* 78 (1992): 78–9. But this provision, like the ban on figural music in general, clearly did not apply to the memorial ceremony, as the first sentence of Sicul's report makes clear. Bach could, however, have had other reasons not to use the organ in the *Trauerode* – if the registers most appropriate to continuo playing, for example, had suffered some sort of damage.

115 See the facsimile of the harpsichord part in NBA IX/2, 110, or I/5, viii, as well as the descriptions and discussion in *ibid.*, KB, 63–4, 72, and 81 (Marianne Helms).

transposed continuo part, containing every movement of the cantata, and an untransposed part containing a keyboard obbligato for the aria "Willkommen will ich sagen."[116] Although this part originally bore no designation – and although an unknown scribe subsequently labeled it "Organo Obligato" – both the notation and the fact that the autograph score assigns the aria to "Hautb[ois] da Caccia e Cembalo obligato" make it clear that Bach must have intended it for harpsichord.[117] But once again, the part includes nothing beyond its single movement, and we have no reason to think that a more extensive harpsichord part might once have existed.[118] Quite the opposite, in fact: for while Bach sometimes added single obbligato movements as inserts to organ parts written at earlier times, what organ parts we have for new works containing obbligato numbers always include these in the context of a continuously written whole.[119]

The example of BWV 27 and 154 opens up a new possibility for understanding the place of the harpsichord in the *Trauerode*: not as an omnipresent continuo, but as a special sonority selectively employed. Such a role, I need hardly emphasize, would seem decidedly appropriate to a work that owes so much of its character to the strategic use of rare instrumental colors. Indeed, one of those rare colors – that of the lutes – may well provide a key both to the very presence of the harpsichord and to the precise extent of its participation.

The association of lutes and harpsichord would appear to have had a long history. In 1619 Michael Praetorius even coined a special term to describe an ensemble of such instruments: "A *Lauten-Chor* is what I call it when you combine harpsichords, spinets, quilled instruments (otherwise just called *Instrument*), theorbos, lutes, pandoras, orpharions, citterns, a large bass lyre, or whatever and however many such fundamental instruments you can bring into play."[120] The term "Lautenchor" occurs in Schütz as well, although with

---

116 See NBA I/23 KB, 105–6. The figuring of the transposed part breaks off after the fourth movement; see also n. 118, below.

117 See Hans-Joachim Schulze, *Studien*, 105, as well as NBA I/23, xii, and KB, 114–15.

118 Admittedly, BWV 27 lacks the principal copy of the continuo part (see NBA I/23 KB, 108 and 111) – the untransposed part in which figuring, if present, would most likely have appeared. But as Bach himself added the figuring to the transposed part, we have no grounds for assuming that the missing part would have contained figures as well. We might note, too, that the organ part leaves "Willkommen, will ich sagen" unfigured – a possible indication that Bach meant the organ to remain silent here, or even that the organist should play the harpsichord obbligato.

119 Integrally copied organ parts including obbligatos survive for BWV 29, 71, and 120a; inserts with organ obbligatos originally scored for other instruments occur in BWV 73, 172, and, in slightly irregular form, 63.

120 Michael Praetorius, *Syntagma musicum*, vol. 3 (Wolfenbüttel, 1619), 168: "Einen Lauten-Chor nenne ich / wenn man Clavicymbel oder Spinetten, Instrumenta pennata, (sonsten in gemein Instrument genant) Theorben, Lauten / Bandoren / Orpheoreon, Cithern, eine grosse Baß-Lyra, oder was vnd so viel man von solchen vnnd dergleichen Fundament-Instrumenten zuwege bringen kan / zusammen ordnet."

a slightly different meaning: for him it refers to a vocal ensemble supported by plucked instruments. But Schütz, too, provides testimony to the lute-harpsichord connection.[121] The continuo part to a polychoral wedding concerto of 1618, "Haus und Güter erbet man von Eltern" SWV 21, bears the legend "Basso continuo, particularly accommodated to the third choir, with which lutes and harpsichords can well be used."[122] The body of the part then signals all the entries of the third choir with the rubric "Lautenchor." Seven years or so after this work, we find a related example in the Psalm "An den Wassern zu Babel" SWV 500. Here, one of the work's two choirs bears the designation "C⁰. 2do di Liuti," and its associated continuo group includes parts for both lutes and harpsichord.[123]

Obviously, a considerable span of time separates these examples from the *Trauerode*, and I have not had the chance to look for evidence to bridge the gap.[124] But even if we cannot yet demonstrate an unbroken continuity for the use of lutes and harpsichord as a particular ensemble, I think we have grounds enough to suspect that the harpsichord appears in the *Trauerode* less as part of Bach's normal bass group than as an adjunct to the lutes. This, of course, would have the practical implication of restricting the harpsichord to at most those movements of the *Trauerode* in which the lutes – and the gambas – also appear.[125] But the matter might not rest there. The cantatas just discussed, after all, did not restrict the harpsichord simply to a handful of movements but to a single aria. It seems worth asking, therefore, if Bach might not have used the harpsichord in only a single number of the *Trauerode* as well.

---

121 For Schütz's use of "Lautenchor," see particularly Werner Breig, "Zu Heinrich Schütz' weltlichem Konzert 'Ach wie soll ich doch in Freuden leben' (SWV 474), II: Überlegungen zur Gestalt der Komposition und zu ihrer Einordnung in Schütz' Frühwerk," *Schütz-Jahrbuch* 9 (1987): 96.

122 *Heinrich Schütz: Sämmtliche Werke*, ed. Philipp Spitta (Leipzig, 1885–94), 14, xiii: "Bassus continuus, Insonderheit auff den dritten Chor, zu welchem Lauten und Clavicimbel füglichen gebraucht werden können, gerichtet."

123 Cf. *Heinrich Schütz: Neue Ausgabe sämtlicher Werke* (Cassel, 1955–), 28, xviii–xix and 238–9; for the dating of the Psalm, see Clytus Gottwald, "Neue Forschungen zu den Kasseler Schütz-Handschriften," *Schütz-Jahrbuch* 12 (1990): 38.

124 Werner Breig, "Zur Werkgeschichte von Johann Sebastian Bachs Cembalokonzert in A-Dur BWV 1055," in *The Harpsichord and its Repertoire: Proceedings of the International Harpsichord Symposium Utrecht 1990*, ed. Pieter Dirksen (Utrecht, 1992), 205–8, has suggested that Bach might have figured the continuo part of the harpsichord concerto BWV 1055 for use by a lutenist, as the "use of two instruments of the same sort in solo and accompanimental function would have . . . seriously obscured the solo part" (207). While tantalizing, the argument strikes me as less than wholly persuasive: the figured continuo line in fact only rarely plays during solo passages.

125 As a further consequence, of course, it would reinforce the understanding of the lutes and gambas as a special sub-entity within an otherwise normal Bach orchestra – which, I need hardly mention, would in turn have consequences for our notion of the forces most appropriate to the *Trauerode*; see Section III, above.

Whether by chance or otherwise, an obvious candidate presents itself. The aria "Wie starb die Heldin so vergnügt" has already figured more than once in our discussion. While not placed exactly at midpoint of the *Trauerode*, this movement arguably forms the affective centerpiece of the work. The text comprises the only verses in Gottsched's poem to focus directly on the moment of the queen's death; and the music stands equally apart, both as the only concerted number in a major key and in silencing all the usual instruments of the orchestra – even the continuo – for the ethereal combination of gambas and lutes. This singularity invites speculation. Might not Bach have added the harpsichord to precisely this aria with a view towards underscoring its distinctive qualities? Other considerations could have argued for the use of the harpsichord here as well. As we saw earlier, a degree of uncertainty surrounds the realization of the bass line by the lutes. However much or little chordal elaboration they would have supplied, augmenting the lutes with harpsichord could have lent welcome fullness to the rich harmonic texture of the movement while maintaining both the homogeneity and the "otherness" of its timbres. The harpsichord would certainly have had no difficulty negotiating the leaps in the bass and could also have had reached the BB in m. 62.[126] Conceivably, rather than doubling the bass line of the score in every particular, it played a more or less abstracted version, omitting some of the details that we have interpreted as particularly lutenistic: the sigh motifs in mm. 2–4, for example, the octave afterbeats in m. 5, or the excursions into the middle register immediately afterwards.

Admittedly, the proposal to add harpsichord to this aria might seem to bring us into conflict with our avowedly literal reading of the specification "2 Viole da Gamb e 2 Liuti" in the autograph. The conflict vanishes, however, if we consider what these words actually meant. While we tend to read such an indication of scoring as a direction for performers, Bach clearly intended it – in the first instance, at least – as something quite different: as a message telling his copyist into which instrumental parts the aria should go.[127] Bach himself would hardly have needed a part to accompany the aria, so he did not have to make any reference to the harpsichord – if he had even thought to include it at the time he composed the movement. He may, of course, have felt it advisable to have a separate harpsichord part for a differentiated bass line of the sort

---

126 Bach's harpsichord writing at the time presupposes an instrument extending down to GG; cf. Alfred Dürr, "Tastenumfang und Chronologie in Bachs Klavierwerken," *Im Mittelpunkt Bach*, 225–6, and David Schulenberg, *The keyboard music of J. S. Bach* (New York, 1992), 276.

127 Notably, Bach did not have to identify the voice, as the copyist could recognize this from the clef; indeed, indications of scoring for arias and recitatives in Bach's vocal autographs leave the voice unspecified more often than not.

proposed in the last paragraph. But creating such a part entailed compositional decisions, which meant that no one but he could have carried it out.

With these speculations, we reach the limits of what the surviving evidence will usefully sustain. I have titled this paper "Some questions of performance," and it has indeed raised more questions than it has provided answers. Both the sources and the music may have brought our choices into better focus; yet they have hardly offered a surefire means of negotiating among them. For this, we have only instinct and intuition, preference and prejudice. None of us can claim Bach's sanction in this regard. But then again, we don't really need to. Bach has unwittingly entrusted his music to us across the ages. We may continue to make of it what we will.

Chapter nine

J. S. Bach's A major flute sonata BWV 1032 revisited

JEANNE SWACK

The first movement of the A major flute and harpsichord sonata of Johann Sebastian Bach, BWV 1032, survives only in part: an autograph fair copy from which Bach excised approximately forty-six to forty-eight measures.[1] The extensive literature on this piece has attempted both to explain Bach's excision in terms of perceived stylistic weaknesses in the movement and to explicate the piece only in terms of its putative earlier versions. Most recently, however, Michael Marissen has proposed that both the unusual layout of the score of the sonata and the reasons for the excision lay not in stylistic or formal problems in the movement itself, but were merely the result of expediency in copying parts simultaneously for both the sonata and the concerto arrangement with which it shares the pages. The first movement and the beginning of the second movement are copied on the three lowest staves beneath Bach's transcription of the Concerto for Two Violins and Strings in D minor BWV 1043 as the Concerto for Two Harpsichords and Strings in C minor BWV 1062, while the continuation of the second movement and the third movement are written on the pages remaining at the end of the concerto.[2]

I am grateful to Joshua Rifkin, Marian Smith, Brian Hyer, Michael Marissen, and Ardal Powell for their helpful comments in the preparation of this essay.

1 SBB Mus. ms. Bach P 612. Hans-Joachim Schulze has shown that Bach himself was responsible for the excision; Foreword to *Johann Sebastian Bach: Konzert c-Moll für zwei Cembali und Streichorchester BWV 1062, Sonate A-Dur für Flöte und Cembalo BWV 1032, Faksimile der autographen Partitur* (Leipzig, 1979), 9 (cited hereafter as *Faksimile*).

2 See Michael Marissen, "A critical reappraisal of J. S. Bach's A-major flute sonata," *Journal of Musicology* 6 (1988): 367–86. Previous discussions of this work include NBA VI/3 KB, 43–7 (Hans-Peter Schmitz); Hans Eppstein, *Studien über J. S. Bachs Sonaten für ein Melodieinstrument und obligates Cembalo* (Uppsala, 1966), 90–102; Schulze, *Faksimile*, 13–9; Robert Marshall, "J. S. Bach's compositions for solo flute," in *The music of Johann Sebastian Bach: the sources, the style, the significance* (New

Marissen has offered a reconstruction of the first movement based in part on physical details in the autograph score itself. Aside from the few but significant details he gleaned from the manuscript, such as the remains of ties and a custos not visible on the facsimile,[3] he invoked further evidence that the manuscript seems to reflect "meticulous local excisions," which he used as additional clues in his reconstruction.[4]

One detail in his treatment of these philological clues requires further elucidation. One must not be misled by either the appearance of the autograph in the facsimile edition or by the present state of the rapidly deteriorating manuscript.[5] When the manuscript was returned to the Deutsche Staatsbibliothek from Poland in 1977, a microfilm was prepared that serves as testimony to the state of preservation of the manuscript at that time. Because the first movement of the sonata was copied on the lowest three staves of the manuscript, Bach excised the missing measures by cutting strips from the bottoms of the pages. The apparent "cut-outs" in the manuscript on pp. 19–20, which one could easily take as "local excisions" that Bach made to preserve the flute line of the sonata, did not exist in 1977.[6] It is clear on the film that this strip was cut straight across. When the facsimile edition was prepared shortly thereafter (published in 1979), Bach's acidic ink was already taking its toll. It was the ink, not Bach, that caused the "excisions" on pp. 19–20, because the notches represent notes in the bottom staff of the double harpsichord concerto, clearly visible on the film, which have literally fallen out of the manuscript. When I had the opportunity to examine the manuscript in March, 1990, the paper had further deteriorated to the point that the paper between the notches was entirely eaten away.[7] Clearly, these notches cannot be taken as proof that Bach

York, 1989), 217–20; Hans Eppstein, "Zur Problematik von Johann Sebastian Bachs Flötensonaten," BJ 67 (1981): 78, 87–9; Alfred Dürr, NBA VI/3 *Ergänzung zum* KB; Michael Marissen, "A trio in C major for recorder, violin and continuo by J. S. Bach?" *Early Music* 13 (1985): 384–90; Willem Kroesbergen and Marijke Schouten, "Bachs triosonates gereconstrueerd," *Tijdschrift voor Oude Muziek* 1 (1986): 115–18; Marianne Betz, "Bearbeitung, Rekonstruktion, Ergänzung: Der erste Satz der Sonate A-Dur BWV 1032 für Flöte und obligates Cembalo von J. S. Bach," *Tibia* 13 (1988): 158–63; and Jeanne Swack, "Quantz and the sonata in E-flat major for flute and obbligato cembalo, BWV 1031," *Early Music* 23 (1995): 44–5.

3 Marissen, "Critical reappraisal," 375–6.
4 *Ibid.*, 375.
5 See Schulze, *Faksimile.*
6 That is, Bach would have cut high into the lowest staff of the double harpsichord concerto to avoid removing high notes in the flute part of the sonata.
7 I am grateful to the staff of the music division of the former Deutsche Staatsbibliothek for allowing me to see the autograph. I imply no criticism of Marissen here. Had I been granted immediate access to the autograph without seeing the microfilm first, I would not have noticed that the notches were of recent origin. I would also like to stress that Marissen culls considerable evidence from philological details in the manuscript that clearly do stem from Bach.

was carefully trying to preserve the flute line of the excised portion of the sonata.[8] Nor can they be of any help in reconstructing the piece.

While the reasons for the excision will probably never be known (although Marissen's proposal is the most compelling), enough of the movement survives to form the basis for a critical reading of the piece, and indeed, several have appeared. Even more numerous are published completions of the movement. But by not taking into account the unique formal processes at work in this movement, or by misunderstanding them, the published completions fail to realize the remarkably consistent, albeit carefully concealed, structure of the movement: a sonata in the form of an Italian concerto.

The purpose of this study is twofold: to propose a critical reading of the surviving portion of the movement that accounts for the textural anomalies of the work, providing the groundwork for a conjectural completion that would be formally consistent with the rest of the movement;[9] and to offer an explanation for the probable transposition of at least the outer movements from a lost model in C major to A major.

Sonata movements based on the form of the Italian concerto can be found in Bach's chamber music in various scorings, including the obbligato sonatas with violin, viola da gamba, and flute, as well as the Sonata for Flute and Basso Continuo in E minor BWV 1034.[10] In each of these sonata movements Bach sets the "ground rules" anew. As I will argue, the surviving portion of the first movement of BWV 1032 maintains a regular alternation of "ritornello" and "solo" sections that functions beneath the surface of the piece. Bach camouflages this regularity by playing upon the listener's expectations as to what constitutes "solo" and "ritornello" material. He carefully sets up the opposition of "ritornello" and "solo" material at the very beginning of the movement, only to confound it.

The movement's structure (mm. 1–62)

Bach's sonatas in the concerted manner, like his concertos, play off the listener's familiarity with the conventions of the Vivaldian concerto. Basic to

---

8   They also cannot, of course, be taken as proof that Bach was not trying to preserve the strip.

9   A summary of some of the more recent completions is given in Betz, "Bearbeitung." To this must be added Michael Marissen's forthcoming edition, Johann Sebastian Bach, *Sonate A-Dur für Flöte und obligates Cembalo BWV 1032* (Carus-Verlag, in press). I am grateful to Michael Marissen for providing me with a copy of his edition.

10 One may also, in this regard, include the second movement of the Fifth Brandenburg Concerto, because it employs a ritornello structure and is in a conventional trio texture; although there are, on the surface, four lines, including two in the harpsichord, the piece never makes use of more than three obbligato parts.

the listener's beliefs about such concertos is the axiom that a portion of the ritornello may represent the entire ritornello after its initial statement. However, I would propose that in this movement each restatement of the ritornello, not just the first, includes all three sections of the ritornello (*Vordersatz, Fortspinnung, Epilog*). The bulk of the "solo" material, in contrast, consists of fragments of the ritornello, largely taken from the *Vordersatz*. In this reading, all of the ritornellos are tonally stable, whereas all of the "solo" sections modulate. So pervasive is the ritornello material in this movement, however, that even the opening "solo" theme in the flute is controlled by the *Vordersatz*, because it comprises in part a simple counterpoint to the statement of the *Vordersatz*, with an altered bass, in the right hand of the harpsichord (mm. 11–13; see Example 9.1 below). Table 9.1 provides a summary of the structure of the surviving portion of the first movement.

Table 9.1. *Structure of the surviving portion of BWV 1032/1*

Section	Measures	Key	Comments
Ritornello 1	1–9/1	A major	Ritornello in cembalo, two parts
Solo 1	9–25/1	A major–E major	*Vordersatz*, with altered bass, in mm. 16–18
Ritornello 2	25–35/3	E major	Feigned 3-part polyphony; real 3 parts only in mm. 33–5
Solo 2	35–46/1	E major–F♯ minor	Largely constructed from ritornello material
Ritornello 3	46–62/1	F♯ minor	In two parts except for interpolation at mm. 49–55. M. 62 is last measure before excision

Both Eppstein and Marissen have taken note of the uncharacteristically thin texture of the surviving portion of the movement. Much of the movement is in only two real obbligato parts. This textural anomaly, as it turns out, is carefully tied to the structure of the movement. For the recurring ritornellos are all in two parts, departing from this texture only when Bach inserts additional material into the ritornello, as he does in the second and third ritornellos. The three sections of the ritornello are not always presented contiguously, although they always occur in their original order. Through these additions to the ritornello, Bach introduces real three-part counterpoint.

To show the consistent alternation between tonally stable ritornellos comprising all three ritornello segments, on the one hand, and modulating solo episodes comprised largely of altered ritornello material, on the other hand, I

Example 9.1   J. S. Bach, Sonata for Flute and Harpsichord BWV 1032/1, mm. 1–9

will proceed with a close analysis of the surviving portion of the movement. Let us consider first the ritornello sections, beginning with the first ritornello, given in Example 9.1, which presents the ritornello in its most pristine form, without interpolations. The "inner part" in the left hand, while seemingly mere harmonic filler, is granted the status of an independent part in later statements of the ritornello, although its contrapuntal worth there is only feigned.[11] This "model" ritornello forms a grid against which to measure subsequent ritornellos.

11   One must wonder about the status of this "filler" part if the left-hand part of the piece was originally a

The elaboration of the second ritornello shows two of Bach's methods of elaborating the ritornello: the simulation of three-part polyphony within an essentially two-part framework, and the addition of a three-voice extension. This ritornello (mm. 25–35), given in Example 9.2a, is in the dominant; its thematic material is presented primarily in the flute. Example 9.2b shows the second ritornello collapsed to its two essential polyphonic parts. Bach introduces real three-part polyphony only in mm. 33–5. He alters the *Epilog* so that it breaks into three parts at the downbeat of m. 33, leading only to an imperfect cadence on the third beat of that measure, and then introduces a two-measure extension in three parts, ending with a perfect cadence in m. 35.[12] But more than simply allowing for three-part polyphony, the extension introduces a subtle quotation from the *Vordersatz* in the bass from the third beat of m. 33 to the second beat of m. 34. This process of elaborating the ritornello plays upon the listener's expectations for the concerto genre by grafting onto the concerto's most distinctive marker – the ritornello itself – gestures more typical of the conventional trio sonata: the trading back and forth of thematic material among the parts and the use of a three-part contrapuntal texture.

The third ritornello, mm. 46–62, given in Example 9.3, has more extensive interpolations.[13] Continuing the plan of rotating the voice that plays the *Vordersatz*, Bach sets it in the bass. This ritornello is in F♯ minor. As Example 9.4 shows, the opening ritornello cannot be transposed to the minor mode without causing a cross relation at the beginning of the *Epilog*.[14] This potential cross relation may have prompted Bach to alter the *Fortspinnung* in mm. 57–9, but he had already begun a subtle elaboration of the ritornello from the second measure of the *Vordersatz* (m. 47) on. This elaboration – or in effect camouflaging – of the ritornello makes the aural recognition of this passage quite difficult, and further mitigates the articulation between ritornello and solo. In addition, it allows further opportunity to introduce three-part writing. In Example 9.3, I have circled the notes of the original *Vordersatz*. Bach adds

---

basso continuo line. The "filler" part is, after all, essential to the piece, since some of it (mm. 3–4) forms the right-hand part in mm. 26–7 in the second ritornello and the flute line in mm. 56–7 in the third ritornello. It is likely that in the original trio-sonata version of the piece this line was not present in Ritornello 1, except as the inevitable result of having realized the basso continuo. In arranging the two lower parts for obbligato harpsichord, Bach may have added this line to the left-hand part of the harpsichord in Ritornello 1 only after having worked it out in Ritornello 2.

12 See also Marissen, "Critical reappraisal," 385.

13 It is instructive, in this regard, to compare this ritornello with the second ritornello of the first movement of the Concerto for Violin in A minor BWV 1041, which Bach expands by introducing solo passages between the three sections of the ritornello proper.

14 See Laurence Dreyfus, "J. S. Bach's concerto ritornellos and the question of invention," *Musical Quarterly* 71 (1985): 341 on problems incurred by changing the mode of concerto ritornellos, an operation Dreyfus calls "MODESWITCH."

Example 9.2a   J. S. Bach, Sonata for Flute and Harpsichord BWV 1032/1, mm. 25–35

Example 9.2b   J. S. Bach, Sonata for Flute and Harpsichord BWV 1032/1, mm. 25–33, hypothetical reduction to two obbligato parts

four beats to the *Vordersatz* by passing the thematic material from the bass to the right hand of the harpsichord, stretching it by adding notes between those that belong to the ritornello proper, and by setting the flute against it with a chain of suspensions.

Following the *Vordersatz*, Bach inserts a "new" *Fortspinnung*, derived from the original, in brief canon in three obbligato parts (mm. 49–55).[15] With its three-part imitative polyphony, this *Fortspinnung* interpolation is more evocative of the conventional trio sonata than it is of the concerto. Bach then presents a version of the original *Fortspinnung*, which proceeds quite literally until the

15   The bass part does not continue the canon in mm. 52–5.

Example 9.3   J. S. Bach, Sonata for Flute and Harpsichord BWV 1032/1, mm. 46–62

Example 9.4   J. S. Bach, Sonata for Flute and Harpsichord BWV 1032/1, hypothetical
ritornello in F♯ minor (connection of *Fortspinnung* to *Epilog*)

Example 9.5   J. S. Bach, Sonata for Flute and Harpsichord BWV 1032/1, mm. 9–25

third beat of m. 57 (the flute takes the top part of the bass in the opening ritornello, while the bass plays the bottom part). Were Bach to continue with this literal repeat of the ritornello, a cross relation would occur at the beginning of the *Epilog* at the end of m. 59, as Example 9.4 shows.

Bach's solution, to transpose the *Fortspinnung* material up a third beginning in m. 58 and to divide it between the right hand of the harpsichord and the flute, allows him to break into a feigned three-part texture, as well as skirt the problem of the accidentals at the beginning of the *Epilog*. The *Epilog* theme transfers to the flute after the first note of m. 60, and a real three-part texture occurs in the final full measure of the *Epilog*, leading to the F♯ minor cadence at the beginning of m. 62, the last measure before the excision. This cadence, of course, marks a major structural division in the piece: the end of the third ritornello.

We have seen thus far that once Bach laid out the initial ritornello material, he subjected the subsequent ritornellos to various kinds of elaborations

involving the insertion of additional material and the feigning of three-part texture. Let us consider now the two surviving solo sections and their interrelationships with the ritornellos. Each of the two solos is marked by thematic borrowing from the previous ritornello, producing a thematic chain extending from formal section to formal section. While the first solo section presents at least a semblance of the traditional contrasting material following the initial ritornello, the second solo section goes much further in blurring the apparent concerto structure of the piece by presenting no contrasting material at all.

In the first solo section, mm. 9–25, shown in Example 9.5, Bach lays out the unmistakable outlines of a "concerto" at the outset by setting off the first solo with a marked thematic contrast and change of texture and scoring. Then, as he often does, he begins to undermine the ritornello-solo opposition by bringing in the *Vordersatz* under the flute solo in mm. 11–13.[16] Note, however,

---

16   Compare, for example, the opening soli section of the first movement of the Fifth Brandenburg
     Concerto BWV 1050, in which Bach further dismembers the *Vordersatz* and uses it to "accompany" the

Example 9.6   J. S. Bach, Sonata for Flute and Harpsichord BWV 1032/1, mm. 35–46

that the bass of the "*Vordersatz*" has been altered, and now features a prominent pedal point on the dominant.

While the accompanimental role of the *Vordersatz* at this point seems evident, since the flute continues the solo begun in m. 9,[17] the return of the *Vordersatz* in mm. 16–19 is more ambiguous. One would expect the entrance of the *Vordersatz* in the harpsichord to signify the awaited ritornello in the dominant. The right-hand part of the harpsichord has up to now been associated with the role of the orchestra, and there is a cadence on the dominant. What ensues, however, is the *Vordersatz* at the original pitch level, but largely under a dominant pedal. Only a fragment of the *Fortspinnung* follows, leading to a restatement of the *Vordersatz* in the dominant in mm. 20–2. This, however, is an inversion of mm. 11–12, and carries the same formal status, that of solo accompanied by *Vordersatz*. The rest of the first solo, mm. 22–5, is a variation of mm. 13–15, and the cadence on the dominant ending the first section corresponds to the cadence at m. 16.

The second solo section, mm. 35–46, given in Example 9.6, is more complex and less clearly differentiated from the surrounding ritornellos than the first solo. Bach increasingly blurs the outlines of the concerto as the movement progresses. Thus, although he had marked the entrance of the first solo by the introduction of a distinct theme, the second solo has no such identifying marker. In fact, it seems designed to issue no signals at all regarding its solo status. All the material in this solo section comes directly from the ritornello, though it presents no segment of the ritornello in its original form.

Bach constructs the second solo section from five thematic segments, three based on the *Vordersatz* and two based on the *Fortspinnung*. Two of the *Vordersatz* segments appear sequentially at the beginning, and this section seems to begin exactly as did the second ritornello, with the material formerly in the flute part now in the right hand of the harpsichord. But both these statements of the "*Vordersatz*" (in mm. 35–9) lack one of the most crucial syntactical elements of the original *Vordersatz*: the last two eighth-notes marking the articulation of the dominant.[18] This is also true of the third "*Vordersatz*" in mm. 41–3, which is an inversion of mm. 37–9. Note also the

soli. The listener's attention is claimed at this point by the three soloists, and he or she is only secondarily aware of the progression of the fragmented beginning of the ritornello. The blurring of the ritornello/solo distinction is frequent in Bach's concertos as a whole.

17 As Michael Marissen has pointed out to me, the dominance of the upper part at this point is less evident when the piece is performed as a trio sonata instead of a sonata with obbligato harpsichord. See also Laurence Dreyfus, "J. S. Bach and the status of genre: problems of style in the G-minor sonata, BWV 1029," *Journal of Musicology* 5 (1987): 62–3 n. 12 for another discussion of this passage.

18 On a similar problem in BWV 1041, see *ibid.*, 61 n. 9.

alteration of the bass in mm. 38–42, and the overall emphasis on extended pedal points not present in the real ritornello. The pedal points do refer back, however, to the version of the *Vordersatz* used to accompany the first solo.

The two *"Fortspinnung"* sections, which continue from the *"Vordersatz"* sections in mm. 39 and 43, begin like the original *Fortspinnung* sections, but continue in an ascending, rather than descending, sequence. The second of these sections begins, of course, as an inversion of the first, since it continues from the end of the *"Vordersatz"* in m. 43 just as the first *"Fortspinnung"* does in m. 39. Bach, however, extends this second section by a full measure and adds a brief cadential section in F♯ minor, setting up the return to the ritornello in that key. Only this two-beat cadential section is in three obbligato parts; all of the second solo section to this point is in two real parts.

How did Bach continue the rest of the movement following the third ritornello? Much hinges upon a reading of m. 62, the last measure before the excision. This measure comprises the cadence that concludes the third ritornello and the beginning of the ensuing section. M. 62 is identical to m. 46, the beginning of the third ritornello, transposed to B minor with the upper parts exchanged. Two possibilities present themselves. First, m. 62 may have initiated a section that is a repetition of the previous ritornello, mm. 46–62, beat 1, now in B minor.[19] This would certainly be in keeping with Bach's customary modular treatment of his musical material, in which sections of a movement recur at various transposition levels, often with exchanged parts. This reading would break with the regular alternation of tonally stable ritornellos and modulatory solos at work in the movement up until this point by presenting two adjacent ritornellos a fourth apart, which, however, could be considered to function as a "composite" ritornello.

Following this double presentation of the ritornello would come another solo section and the final ritornello. The last two measures of the end of the *Epilog* are left at the end of the movement.[20] This is a transposition of mm. 32–3, with the two upper voices exchanged in the last measure and a root-position tonic instead of a first-inversion tonic at the end to form the final cadence (at this point in the second ritornello, a second *"Epilog"* occurred to provide a more extended passage in three-voice texture for the end of the ritornello).[21]

19 Marissen's completion follows this reading of m. 62: mm. 62–78, beat 1 are a transposition of mm. 46–62, beat 1.
20 Bach had originally removed the strip containing these two measures (at the bottom of pp. 29–30 of the autograph score). But, perhaps upon realizing that to excise this strip would mean destroying the beginning of the second movement on the other side, he carefully glued it back in.
21 This voice exchange is even more complicated than it seems at first, because on the downbeat of the final measure the right hand of the harpsichord has the bass figure from the first beat of m. 33.

Working backward, one could thus transpose mm. 25–34 to the tonic, substituting the ending remaining in the manuscript for mm. 32–3, to provide the final ritornello.[22] The movement would thus have the structure shown in Table 9.2.[23] In this case, it is the third solo that is problematic, because there is no way to tell whether this solo would have been a restatement of previous material, or, if so, how such a restatement was organized.

Table 9.2. *Possible completion of BWV 1032/1 with two adjacent ritornellos*

Section	Measures	Key	Comments
Ritornello 1	1–9/1	A major	[As in Table 1]
Solo 1	9–25/1	A major–E major	"
Ritornello 2	25–35/3	E major	"
Solo 2	35–46/1	E major–F♯ minor	"
Ritornello 3	46–62/1	F♯ minor	"
Ritornello 4	62–?	B minor	
Solo 3	?	B minor–D major?–A major	
Ritornello 5	?	A major	= Ritornello 2

A second possible completion is based on the premise that Bach continued the regular alternation of ritornellos and solos at work until the downbeat of m. 62. In this reading, the material following m. 62 does not continue as a literal transposition of mm. 46–62, beat 1, but rather m. 62 initiates a modulatory solo section. Because the preceding two solo sections had borrowed extensively from ritornellos that they immediately followed, the third solo may have likewise drawn upon parts of the preceding ritornello, in this case at least its opening. If one continues the process whereby the solo and ritornello sections become progressively longer, then it is possible that the third solo section was fairly extended, longer than the ten and one-half measures of the second solo.

22 Marissen's completion also uses this ending. For the solo section between the B minor ritornello and the final ritornello he uses a transposition of the first part of the opening solo section, now in B minor (that is, mm. 9–16 transposed to B minor), and then a restatement of the entire opening solo section in D major with the upper parts exchanged (that is, mm. 9–25 transposed to D major). This then leads to the final ritornello, a transposition of the second, just as the first solo leads to the second ritornello. As Marissen states in the preface to this edition, however, this version is probably slightly too short. See Marissen, *Sonate A-Dur für Flöte und obligates Cembalo BWV 1032*, vi n. 10, and "Critical reappraisal," 375.

23 The continuation of the piece after Ritornello 3 in Table 2 is identical with Marissen's completion, even though his reading of the piece up to the point of excision differs from mine. See Marissen, "Critical reappraisal," 383.

Because one needs to account for approximately forty-six to forty-eight missing measures, this reading would require a total of five ritornellos. The completion would thus comprise a fourth ritornello in a non-tonic key, perhaps a version of the first ritornello with extended three-voice interpolations, a fourth solo section, and a fifth ritornello. As in the first suggested solution, the fifth ritornello was probably a transposition of the second ritornello. Again working backward from the end, the fourth solo could be a transposition of the first solo, modulating from the subdominant to the tonic (D major–A major), as the first solo modulated from the tonic to the dominant (A major–E major). The fourth ritornello in this case would be in the subdominant, and the third solo would modulate from the supertonic minor (B minor) to the subdominant (D major, its relative major). This reading has the advantage of providing a consistent continuation of the musical processes at work in the first sixty-two measures. The overall structure of such a movement is given in Table 9.3.

Table 9.3. *Possible completion of BWV 1032/1 with five non-adjacent ritornellos*

Section	Measures	Key	Comments
Ritornello 1	1–9/1	A major	[As in Table 1]
Solo 1	9–25/1	A major–E major	"
Ritornello 2	25–35/3	E major	"
Solo 2	35–46/1	E major–F♯ minor	"
Ritornello 3	46–62/1	F♯ minor	"
Solo 3	62–?	B minor–D major?	
Ritornello 4	?	D major?	variant of Ritornello 1?
Solo 4	?	D major?–A major	=Solo 1?
Ritornello 5	?	A major	=Ritornello 2

To sum up: the surviving portion of the movement presents a regular structure based on the alternation of tonally stable ritornellos with tonally unstable solo sections, which, however, derive most of their thematic material from the ritornellos. Because of the lack of true thematic contrast in all but the opening solo, the outlines of the "concerto" are well-disguised. As alternatives to the completions published to date, I have suggested two possibilities for conjectural completions that continue this regular alternation while maintaining the web of interconnections from section to section present in the rest of the movement.

The transposition of the outer movements

I would like to consider a possible reason for the preparation of the 1736 score. Although the work may well have been performed by the Leipzig Collegium musicum, it is worth exploring further a possible Dresden connection for the work's performance. In his preface to the facsimile edition of BWV 1032 and BWV 1062, Hans-Joachim Schulze speculates that Bach had copied out the two works for a performance in Dresden in conjunction with the organ concert that he presented at the Frauenkirche on December 1, 1736. Schulze further postulates that Bach's partner in the double harpsichord concerto would have been his eldest son Wilhelm Friedemann Bach, then organist at Dresden's Sophienkirche. But his second suggestion – that the principal flutist at the Dresden *Hofkapelle*, Pierre-Gabriel Buffardin, had been the flute soloist – requires further scrutiny.[24]

As I have shown elsewhere, Bach's models for the *Sonate auf Concertenart* probably included at least one of the three surviving examples of the genre by the Dresden flutist Johann Joachim Quantz.[25] Quantz's Eb major trio QV2:18 most likely served as the model for the Sonata in Eb Major for Flute and Harpsichord BWV 1031 attributed to Bach. While the attribution of BWV 1031 to Bach is uncertain, the surviving sources for the work ultimately stem from Bach's household, and he was at least the owner of the work.[26] At any rate, BWV 1031 is a work with clear connections to Quantz.

On a more specific level, BWV 1032 seems to be indebted to BWV 1031 for a number of its details. First, in the first movement of BWV 1032, the opening ritornello is stated by the harpsichord alone, without the solo flute. This opening gambit (with a solo violin or harpsichord ritornello, depending on the scoring) is common to BWV 1031 and all three of Quantz's sonatas in the concerted manner.

Second, the first movement of BWV 1032 is closely related to the opening movement of BWV 1031 in the shape of its opening ritornello and some of the opening solo material. The respective third movements share similar motivic material (compare the motive presented in two-part imitation in mm. 78 ff. in BWV 1031/3 with a passage treating a very similar motive in three-part

---

24 Schulze, *Faksimile*, 18.
25 Jeanne Swack, "Quantz and the sonata in E-flat major" and "On the origins of the *Sonate auf Concertenart*," *Journal of the American Musicological Society* 46 (1993): 391–3.
26 If BWV 1031 is a work of Bach, then it shows Bach's clear acquaintance with QV2:18, to which it is indebted for the structure of the outer movements and some of its thematic material. If, on the other hand, BWV 1031 is a work of Quantz (its style and technique is consistent with Quantz's examples of the *Sonate auf Concertenart*), then Bach was still acquainted with the work, since he owned the manuscript.

imitation in BWV 1032/3 at mm. 52 ff. and in subsequent passages).[27] Because BWV 1031 is modeled on QV2:18, BWV 1032 bears a connection to at least one of Quantz's trios.

If BWV 1032 is ultimately inspired by Quantz's trio sonatas *auf Concertenart*, then it seems more likely that Bach's partner in the work, if Schulze's posited Dresden performance really took place, would have been Quantz rather than Buffardin.[28] While this is speculative, Quantz's participation in the piece would help to explain one of the more puzzling aspects of the autograph: the transposition down a minor third of the outer movements, and possibly the middle movement as well.[29]

The transposition, after all, is not necessary for the performance of the piece in the transmitted scoring for flute and cembalo. The piece can be played perfectly well in C major on at least some transverse flutes, and Bach could have saved himself the trouble of copying the work out again in the new key.[30] In fact, transposing the outer movements back to C major eliminates the technically most difficult passage for a one-keyed flute: the approach to the F♯ minor cadence in m. 61 of the first movement.

But consider, for a moment, the possibility that the transposition was carried out at the request of the flutist. The piece presents one problem in C major,

---

27 A more detailed comparison of BWV 1031 and BWV 1032 is in Swack, "Quantz and the sonata in E-flat major, 44–5."

28 Robert Marshall expressed a similar opinion in his response to my paper "Quantz and the sonata in E-flat major for flute and obbligato cembalo, BWV 1031," presented at the National Meeting of the American Musicological Society, Chicago, November 9, 1991.

29 The autograph score offers a number of clues that the outer movements of the work were originally in C major and transposed down to A major in the 1736 score. Hans Eppstein had been the first to suggest that the outer movements of the piece had originally been in C major. See Eppstein, *Studien*, 92–8. Although Alfred Dürr had argued that the corrections in the autograph did not prove the existence of a C major version (NBA VI/3 *Ergänzung zum KB*, 12–4), an analysis of irregularities of voice leading, as presented in Eppstein, supports the C major hypothesis. Marshall, "The compositions for solo flute," 217–19, and Marissen, "A trio in C major," 386–7, both cite corrections of a third in the autograph as supporting the case for the C major version. In his preface to *Johann Sebastian Bach: Sonata in C Major for Recorder, Violin, and Basso Continuo (probable early version of the A-major flute sonata, BWV 1032)* (Carus-Verlag, in press), i, Marissen argues for C minor as the original key for the second movement.

30 Marissen, "Critical reappraisal," 372, argues that the original clefs in the C major version were French violin clef (top line, for recorder), treble clef (second line, violin), and bass clef (bottom line, basso continuo). Thus Bach would have simply substituted a treble clef for the French violin clef on the top line and a soprano clef for the treble clef on the middle line, adjusting the key signature and accidentals. Only the bass line would require moving the position of the notes on the staff. Thus most of the work of transposition would have been carried out by the change of clefs. As Marissen has pointed out to me, Bach did not expect his traverso players to perform from parts in French violin clef. Thus, he would have recopied the top part into the treble clef. The downward transposition of a minor third greatly expedites this, since it is effected by the change in clef. Copying the piece for transverse flute in C major would have thus been more trouble than copying it in A major. Still, for some flutists it would certainly have been advantageous to have the outer movements copied in C major. The second movement, however, is considerably more idiomatic to a one-keyed flute in A minor than in C minor.

the use of f'''. This f''' can be a weak note on some flutes, and appears only infrequently in the flute literature of the time. In C major, the flute part would have contained one f''' in the surviving portion of the first movement (m. 54) and five in the last movement (mm. 115, 180, 237, 239, 240). And if, as is a distinct possibility, the middle movement was originally in C minor, instead of A minor as in BWV 1032, it would have required a prominent, indeed climactic f''' at m. 26. In addition, the third movement would have required f♯''' and g''', notes that do occur, although infrequently, in Bach's Leipzig flute parts. But while Bach's flute parts do not shy away from the high range, Quantz's Dresden flute parts do their best to avoid it. Relatively few of the flute parts in his approximately 45 Dresden trios require e''', and several do not rise above c'''.[31]

At least two eighteenth-century accounts of Quantz's preferred style of flute attest that Quantz preferred wide-bored flutes that favored the lower octaves at the expense of the third (highest) register. In the article that F. D. Castilon supplied to the third volume of the Supplément of Diderot's *Encyclopédie* (1777), the author seems to have a first-hand acquaintance with the flutes Quantz produced in Berlin: "Firstly, Quantz's flutes are longer, of wider bore and thicker in the wood than ordinary flutes. Consequently they have a tone of more weight, lustiness and sonority, but a more limited compass."[32] And an eyewitness account by the late eighteenth-century flutist and pedagogue Johann George Tromlitz also refers to Quantz's limited range:

Quantz says in his book [the *Versuch*]: one should draw the lips gradually away from the teeth the most easily to obtain the high register. This can only happen if the mouth and its opening are rounded; but in this way I cannot make the high notes work, and I do not think they can for Quantz either. I have often heard him play, but since he only went as high as E''' and never any higher, I was unable to find out; but one of his students has assured me that his high register was not good.[33]

Although these descriptions pertain to the flutes Quantz made for his own use and for Frederick the Great in Berlin, the limited range of the flute parts of most of the Dresden trios indicates that Quantz also preferred to play wide-bored flutes in Dresden. Such flutes were typical of the Parisian instruments that Quantz encountered during his stay in Paris in 1726, which

31 Both the Sonata in E♭ major, BWV 1031 and its parent sonata, Quantz's Trio Sonata in E♭ major, QV 2:18, rarely exceed c'''. The range of BWV 1031 is typical of Quantz's flute writing, but not Bach's.

32 Quoted in Edward Reilly, *Quantz and his* Versuch: *three studies* (New York, 1971), 98. The translation is from Eric Halfpenny, "A French commentary on Quantz," *Music and Letters* 37 (1956): 65.

33 Johann George Tromlitz, *Ausführlicher und gründlicher Unterricht die Flöte zu spielen* (Leipzig, 1791), trans. Ardal Powell as *The Virtuoso Flute-Player* (Cambridge, 1991), 49. I am grateful to Ardal Powell for pointing this passage out to me and for the information on Quantz's flutes in the ensuing discussion. Surviving examples of Quantz's instruments are of the wide-bore type.

provided him with the models for constructing his own instruments. These Parisian instruments typically have a rich low register at the expense of the upper register. The outer movements of BWV 1032 may have been transposed down to suit Quantz's flute playing.

The dating of the original version of BWV 1032, like the dating of all of Bach's sonatas *auf Concertenart*, remains problematic, other than the establishment of 1736, the date of the autograph score, as a *terminus ante quem*. I would like to suggest, however, that the work dates from the period *c.* 1730 to 1736, because the parallels that it shows with BWV 1031 – regardless of the assignment of the work to Bach or Quantz – seem to reflect a familiarity with Quantz's sonatas *auf Concertenart*, whose sources date from around 1730–5.[34]

My reading of the structure of the first movement of BWV 1032 should lay to rest any discomfort with the construction of the surviving portion of the first movement. The formal process underlying the movement is unique, and the "redundant cadences" and lack of thematic contrast are part of the intellectual construct of the piece. In this regard I am also more inclined to believe Marissen's scenario that Bach made the excision for the sake of expediency in copying over an explanation based upon Bach's dissatisfaction with formal weaknesses in the piece.

If my reading departs from previous readings, it is because it takes as its starting point the belief that the work reflects a systematic and consistent working out of the tonal and thematic properties of the ritornello, and that this working out is at a structural level that is meant to be inaudible. The listener's attention is focused on the "surface" structures of the piece, which are designed at least initially to convey the contrast of *tutti* and solo material inherent in the Vivaldian concerto. Although this play on the expectations of the genre is to some degree part and parcel of the genre of *Sonate auf Concertenart*,[35] the process at work in the first movement of BWV 1032 is remarkable for the complexity and subtlety of the treatment of ritornello and solo materials. The governing principle beneath this complexity – the consistent alternation between tonally stable and tonally unstable sections – is ultimately not tied to the dichotomy between ritornello and solo material apparently established at the outset of the movement. This dialectic between thematic material and its expected function on the one hand, and tonal structure on the other has made an understanding of the surviving portion of this movement so elusive.

34 See Swack, "Quantz and the sonata in E-flat major for flute and cembalo," 41–2 and "On the origins of the *Sonate auf Concertenart*," 391–2 for a discussion of the dating of Quantz's trios *auf Concertenart* and for a comparison of BWV 1031 and BWV 1032.

35 A fuller treatment is in Swack, "On the origins of the *Sonate auf Concertenart*," 411–13.

Chapter ten

Rhetoric, the ricercar, and J. S. Bach's *Musical Offering*

PAUL WALKER

Humanism, the revival of classical Roman and Greek culture primarily through the study of ancient Latin literary texts, was the predominant intellectual movement in Europe during the fifteenth and sixteenth centuries.[1] Its influence has survived down to the present day in our liberal arts education and study of the Humanities. Intellectuals such as Erasmus of Rotterdam welcomed this revival as an antidote to the late-medieval tradition of scholasticism, which they characterized as dry, formalistic, and lost in the endless sophistry of hair-splitting logic based on Aristotle and the early church fathers. In place of logic, fifteenth- and sixteenth-century intellectuals preferred another of the seven liberal arts, rhetoric, the art of writing and speaking persuasively and elegantly in classical Latin. Their heroes were Cicero, whose style they sought to emulate, and Quintilian, who taught them how to emulate it. In the north, this revival accompanied a freer, somewhat less orthodox approach to Christianity (orthodoxy retaining to some degree its association with scholasticism) and humanistic education was eagerly adopted into the Protestant grammar school or *Lateinschule*. However far it eventually strayed from Quintilian's original, some form of classical Latin grammar and rhetoric greeted generations of northern European schoolboys – including Johann Sebastian Bach – in their earliest years of training.

The author would like to thank David Fuller, Kerala Snyder, Eva Linfield, Daniel Melamed, and the late Howard Brown for their helpful advice and comments on this and earlier versions of this paper.
1 Many texts could be cited on this topic. An excellent summary by one of the leading international scholars on the subject is Paul Oskar Kristeller, *Renaissance thought and the arts*, expanded edn. (Princeton, 1990). Many of these essays date from the 1950s and 1960s. For an overview of more recent thinking on the topic, see *The impact of humanism on Western Europe*, ed. Anthony Goodman and Angus MacKay (London, 1990). On the topic of humanistic education, see Anthony Grafton and Lisa Jardine, *From humanism to the humanities* (Cambridge, Mass., 1986).

Similarly, one might call the period of music from Josquin des Prez to Bach the period of musical humanism. Despite the dramatic changes that took place in compositional techniques during this period of nearly 250 years, the primary aim of vocal music remained for nearly all musicians that of expressing the text through both proper declamation of the words and the use of appropriate means of musical expression. In *Le istitutioni harmoniche*, the classic work on the high-Renaissance style, Gioseffo Zarlino wrote,

the fact is that Plato places the words before the other components [that is, harmony and rhythm] as the principal thing, and considers the other two components to be subservient to it . . . And so it should be. For if a text, whether by way of narrative or imitation, deals with subjects that are cheerful or sad, grave or without gravity, and modest or lascivious, a choice of harmony and rhythm must be made in accordance with the nature of the subject matter contained in the text, in order that these things . . . may result in music that is suited to the purpose.[2]

In fact, although advocates of the *stile moderno* in the years around 1600 accused the earlier musicians of showing no regard for text, the Artusi-Monteverdi controversy was not about whether music should express a text but to what extent this end justified the breaking of well-established rules of counterpoint and mode. In this light, it is not surprising that writers about music in both the Renaissance and the Baroque period recognized an analogy between the orator and the composer. The language of the orator may have been classical Latin, that of the composer counterpoint, but the goal of effectively and persuasively communicating an idea or mood to the listener remained the same.

Although Italy was the birthplace of Humanism, both in general and in musical thought, it was in Germany that a host of writers about music explored this analogy in some detail.[3] In broadest terms, these theorists applied the analogy to three specific parts of the creative process: (1) the invention of a subject for presentation and of the arguments supporting it

2 Gioseffo Zarlino, *On the modes. Part IV of Le istitutioni harmoniche, 1558*, transl. by Vered Cohen (New Haven, 1983), 94.

3 Concerning Italy's role in musical humanism, see Claude V. Palisca, *Humanism in Italian Renaissance musical thought* (New Haven, 1985). The reason for the considerable interest in the rhetorical analogy among German theorists and its almost complete absence from the writings of Italians has long been the topic of speculation, although no widely agreed upon answer has ever been put forth. For a summary of traditional twentieth-century thinking on the topic, see George J. Buelow, "Rhetoric and music," *New Grove*. A more recent approach – and in this author's opinion a more sensible one – is set forth in Arno Forchert, "Musik und Rhetorik im Barock," *Schütz-Jahrbuch* 7/8 (1985/86): 5–21. Of particular relevance for Bach is Arno Forchert, "Bach und die Tradition der Rhetorik," in *Alte Musik als ästhetische Gegenwart: Bach, Händel, Schütz. Bericht über den internationalen musikwissenschaftlichen Kongreß Stuttgart 1985*, ed. Dietrich Berke and Dorothee Hanemann, vol. 1 (Cassel, 1987), 169–78.

(*inventio*), (2) the proper ordering of these arguments (*distributio*, consisting at the most basic level of beginning, middle, and end [*exordium, medium,* and *finis*]), and (3) the means of presenting the arguments skillfully and persuasively (*elocutio*). The last of these – with its emphasis on effective figures of speech and the analogous figures of music – received the most attention from rhetoricians and music theorists of the Renaissance and early Baroque. It was also the first to attract twentieth-century music historians. Since the early part of this century, the relationship between music and rhetoric has remained a significant – one might even say a dominating – component of our thinking about Baroque music.

It is probably safe to say, however, that of all the ideas to come out of this area of inquiry none has generated quite the controversy or captured the attention to quite the same extent as the thesis put forward by Warren and Ursula Kirkendale in the late 1970s that J. S. Bach wrote his *Musical Offering* BWV 1079 under the direct influence of Quintilian's *Institutio oratoria.* In the first of a pair of articles, Warren Kirkendale argued that the genre of ricercar had been intended throughout the period to serve a preludial function analogous to the *exordium* – and thus, by extension, that the two ricercars of the *Musical Offering* were intended to serve as double exordium to the collection.[4] Ursula Kirkendale then followed up by attempting to demonstrate that all of the movements of the *Musical Offering* were intended to be ordered according to Quintilian's *dispositio*, not according to the order deduced by Christoph Wolff from study of the original print and manuscript copies.[5]

Because the first of these two articles forms the foundation for the second, it is on its arguments that the present article will focus. There is no question that when Bach, for the first and only time in his career, chose the word *ricercar* as the title for the two extended fugal works of the *Musical Offering* he was turning to a word that by the 1740s had largely fallen from use and that brought with it certain archaic connotations. Why he called these pieces *ricercar* rather than the much more common *fugue* has remained an unsolved puzzle to this day. In his search for the source of Bach's inspiration, Warren Kirkendale sheds much valuable light on the earliest musical uses of the word *ricercar* and the analogies that musicians drew between the preludial, improvisatory function of these early ricercars for lute and the *exordium* of classical rhetoric. The weight

4 "Ciceronians vs. Aristotelians on the ricercar as exordium, from Bembo to Bach," *Journal of the American Musicological Society* 32 (1979): 1–44.

5 Ursula Kirkendale, "The source for Bach's *Musical Offering*: the Institutio oratoria of Quintilian," *Journal of the American Musicological Society* 33 (1980): 88–141. Christoph Wolff's arguments are set forth in "New research on Bach's *Musical Offering*," in his *Bach: essays on his life and music* (Cambridge, Mass., 1991), 239–58.

of historical evidence, however, suggests that this rhetorical analogy was probably not in the end Bach's inspiration, as Kirkendale argues. Rather, a second, more purely musical tradition of the imitative ricercar for keyboard, with emphasis on Renaissance-style counterpoint and learned contrapuntal devices but without preludial implications, seems a more likely candidate. This conclusion places into doubt Ursula Kirkendale's thesis concerning the *Musical Offering*, because it removes the principal piece of evidence in support of a rhetorical analogy for the entire collection.

Warren Kirkendale's argument proceeds as follows: first, he notes that Aristotle, in his *Rhetoric*, draws an analogy between the introduction or *proem* of a speech and the sort of prelude executed by an aulos player before continuing with the main piece at hand. Next Kirkendale observes that beginning in 1548, Italians who translated this passage frequently added that the modern equivalent to Aristotle's proem was the ricercar. Here is the earliest such Italian translation (by Felice Figliucci, published in 1548) as rendered in English by Kirkendale (note that string players have replaced flutists by this time):

the proems of epideictic orations are similar to the ricercars of the instrumentalists before they begin to play, since they, when they must play some good dance, first run over the frets of the strings which prevail in the dance they intend to play, then continuing they begin to play distinctly everything which they have run through. And thus it happens in epideictic orations, because first one lets the listeners hear briefly the theme of the oration, about which one intends to praise or censure.[6]

It is well known that the first surviving pieces called *ricercar*, from the early sixteenth century, fit this description well. Most of these pieces appeared in collections of music for lute, beginning with the five books of lute music published between 1507 and 1511 by Petrucci and including the various collections of the works of Francesco da Milano published in the 1530s and 1540s.[7] All of these collections contain both free works and intabulations of

6   "Lo proemio si è lo principio de l'oratione . . . come . . . nel sonar de la lira quel primo toccar de le corde . . . Et spetialmente li proemii de le orationi dimostrative sono somiglianti le ricercate de li sonatori prima che comincino il suono. Percioche essi quando debbono sonare alcuna buona danza, allhora primamente corrono per li ponti de le corde, lequali sono principali ne la danza, laquale intendono di sonare, et continuando appresso cominciano sonare distintamente tutto cio, che haveano trascorso. Et cosi avviene ne le orationi dimostrative, perche primamente in brevita di parole si da ad intendere li auditori il tema de l'oratione intorno al quale intende di laudare o di biasmare." [Felice Figliucci], *Tradottione antica de la rettorica d'Aristotile, nuovamente trovata* (Padua, 1548), ff. 167r–167v. Quotation and translation from W. Kirkendale, "Ricercar as exordium," 4.

7   The Petrucci volumes comprise Francesco Spinacino, *Intabolatura de lauto, Libro primo* and *Libro secondo* (1507_1 and 1507_2), Joan Ambrosio Dalza, *Intabulatura de lauto, Libro quarto* (1508_2), and Franciscus Bossinensis, *Tenori e contrabassi intabulati . . . per cantar e sonar col lauto, Libro primo* (1509_1) and *Libro secondo* (1511_1). Publications of Francesco's music include *Intabolatura di liuto*

vocal works; some also include dances. The free works are generally grouped together, either in the front or the back of the volume, and are called either *ricercar* or *fantasia*, occasionally both.[8] They are brief pieces in which chords alternate with fast passagework rather in the manner of an improvisation.[9] The works of Francesco are frequently longer and sometimes proceed as an alternation between free, improvisatory sections and points of imitation.[10] Even in these works, however, the counterpoint is freely handled, doubtless because of the nature of the instrument. Similarly improvisatory are contemporary ricercars for viola da gamba, for instance, those in Silvestro di Ganassi's *Regola Rubertina* (Venice, 1542) and *Lettione seconda* (Venice, 1543) and Diego Ortiz's *Trattado, Libro primo* (Rome, 1553). In these pieces the writing is unabashedly monophonic, with little attempt to evoke imitative or strict counterpoint.

A quite different type of ricercar made its first appearance in 1540 in a publication entitled *Musica nova* and containing almost exclusively pieces called *ricercar*.[11] Most of these are the work of Julio Segni, represented by thirteen ricercars, or Adrian Willaert, represented by three, and their pieces and the collection as a whole differ from their lute counterparts in nearly every respect. Not only does *Musica nova* include no vocal intabulations with which the ricercars might be paired, but it was printed in three partbooks and was said on its title page to be intended for organ or other instruments. These pieces are considerably longer than the ricercars for lute, and they are based without exception on the technique of imitative counterpoint carried through in more or less systematic fashion.

The volume includes no statement about the purpose for its ricercars, but all of its composers seem to have been associated in some way with Willaert, and

(1536₃), *Intabolatura de lauto, Libro secondo* (1546₇), *Intabolatura de lautto, Libro settimo* (1548₄), and, in collaboration with Perino Fiorentino, *Intabolatura de lauto, Libro terzo* (1547₂). The subscripts after the publication dates are from Howard Mayer Brown, *Instrumental music printed before 1600: a bibliography* (Cambridge, Mass., 1965).

8   In 1546₇ and 1547₂, Francesco's title pages speak of "motetti, recercari, and canzoni francese," but each of the free pieces is actually entitled "fantasia" in the volume itself.

9   Incipits of all of these early lute ricercars can be found in H. Colin Slim, "The keyboard ricercar and fantasia in Italy, *c.* 1500–1550, with reference to parallel forms in European lute music of the same period" (Ph.D. diss., Harvard University, 1960), 434–49. Two examples are transcribed in the *Historical anthology of music*, ed. Archibald T. Davison and Willi Apel, rev. edn., vol. 1 (Cambridge, Mass., 1949), 101.

10 See the complete edition by Arthur Ness (Cambridge, Mass., 1970).

11 A modern edition of the complete contents was prepared by H. Colin Slim, ed., *Musica nova*, Monuments of Renaissance music 1 (Chicago, 1964). Only the bass partbook survives from the original publication, but a later reprinting of the pieces in different order and with added dances appeared under the title *Musique de joye* published by Jacques Moderne. The only piece in *Musica nova* not called ricercar is a contrapuntal setting of the plainchant "Da pacem"; its musical style differs from that of the surrounding ricercars only in its incorporation of a long-note cantus firmus.

one could reasonably speculate that the pieces were gathered for the purpose of recording the activity of Willaert's private teaching studio.[12] In fact, a first guess might be that this is a collection of works intended as a teaching or study tool, that is, a demonstration of the possibilities inherent in that most sophisticated of compositional devices, imitative counterpoint, and without any constraints of vocal text. *Musica nova* was the first of a large number of such collections, all based on the technique of imitative counterpoint, which generally increased in severity of contrapuntal style as the century progressed. A great many of these works were composed by organists of St. Mark's, Venice: particularly worthy of note are those by Jacques Buus (1547 and 1549), Annibale Padovano (1556), Claudio Merulo (1567, 1574, 1607, and 1608), and Andrea Gabrieli (1589, 1595, and 1596). Meanwhile, as these imitative keyboard ricercars became progressively more sophisticated and rose in prominence, the improvisatory lute ricercar faded. In fact, by century's end the designation *ricercar* had disappeared from lute music altogether, replaced by the designation *fantasia*. The ricercar had found its new home among organists.

Scholars have long puzzled over the use of the term *ricercar* for both the free, improvisatory lute and gamba pieces and the more familiar, strictly imitative type written for keyboard or instrumental ensemble. The traditional explanation has been that each type involves something that is being "studied or researched:" in the first instance, the instrument itself and the mode of the piece to follow; in the second, the potential of the thematic material presented at the beginning.[13] Kirkendale offers a different explanation: namely, that the word *ricercar* was used consistently during the sixteenth, seventeenth, and eighteenth centuries as a replacement for the word *prelude* and that all ricercars, including the imitative type, were intended by their composers as preludes to other pieces. He then proceeds to discuss Cicero's two distinct types of exordium, one in which the speaker begins boldly and directly (called the *principium*) and one in which he begins circuitously and indirectly (called *insinuatio*). Musicians, according to Kirkendale, consistently associated the improvisatory type of ricercar with the direct *principium* and the imitative type with the circuitous *insinuatio*. Having brought the imitative ricercar into the rhetorical analogy, he maintains that Bach must have chosen the term *ricercar* under the influence of this analogy and thus was indicating an exordial function for the three- and six-voice ricercars. Although a speech would ordinarily only have one exordium, Quintilian "taught that a second exordium can be inserted before

---

12 This is at least hinted at in Slim's preface to the edition of *Musica nova*, xxxv–xxxvi.
13 See, for example, the entry "Ricercar(e)" in Willi Apel, ed., *Harvard Dictionary of Music*, 2nd edn. (Cambridge, Mass., 1973).

the *argumentatio*, parallel to the first one before the *narratio*."[14] Kirkendale concludes, therefore, that Bach's two ricercars were intended to serve the role of double exordium to the *Musical Offering* and, by extension, that the entire collection was deliberately organized according to the Quintilian *dispositio*.

This chain of reasoning seems sound at first glance, but it unfortunately includes one weak link, on which we must now focus. There is no question that the free, improvisatory type of ricercar could – and did – quite naturally serve a preludial function. The problem is this: Did the imitative type of ricercar likewise serve this function? Let us examine the evidence more closely.

First of all, it is by no means obvious that every imitative ricercar is well suited to hint in a circuitous and indirect manner at something that is then more boldly stated by a musical movement or piece to follow, as Quintilian's description of the *insinuatio* would suggest. One might think, for instance, of the ricercars of Jacques Buus.[15] Buus's ricercars proceed as a series of points of imitation and are frequently enormous, several over 300 measures long. One of them, no. 8 of Book II, begins with its first theme treated fifty-six times in the opening point of imitation; its seventh theme appears forty-three times. Such treatment hardly elicits thoughts of "insinuating" or "hinting at" something to follow. Quite the contrary: the themes are exhausted by the time the final cadence sounds.

Other ricercars likewise resist obvious classification as "preludial." In the 1660s and 1670s musicians in Hamburg and Lübeck – including Matthias Weckmann, Johann Adam Reinken, Christoph Bernhard, and Dieterich Buxtehude – began to experiment with the incorporating of elements of invertible counterpoint into the writing of fugue. These experiments led to the late-Baroque fascination with the countersubject in fugal writing and to the permutation fugue, and they were eagerly adopted by composers in central Germany.[16] There are, for instance, pieces by Johann Krieger (1696) and Johann Heinrich Buttstedt (1713) in which several themes are treated, first separately in individual fugues, then all together in one final fugue; both are almost certainly intended to be studies in the combining of fugue with invertible counterpoint.[17] Krieger titled each item separately: "Fugue in C on Theme 1,"

14 W. Kirkendale, "Ricercar as exordium," 40.
15 *Ricercari, Libro primo* (1547$_1$) and *Libro secondo* (1549$_5$) and *Intabolatura d'Organo* (1549$_4$). Modern editions of the first and third, prepared by Thomas Daniel Schlee for keyboard, are published by Universal Edition (Vienna, 1982 and 1980, respectively); another edition of the first, by Donald Beecher and Bryan Gillingham for consort, is published by Dovehouse Editions (Ottawa, *c.* 1983). A modern edition of the second, edited by James Ladewig, is published by Garland Press (1993).
16 This topic is explored in detail in Paul Walker, "From Renaissance *fuga* to Baroque fugue: the role of the Sweelinck theory manuscripts," *Schütz-Jahrbuch* 7/8 (1985/86): 93–104.
17 Johann Krieger, *Anmuthige Clavier-Übung* (Nuremberg, 1698); modern ed. by Max Seiffert in Denkmäler der Tonkunst in Bayern 18, 46–52. Johann Heinrich Buttstett, *Musicalische Clavier-Kunst und Vorrathe-Kammer* (Leipzig, 1713), 16–21.

etc., ending with a "Fugue in C with Four Subjects;" Buttstedt chose one title for the whole complex of three pieces: he called it "Ricercar," with each separate piece labeled "Stanza 1," "Stanza 2," and "Stanza 3." This work is yet another ricercar that at least on the surface appears not to fulfill a preludial function.

If, puzzled by such examples, one then begins to search in Kirkendale's article for evidence of imitative ricercars that were explicitly linked by their composers to particular vocal pieces, one discovers that the author is unable to cite a single unequivocal example. Instead, imitative ricercars were generally grouped together, frequently but not always organized according to mode, and often in self-contained collections with no indication of preludial function at all.[18] Kirkendale argues that the link between the non-imitative and the imitative ricercar, i.e., the inspiration for drawing the imitative type into the rhetorical analogy, is Pietro Bembo, the noted Italian humanist and man of letters. Many biographical details connect Bembo with important early composers of the keyboard ricercar, especially Andrea Gabrieli and the two Cavazzonis, father and son. Kirkendale focuses his reasoning on the Cavazzonis. In 1523, the elder Cavazzoni, Marc Antonio, published a collection of keyboard works entitled *Recerchari, motetti, canzoni*, which included two non-imitative ricercars. Each precedes a vocal composition, and a preludial intent seems clear. Twenty years later the younger Cavazzoni, Girolamo, published four imitative ricercars as part of a keyboard volume entitled *Intavolatura, cioe recercari, canzoni, himni, magnificati* and dedicated to Bembo. Kirkendale maintains that the dedication to a noted Ciceronian ensures that these ricercars were likewise conceived within the same rhetorical analogy and thus that they were also intended to serve, like the non-imitative ones of his father, as preludes.

For every bit of evidence in favor of this interpretation, however, an equally convincing bit can be cited against it. In the first place, despite a flowery preface addressed to Bembo, Girolamo nowhere mentions such an analogy or function for his ricercars. Furthermore, the ricercars are no longer interspersed among vocal works, as they were in his father's print. Rather, all four of them are grouped together at the beginning of the volume. It is true that the dedication to Bembo suggests possible humanist intent; nevertheless, it also seems significant that the younger Cavazzoni replaced his father's non-imitative type of ricercar with imitative works of the sort found in *Musica nova* of three years

18 The most recent studies of this repertory have been by Anthony Newcomb. See his article "The anonymous ricercars of the Bourdeney Codex," in *Frescobaldi Studies*, ed. Alexander Silbiger (Durham, N. C., 1987), 97–123, and the preface to his edition *The ricercars of the Bourdeney Codex: Giaches Brumel [?], Fabrizio Dentice, Anonymous*, Recent researches in the music of the Renaissance 89 (Madison, 1991), which also contains a comprehensive list of collections of four-voice imitative ricercars from 1540 to 1615, x.

earlier at the same time that he chose no longer to distribute these pieces among vocal works, as his father had done. Further, if the "Hieronimo da bologna" who contributed one imitative ricercar to *Musica nova* is Girolamo himself, as many have concluded,[19] then one might speculate that the young Cavazzoni had a direct connection with Willaert, possibly even a student-teacher relationship.[20] Given the stylistic resemblances between Girolamo's ricercars and those of Willaert, the latter's influence might have been stronger in more purely musical matters than would that of the humanist Bembo. One could therefore argue that as soon as composers began to think of the ricercar as a genre concerned with the imitation of thematic material, they ceased to think of it as preludial.

In fact, Kirkendale fails to cite even one example of an imitative ricercar, either in manuscript or printed source, that is paired with a vocal work intended to follow it in performance. One cannot, of course, automatically dismiss any thought that a preludial function was intended. Kirkendale explains the lacuna by noting the practice among orators of collecting exordia and publishing them separately. Presumably, then, the after-dinner speaker would select an appropriate introduction to his talk from his favorite book of introductions. Likewise, the performer could select an appropriate ricercar from his favorite collection whenever he wished to introduce a vocal composition. If the collection comprised one ricercar per mode, as so many of them do, the performer would always be sure to find one in the proper mode.

Kirkendale is unable, however, to find a single such collection whose preface indicates a preludial intent, and he discusses only one collection that appears to match up with particular vocal works. This is a set of monothematic ricercars published in 1549 under the title *Fantasie et ricercari a tre voci* by Giuliano Tiburtino and based on themes taken from works of Josquin des Prez. Like Girolamo Cavazzoni's, however, Tiburtino's collection includes not the slightest suggestion that the ricercars were intended as preludes to the Josquin pieces. Tiburtino actually suppresses both Josquin's name and the identity of the pieces from which his themes are drawn. This may mean only that the themes were well known and required no identification, but it would not have been a strong marketing ploy for a volume of pieces whose purpose is supposed to be preludial. Tiburtino makes no statement about the function of his ricercars, and there is no reason to think that they were intended as preludes to vocal works of Josquin.[21]

19 See Slim, *Musica nova*, xxix, especially n. 46

20 Such a relationship has in the past frequently been taken for granted. See Gustav Reese, *Music in the Renaissance*, rev. edn. (New York, 1959), 535, where it is stated as fact.

21 For more on this collection, see James Haar, "The *Fantasie et recerchari* of Giuliano Tiburtino," *The*

If the lack of evidence from the sources themselves seems worrisome, Kirkendale presumably feels that the validity of his thesis rests most securely on theoretical writings of the period. These are predominately German, of course, but German musicians made use of the word *ricercar* only infrequently and preferred instead to designate improvisatory-type pieces with the words *praeambel, praeludium* or *toccata*[22] and imitative pieces with the word *fugue*. When Kirkendale tries to equate the latter word with *ricercar*, however – i.e., Italian ricercar = German fugue – he ignores the multiple meanings of the latter word and as a result misinterprets several key pieces of evidence. He first recalls Michael Praetorius's well-known definition of fugue and ricercar from Part III of his *Syntagma musicum* of 1619:

Fugue: Ricercar

Fugues are nothing more than . . . repeated echoes of the same theme on different degrees [of the scale], succeeding each other through the use of rests. . . . In Italy they are called ricercars. RICERCARE is the same thing as "to investigate," "to look for," "to seek out," "to research diligently," and "to examine thoroughly." For in constructing a good fugue one must with special diligence and careful thought seek to bring together as many ways as possible in which the same [material] can be combined with itself, interwoven, duplicated, [used] in direct and contrary motion; [in short,] brought together in an orderly, artistic, and graceful way and carried through to the end.[23]

Here we are told that what the Italians call ricercar, the Germans call fugue. Praetorius's statement is not the same, however, as saying that "whenever the Germans call something fugue, they refer to that which the Italians call ricercar," as Kirkendale wishes to do. As I have written elsewhere, Praetorius's use of

Musical Quarterly 59 (1973): 223–38. Tiburtino was principally known in his day as a performer rather than as a composer, and Haar expresses the opinion that what his ricercars "are all about" is the taking of a pre-existent tune and improvising a piece on it "in regular fashion," much as candidates for the organist posts at St. Mark's, Venice, were expected to do as a part of their audition. See pp. 235–6.

22   Hans Judenkünig (1523$_2$) employed the designation "Priamell," Hans Gerle (1532$_2$ and 1533$_1$) "Priambel" or "Preambel," and Hans Newsidler (1536$_6$ and 1536$_7$) "Preambel." The first German lutenist working primarily in Germany to publish a collection that included the genre designation *ricercar* was Wolf Heckel in 1556. (Simon Gintzler, who included a few ricercars in his *Intabolatura de lauto* of 1547 appears to have been active principally in Italy.)

23   "Fuga: Ricercar. Fugae nihil aliud sunt, ut ait Abbas D. Ioannes Nucius, quam ejusdem thematis per distinctos locos crebrae resultationes Pausarum interventu sibi succedentes. Dictae sunt autem a fugando, quia vox vocem fugat, idem melos de promendo. Italis vocantur Ricercari: RICERCARE enim idem est, quod investigare, quaerere, exquirere, mit fleiss erforschen / unnd nachsuchen; Dieweil in tractirung einer guten Fugen mit sonderbahrem fleiss unnd nachdencken aus allen winckeln zusammen gesucht werden muss / wie unnd uff mancherley Art und weise dieselbe in einander gefügt / geflochten / duplirt, per directum & indirectum seu contrarium, ordentlich / künstlich und anmuthig zusammen gebracht / und biss zum ende hinaus geführt werden könne. Nam ex hac figura omnium maxime Musicum ingenium aestimandum est, si pro certa Modorum natura aptas Fugas eruere, atq; erutas bona & laudibili cohaerentia rite jungere noverit." Michael Praetorius, *Syntagma musicum*, vol. 3 (Wolfenbüttel, 1619;) 21–2 [the latter misnumbered 24]. The translation is my own, as are all translations in the present article unless otherwise noted.

fugue as a genre designation is the first such use of the term by a musical theorist (aside from its medieval meaning of "canon"), but he in no way implied by this designation that the more traditional meanings of the word were suddenly obsolete.[24] In *Syntagma* III Praetorius himself used the word in the more usual sense of "a point of imitation," as well as "a theme to be imitated in such a point." For German writers of the late Renaissance and early Baroque, the word "fugue" nearly always designated either the compositional technique of imitative counterpoint or the most important manifestation of that technique, namely the point of imitation.

We can best understand their usage by thinking about our modern use of the word *canon*. We refer to a compositional technique when we say "Bach makes extensive use of canon in the *Goldberg Variations*"; we refer to a piece of music when we say "Bach's *Musical Offering* contains several canons." In the first sense, German theorists from Gallus Dressler and Johannes Nucius to Athanasius Kircher wrote that any composer worth the name had to be able to incorporate fugue into his music.[25] In the second sense, Praetorius (in *Syntagma* III) characterized the vocal motet as an alternation of "harmonies and fugues" [*Harmoniae et fugae*], a description that must be understood as points of imitation alternating with homophonic passages.[26]

A key piece of evidence for Kirkendale's thesis comes from the manuscript treatise *Praecepta musicae poeticae* written by Gallus Dressler and dated 1563.[27] In this treatise, perhaps the first to take the musico-rhetorical analogy as the basis for its entire text, Dressler defines the exordium of a composition as the opening section up to the first important cadence. He then defines two types: the full [*plenum*], in which all voices enter together, and the bare [*nudum*], in which they enter one by one in fugue. These two match very neatly with Cicero's *principium* and *insinuatio* (Dressler himself does not mention such an analogy), but they do not support Kirkendale's argument. Dressler's "fugue" is a compositional technique or a point of imitation, never a piece of music. When he discusses the *exordium, medium,* and *finis,* he makes clear that the repertory of which he speaks is the vocal motet repertory, exemplified most perfectly by the works of Clemens non Papa. Dressler's description can be applied nicely to

24 Paul Walker, "Fugue in German theory from Dressler to Mattheson" (Ph.D. diss., State University of New York at Buffalo, 1987), 190–9.
25 This point is discussed in detail in Walker, "Fugue in German theory," *passim.*
26 Praetorius, *Syntagma musicum,* 3:6.
27 Gallus Dressler, *Praecepta musicae poeticae,* ed. Bernhard Engelke, *Geschichtsblätter für Stadt und Land Magdeburg* 49–50 (1914–1915): 213–50. Dressler's treatment of the word *fugue* and his analogies between rhetoric and imitative counterpoint are discussed at greater length in Walker, "Fugue in German theory," 81–114.

the imitative ricercar, but not in the way suggested by Kirkendale. Such a piece – like its vocal counterpart, the motet – begins with a "bare fugal exordium" (that is, an opening point of imitation), proceeds with a medium consisting of additional sections that may be handled more freely with respect to mode and thematic material, and closes with a strong reaffirmation of the original mode. Dressler himself said nothing about an analogy between an entire composition such as the ricercar and an individual portion of the classical *dispositio*, nor does he mention two or more pieces or movements that work together to recreate the *dispositio*. Dressler's "fugue as exordium" tells us nothing about Kirkendale's "ricercar as exordium."

Later German writers did discuss the genre of ricercar, but not within the context of rhetorical analogy. Furthermore, the testimony offered by Praetorius, the first German theorist to mention the ricercar, proves extremely damaging to Kirkendale's thesis. Praetorius's descriptions of the fugue/ricercar and the vocal motet cited above appear in a portion of *Syntagma* III (16–26) devoted to the various genres of music, with emphasis on the latest Italian practice. The genres are divided into several categories: for vocal music, those with sacred or serious texts and those with secular texts; for instrumental, two categories of dances, preludes to dances, preludes to motets or madrigals, and independent pieces (which Praetorius calls *praeludiis vor sich selbst*). Praetorius assigns the ricercar/fugue not to one of the preludial categories, but to the category of independent pieces, together with fantasies, sinfonias, and sonatas. Only the toccata appears under the category of preludes to motets or madrigals. We even learn at this point that a toccata may precede the performance of a fugue: "Toccata is [the same] as a Praeambulum or Praeludium which an organist, when he first puts his hands to the keyboard and before he begins a motet or fugue, invents out of his head with simple chords and fast passagework."[28]

Also of interest in Praetorius's book is the inclusion of sinfonia under the independent category (22 [misnumbered 24]). Praetorius adds that these can likewise be used as preludes, but he makes no such comment for the ricercar/ fugue. Alexander Silbiger notes a source in which each of several brief, preludial pieces entitled *entrata* is followed by a ricercar in the same key.[29] Buttstedt's ricercar mentioned above is also preceded by a praeludium in the same key. Praetorius's description makes it seem quite plausible, although it is by no means certain, that both are examples of prelude/fugue pairs.

28 "Toccata, ist als ein Praeambulum, oder Praeludium, welches ein Organist / wenn er erstlich uff die Orgel / oder Clavicymbalum greifft / ehe er ein Mutet oder Fugen anfehet / aus seinem Kopff vorher fantasirt, mit schlechten enzelen griffen und Coloraturen, &c." 23 [misnumbered 25].
29 *Italian manuscript sources of seventeenth century keyboard music* (Ann Arbor, 1976), 34.

Not only is Praetorius's pairing of toccata and fugue extremely interesting in light of its importance for the later genre of "prelude and fugue," but it reveals the weakness in Kirkendale's argument. That is, once a musician as influential as Praetorius can be found who assigns explicitly non-preludial functions to the ricercar and thus reveals himself ignorant of any implied rhetorical analogy, then it is manifestly untrue to say that every ricercar during the period 1500–1750 was intended to serve as an analogy to the exordium. In the absence of a universal and unbroken tradition of ricercar as exordium extending from Renaissance Italy to late-Baroque Germany, we must examine every ricercar or collection of ricercars on its merits to determine whether its author had some sort of rhetorical analogy in mind.

Despite the enormous authority enjoyed by Praetorius's writing among German musicians and the Germans' leading role in the writing of imitative keyboard ricercars of the learned type, the original preludial, improvisatory sense of the word *ricercar* did not die. In his dictionary of 1703, the French lexicographer Sebastien de Brossard gave the following definition:

RICERCATA means "search." It is a type of prelude or fantasy played on the organ, harpsichord, theorbo, etc., in which it appears that the composer searches out the harmonic ideas that he wishes to use in the stricter pieces that are to be played after it. This is ordinarily done *ex tempore* and without preparation and as a result it requires a great deal of skill.[30]

Brossard offers us a possible clue to the disappearance of short, improvisatory pieces entitled "ricercar" from manuscripts and prints of the seventeenth century: musicians now generally improvised them and no longer wrote them down. Although by Brossard's time the word *fugue* had become perhaps the most widely used genre designation for pieces based principally on imitative counterpoint, he relates the ricercar not to it, but to the genres of prelude and fantasy.

In his *Musicalisches Lexicon* of 1732, Johann Gottfried Walther placed Praetorius's and Brossard's definitions one after the other for the entry "ricercar."[31] Christoph Wolff has argued that Bach was influenced by these two definitions to apply the designation to the two pieces in the *Musical Offering*: that is, the three-voice ricercar represented the piece that he improvised for the

---

30 "RICERCATA. veut dire, RECHERCHE. E'est un espece de Prelude ou de fantaisie qu'on joüe sur l'Orgue, le Clavessin, le Théorbe, &c. où il semble que le Compositeur Recherche les traits d'harmonie qu'il veut employer dans les pieces reglées qu'il doit joüer dans la suite. Cela ce fait ordinairement sur le champs & sans preparation, & par consequent cela demande beaucoup d'habilité." Sebastien de Brossard, *Dictionaire de musique* (Paris, 1703). Complete translation by Albion Gruber, *Dictionary of Music – Dictionaire de Musique: Paris 1703* (Henryville, Penn., 1982).
31 Johann Gottfried Walther, *Musicalisches Lexicon* (Leipzig, 1732), 525.

king, the six-voice ricercar the one that he politely declined to improvise but worked out back in Leipzig.[32] Whether or not this was the case, Walther's two definitions leave us once again with an association only between the short, improvisatory ricercar and the prelude. Neither in Walther's copying of the Praetorius definition nor in the story of Bach's improvising before Frederick the Great do we encounter any mention of an imitative ricercar that is intended to precede or introduce another piece.

Whereas no direct evidence links the imitative ricercar with preludial function, considerable evidence does connect it with non-preludial functions. One such is Praetorius's combination of the toccata-ricercar pair mentioned above. Another involves the substitution of ricercars and other instrumental compositions for liturgical items in the Mass and Office.[33] Frescobaldi, for instance, in his *Fiori musicali* of 1635, includes three ricercars that, he states, are to be played *dopo il Credo* (after the Credo), that is, in place of the Offertory. Giovanni Battista Fasolo, in a book of 1645 entitled *Annuale* and directed to church organists, remarks: "If the Graduals [or] Offertories will [prove to] be too short, a ricercar or one of the canzoni in the eight tones can be played."[34] Such liturgical use of the ricercar suggests another conceivable explanation for the grouping of ricercars into collections with one per mode: the organist could always find one in the appropriate mode to ensure smooth transitions in the liturgy.

By far the most common purpose for the imitative ricercar, however, seems to have been as a study in learned counterpoint. Praetorius's definition already stresses this aspect of the genre's character, as we have seen, and in the works of Praetorius's contemporaries Hans Leo Hassler and Christian Erbach we find both fugues and ricercars that are severe in contrapuntal style, extended in duration, and full of the sorts of learned devices described by Praetorius.[35]

---

32   See his "Der Terminus 'Ricercar' in Bachs Musikalischem Opfer," *BJ* 53 (1967): 70–81, and "Apropos the *Musical Offering*: the Thema Regium and the term *Ricercar*," in *Essays*, 328–31.

33   Stephen Bonta, "The uses of the *Sonata da Chiesa*," *Journal of the American Musicological Society* 22 (1969): 54–84.

34   Bonta, "The uses of the *Sonata da Chiesa*," 65.

35   The Turin keyboard tablatures of *c.* 1630 ascribe to Hassler seventeen pieces entitled ricercar and eleven pieces entitled fugue. For a description and inventory of these manuscripts see Oscar Mischiati, "L'Intavolatura d'organo tedesca della Biblioteca Nazionale di Torino," *L'Organo* 4 (1963): 1–154. Concerning problems of attribution in these sources, see Vincent J. Panetta, Jr., "Hans Leo Hassler and the keyboard toccata: antecedents, sources, style" (Ph.D. diss., Harvard University, 1991), esp. 42–51. Also containing ricercars and fugues attributed to Hassler are the second edition (1612) of the composer's published collection *Sacri concentus*, Padua, Biblioteca universitaria, Ms. 1982, and Munich, Bayerische Staatsbibliothek, Ms. 1581. For a description and inventory of the latter two sources, see Lydia Schierning, *Die Überlieferung der deutschen Orgel- und Klaviermusik aus der ersten Hälfte des 17. Jahrhunderts*, Schriften des Landesinstituts für Musikforschung Kiel 12 (Cassel, 1961), 50–3 and 55–60. Most of the ricercars and fugues attributed to Hassler are not to my knowledge available in modern

Hassler is perhaps most likely to have acquired his interest in such pieces from his teacher Andrea Gabrieli, whose ricercars are often cited as the first truly learned examples of the genre.

The association of ricercar/fugue with learnedness and study strengthened as the seventeenth century progressed. In defiance of the stylistic experimentation of the early and mature Baroque, the imitative ricercar stubbornly retained its strict counterpoint and *stile antico* part-writing.[36] The most prominent examples can be found in seventeenth-century Germany, including works by such composers as Johann Ulrich Steigleder, Johann Jacob Froberger, Alessandro Poglietti, Johann Krieger, Johann Pachelbel, Johann Caspar Ferdinand Fischer, Nicolaus Adam Strunck, and Johann Heinrich Buttstedt. Not only do their pieces stress learned contrapuntal devices and severe style, but they are almost all notated, uncharacteristically for most keyboard music of the time, in open score, a format often intended to facilitate study or teaching.[37]

The pairing of toccata with fugue/ricercar in Praetorius's treatise and in Italian keyboard manuscripts; Frescobaldi's and Fasolo's use of the ricercar as a substitute for the Offertory of the Mass; the genre's learned nature as implied by Praetorius's definition and its frequent appearance in open score notation; all of these suggest ways in which composers might – indeed, in the first two cases, did – think of the imitative ricercar. One cannot state with absolute certainty that the primary purpose of these pieces was not to serve as preludes, but the weight of evidence points strongly away from such an interpretation. If one restricts Kirkendale's arguments to the improvisatory ricercar as cultivated particularly by Italian lutenists of the High Renaissance, his thesis stands without qualification. As soon as one attempts to extend the rhetorical analogy

edition, although Adolf Sandberger, ed., *Werke Hans Leo Hasslers*, Denkmäler deutscher Tonkunst in Bayern IV/2 (Leipzig, 1903) contains three (two on 55–65, one on 82–7) and Joseph Auer, ed., rev. Russel Crosby, *Hans Leo Hassler. Sacri Concentus*, Denkmäler deutscher Tonkunst 24–25 (Leipzig, 1961), contains one (255–64). Another Hassler fugue is edited by Georges Kiss in *Hans Leo Hassler, Ausgewählte Werke für Orgel* (Mainz, 1971), 34–41. The known pieces of this type by Erbach can all be found in his *Collected keyboard compositions*, vol. 1–3, ed. Clare G. Rayner, Corpus of early keyboard music 36, nos. 1–3 (n. p.: American Institute of Musicology, 1971).

36   Alexander Silbiger has characterized the seventeenth-century Italian ricercar in general as "in the style of the *stile antico*." See *Manuscript sources*, 34.

37   See Friedrich Wilhelm Riedel, *Quellenkundliche Beiträge zur Geschichte der Musik für Tasteninstrumente in der zweiten Hälfte des 17. Jahrhunderts* (Cassel, 1960), 34 and 38–9. Riedel cites two contemporary publications to support his assertion that the use of open score signaled the composer's (or copyist's) recognition of a pedagogical function. First, a set of Rore madrigals published in 1577 in open score (the first known publication using this notation) is said by its publisher to be "spartiti . . . per qualunque studiosi di Contrapunti" (scored out . . . for the sake of all students of counterpoint). Second, the Dresden composer and music publisher Johann Klemm remarked in the preface to his *Partitura seu tabulatura italica*, a collection of fugues notated in open score and published in 1631, that Heinrich Schütz taught counterpoint to his students using open score notation.

to the imitative ricercar for keyboard, however, problems arise. There is no evidence unequivocally linking this type of ricercar with the exordium, the musical style of these pieces stands diametrically opposed to anything introductory or preliminary, and several explicit statements exist to the effect that at least some composers conceived their ricercars with non-preludial uses in mind. In short, the imitative ricercar very probably never joined its improvisatory cousin in the rhetorical analogy, and Kirkendale's thesis that the ricercar was universally and always understood to be preludial must be abandoned.

We return at last to Bach and the *Musical Offering*. Seriousness of purpose and severity of style – characteristics that describe well nearly all keyboard ricercars from Willaert, Padovano, and Gabrieli to Krieger, Fischer, and Buttstedt – also describe well both the occasion of Bach's visit to Sans Souci and the two fugal works published as a result of that visit. Indeed, would not a composer who had devoted his life's work to the cultivation of seriousness and sophistication but who had more recently watched those goals fade before the onslaught of the galant naturally respond to a genuine show of respect from the King of Prussia (known to be a lover of the traditional in music) by offering something that emphasized those characteristics in their truest form? Bach had never in his life chosen the designation *ricercar*, and he could have given the two pieces of his *Musical Offering* the more usual designation *fugue* (as he did in fact refer to them in a letter to his cousin Johann Elias Bach in the year after its publication).[38] Instead, he chose a title that although rather archaic for the 1740s, brought with it all of the appropriate connotations for the dedicatee and the occasion of the pieces' genesis.

In the end, we cannot be certain why Bach selected a designation that he had never used before. Perhaps more interesting is the question of why Bach, who could scarcely have been ignorant of ricercars by earlier composers, had never before employed that term for fugal pieces in severe style. The answer to these questions will probably never be known, but the preponderance of the evidence forces us to conclude that the keyboard ricercar's traditional role as a paradigm of imitative writing incorporating the strictest contrapuntal rules must have played a significant role in Bach's decision to employ that word for the first and only time late in his career. In contrast to the many strands that converge to support this conclusion, the credible supporting evidence for a

38 The word *fugue* was also used in the Berlin newspaper account of Bach's visit, in an advertisement in the *Leipziger Zeitungen* of September 30, 1747 announcing the collection's availability, and by Bach's student Lorenz Christoph Mizler, who described speaking about the two pieces with Bach himself. See *Dok* I/49 (Bach's letter to Johann Elias), *Dok* II/554 (account of the Potsdam visit), *Dok* 3/558a (Leipzig newspaper advertisement), and *Dok* 2/557 and 580 (reports of Mizler).

rhetorical analogy to the exordium and an inspiration from Quintilian's *Institutio oratoria* turns out to consist almost exclusively of an Italian translation of Aristotle published nearly two centuries before Bach at a time when the improvisatory lute ricercar was at its zenith and the imitative ricercar for keyboard was in its merest infancy.

Finally: if one removes from Ursula Kirkendale's article the premise that Bach intended the two ricercars to function as exordia, then one discovers that no other solid evidence links the creation of the *Musical Offering* with rhetorical analogy or Quintilian. Furthermore, as was the case with the earlier article, a great many of the conclusions that are derived from this premise are anything but intuitively obvious.[39] We are told, for instance, that the second half of the collection comprises a second introduction (*exordium*), the principal arguments (*argumentatio*), consisting of questions and accusations with their refutation, and a conclusion (*peroratio*).[40] To a speechwriter this suggests a main body of text introduced and concluded with a paragraph or two each. As Ursula Kirkendale applies this plan to the *Musical Offering*, however, we are offered a main body that is tiny – a mere four canons – and is dwarfed by the gigantic six-voice ricercar that introduces it and the equally substantial four-movement trio sonata that concludes the piece. It is difficult to see how a scholar not already disposed for other reasons to find rhetorical analogies would be led from this kind of evidence to postulate such an analogy. In fact, given that Bach himself made no mention of such a purpose for the collection, given that his choice of the genre designation *ricercar* implies no such purpose, and given that such an analogy can scarcely be considered obvious from study of the score, this thesis must now suffer the fate of the earlier one. Until some sort of generally acceptable evidence is forthcoming, there is no reason to think that any such rhetorical analogy was ever conceived. We were, it turns out, right all along: the two types of ricercar were given the same title despite their different natures because each incorporated "research" or "investigation" in some way. When Bach chose the word *ricercar*, he was harking back not to a rhetorical tradition, but to a long musical tradition of contrapuntal writing in its purest and most distinguished form.

---

39 For more thorough consideration of the problems arising from Ursula Kirkendale's analogies, see Peter Williams, "The snares and delusions of musical rhetoric: some examples from recent writings on J. S. Bach," *Alte Musik: Praxis und Reflexion*, ed. Peter Reidemeister and Veronika Gutmann (Winterthur, 1983), 230–40; "Encounters with the chromatic fourth . . . or, More on Figurenlehre," *The Musical Times* 126 (1985): 276ff.; and Christoph Wolff, postscript to "New research on the *Musical Offering*," *Essays*, 421–3.

40 There are actually two conclusions, but she suggests that only one of them might be included in any given performance. See U. Kirkendale, "The source for Bach's *Musical Offering*," 121 and 131.

Chapter eleven

J. S. Bach and the legacy of the seventeenth century

CHRISTOPH WOLFF

In memoriam Paul Henry Lang

We do not have much concrete evidence regarding Johann Sebastian Bach's views on musical styles, let alone value judgments of compositional traditions. Based on his copies and arrangements of works by other composers, representing an unusually broad spectrum of several generations and a wide geographical distribution, we know, of course, that he studied, appreciated, and in various ways used pieces from contemporary and retrospective repertoires. Yet from the selections Bach made for various purposes, it is difficult to establish criteria for an aesthetic choice on his part.

There exists, however, an illuminating statement Bach put forth in 1730: "Now . . . the state of music is quite different from what is was, since our artistry has increased very much, and the taste has changed astonishingly, and accordingly the former style of music no longer seems to please our ears . . ."[1] The wording suggests clearly that Bach believed in the progress of musical taste and style and that he joined forces with those unfavorably disposed towards "the former style of music." That included particularly the church music of his predecessors in the St. Thomas cantorate, seventeenth-century music in general, and possibly even his own works from the early Weimar and pre-Weimar periods whose old-fashioned design and sound he himself would doubtless have acknowledged in the 1730s.[2]

This essay was originally presented as the keynote address at the joint meeting of The American Bach Society and The American Schütz Society, April 24–26, 1992, at Columbia University, New York. The lecture followed a memorial service for Paul Henry Lang (1901–1991) at Columbia's St. Paul's Chapel. My paper pays but a modest tribute to Paul, unforgettable mentor and wonderful friend to whom I owe an enormous and lasting debt of gratitude.

1 Memorandum to the Leipzig town council, August 23, 1730. *Dok* I/22; *BR*, 123.
2 For example, Leipzig re-performances of Bach's earliest vocal works (e.g., "Gott ist mein König"

At the same time, the continuation of the statement just quoted reveals Bach's actual intentions: ". . . the former style of music no longer seems to please our ears, and considerable help is therefore all the more needed, in order to choose and appoint such musicians as will satisfy the present musical taste, master the new kinds of music, and thus be in a position to do justice to the composer and his work . . . ."[3] Understandably, Bach wanted to present in his memorandum to the Leipzig authorities a strong case. His "Short But Most Necessary Draft for a Well-appointed Church Music" included, therefore, "certain modest reflections on the decline of the same."[4] He basically had no choice but to portray a situation that was out of line with progress, and by appealing to the local pride of the town councilors Bach hoped to persuade them to give him the much-needed support. Any expression of interest in the old "musical taste" would surely have been counterproductive. Hence, the statement in the 1730 memorandum is of limited use indeed. On the other hand, it cannot be interpreted to mean the opposite either, namely that Bach had a particular predilection for "the former style of music" that he did not want to admit to the town council. Whatever tangible evidence of Bach's actual involvement with earlier repertoires we have points in a different direction: Bach's extreme selectivity regarding both modern and older musical composition, with no particular preference given to any type of repertoire – for example, German music.

It took hardly more than a couple of decades after Bach's death until he was recognized as the "father of [musical] art,"[5] "the greatest harmonist of all times and peoples,"[6] "Albrecht Dürer of German music,"[7] or – in Ludwig van Beethoven's famous dictum – "the *Urvater* of harmony."[8] Thus from the perspective of professional musicians in late eighteenth-century Germany, Bach's pre-eminent and seminal stature in the history of musical composition was firmly established. But what about his musical parentage? To be specific, what about his relationship to Heinrich Schütz whose tombstone, after all, bore the words "seculi sui musicus excellentissimus"[9] [the most excellent

---

BWV 71, "Gottes Zeit ist die allerbeste Zeit" BWV 106, "Aus der Tiefen" BWV 131, "Nach dir, Herr, verlanget mich" BWV 150, "Der Herr denket an uns" BWV 196) cannot be documented; the only exception seems to be a performance in 1724 of the chorale cantata "Christ lag in Todes Banden" BWV 4 in a revised version.

3 See n. 1.
4 See n. 1.
5 Johann Gottlob Immanuel Breitkopf, 1781, *Dok* III/849.
6 Johann Friedrich Reichardt, 1781, *Dok* III/853.
7 Friedrich Rochlitz, 1798, *Dok* III/1009.
8 In an 1801 letter to Franz Anton Hoffmeister, publisher of the first complete edition of Bach's keyboard works.
9 Kurt Gudewill, "Schütz, Heinrich," *MGG*.

musician of his century – the seventeenth century] and who in 1657 was referred to as "parentem nostrae musicae modernae"[10] [father of our modern music], curiously enough by an applicant for the St. Thomas cantorate in Leipzig. We know virtually nothing about Bach's relationship to Schütz, although it is safe to assume that Bach must at least have been aware of the stature and general significance of this greatest master of seventeenth-century German music, who for two generations had served the Dresden court as *Obercapellmeister*. Schütz simply was too well known a figure and as such prominently represented, for instance, in Johann Gottfried Walther's *Musicalisches Lexicon* (Leipzig, 1732) or among the biographical reports of Johann Mattheson's *Grundlage einer Ehren-Pforte* (Hamburg, 1740). Of course, the St. Thomas School's music library kept in the cantor's office provided Bach with easy access to a number of key works by Schütz.[11] After all, the *Geistliche Chor-Music* of 1648 was dedicated to the Leipzig Town Council and the St. Thomas choir. Because we can document Bach's selection of some items (for example, Johann Caspar Kerll's *Missa superba*) from the rich collections of the St. Thomas School's library for his own use,[12] and because we also have reason to assume that Bach did some research in this very collection as a collaborator of Johann Gottfried Walther in preparation for the latter's musical dictionary,[13] it would be hard to imagine that Bach continually bypassed the works of Schütz. But again, we have no concrete information about Bach having ever studied, let alone performed a piece by the Dresden master. It is all the more interesting to note, however, that a copy of *Heinrich Schützens Lebenslauf*, the biographical appendix to Martin Geier's funeral sermon (Dresden, 1672), was in the possession of Carl Philipp Emanuel Bach – an item that may well have come from his father's library.[14]

The question of Bach's relationship with seventeenth-century traditions, which can hardly be pursued by focusing on individual composers or repertoires, calls for broadening the scope of inquiry. Today's historians generally describe the seventeenth century as the beginning of "modern" times, a century that saw the conclusive end of the medieval society, the emergence of the administrative state, the transformation of the economy and financial systems, a new scientific understanding of the universe, revolutionary developments in

10   Elias Nathusius, 1657, cited in Gudewill, "Schütz, Heinrich."
11   Arnold Schering, "Die alte Chorbibliothek der Thomasschule in Leipzig," *Archiv für Musikwissenschaft* 1 (1918–19): 275–88.
12   Hans T. David, "A lesser secret of J. S. Bach uncovered," *Journal of the American Musicological Society* 14 (1961): 199–223.
13   Konrad Küster, "Bach als Mitarbeiter am 'Walther-Lexikon'?," *BJ* 77 (1991): 187–92.
14   Ulrich Leisinger, "Die 'Bachsche Auction' von 1789," *BJ* 77 (1991): 121.

mathematics, mechanics, technology, and philosophical skepticism, and the overcoming of large-scale religious conflict. Countries with a strong national identity, most notably England, Holland, France, and Spain, experienced the seventeenth century as a period of unprecedented growth, strength, and affluence, in many ways a "golden age." The situation in the German lands was very different, though, at least in terms of general economic, political, and even social conditions. The Thirty Years' War in particular had left its deep and lasting mark, and the badly splintered political landscape prevented a coordinated consolidation into larger geographical units. As a consequence, political, cultural, and religious life in the German lands developed in a manner of fragmented competition, more often than not with counterproductive repercussions.

Musically speaking, however, the situation must not be seen in a prevailingly negative light, for it led in many ways to unique developments that had a profound influence on the entire eighteenth century. The German situation might best be described as one of anti-uniformity or anti-standardization. To provide some specific examples, each of which could easily be expanded in various directions: (1) In the area of instrument technology, the German church organ resisted any tendency toward standardization, unlike in France; similar observations can be made regarding the making of wind and string instruments or the make-up of instrumental ensembles. (2) In the area of compositional technique, we find a clear predilection for the coexistence of diverse formal and stylistic models, combined with a tendency towards developing mixed features. (3) In the area of music theory, we see a deliberate and scholarly integration of speculative and philosophical thinking on the one hand, pragmatic compositional and performance-oriented craftsmanship on the other. Taken together, these developments indicate a genuinely individualistic approach that ultimately paved the way for the emergence of the eighteenth-century concept of the "original genius."

The young Johann Sebastian Bach was strongly influenced by a situation unique in seventeenth-century Europe – the same is true of Georg Friedrich Handel, for that matter. Their exact contemporary Domenico Scarlatti, for instance, grew up in Naples, where he had virtually no access to French or German keyboard repertoire. How different was the scene in late seventeenth-century Thuringia and Saxony where the so-called Andreas Bach Book and the Möller Manuscript – two keyboard albums compiled by Johann Sebastian Bach's elder brother, Johann Christoph Bach – happen to provide a case in point.[15]

15   *Keyboard music from the Andreas Bach Book and the Möller Manuscript*, ed. Robert Hill, Harvard Publications in Music 16 (Cambridge, Mass., 1991).

Representing the most important German manuscript collections of keyboard music from the time around 1700 they also belong generally among the most prominent sources that illuminate the extraordinarily rich and varied musical culture institutionally sustained by the towns, churches, and courts in seventeenth- and early eighteenth-century central Germany. Thuringia, especially, the traditional Lutheran heartland and then one of the most densely populated areas in Europe, dotted with countless towns in a politically fractured landscape of numerous principalities, had developed into an economically and culturally vigorous area. Some of the most important crossing-points of the East–West and South–North continental trade routes made the area particularly susceptible to influences from other regions, in the arts most notably from Italian and French traditions. Here the manifold European trends met, merged, and thus determined a unique musical climate.

Manuscript and printed collections originating in South and North Germany, and especially in Italy, France, and England are fundamentally different from Johann Christoph Bach's albums. They feature largely homogeneous, often parochial collections, without regard for a broader, let alone "international" spectrum. As their varied contents make abundantly clear, the Andreas Bach Book and Möller Manuscript present a highly sophisticated, multifaceted, and unbiased keyboard repertoire that offers welcome insights into the musical environment of the young Johann Sebastian Bach. Indeed, the two manuscript sources reveal the composers, genres, and styles that formed a decisive and challenging background into which he was born and that gave him the unique opportunity to aim at a consolidation of influences and to lay the foundations of a highly individualized musical language early in his career. In other words, the phenomenon we might refer to as Bach's hereditary aesthetic disposition was largely determined by a contextual situation that formed an essential part of seventeenth-century German traditions.

Naturally, Georg Philipp Telemann, Handel, and indeed many of Bach's contemporaries can claim a very similar background. Yet in most instances it would be difficult to make a strong case for the notion that any of them exhibited specifically the legacy of the seventeenth century. In this regard, Bach's upbringing as such may not play the strongest role either. As a matter of fact, he shared that with many of his musician colleagues. Of much greater importance seem to be some particular interests shown, and deliberate choices made, in part at an early point. While resisting the temptation here to draw a synthetic character portrait of Bach, emphasizing a few points regarding Bach and seventeenth-century traditions may help to shed light on his artistic personality.

There exists, above all, the ideal of the "universal" musician that is basically identical with the personified concept represented in Mattheson's treatise *Der vollkommene Capell-Meister* (Hamburg, 1739). Michael Praetorius embodied the prototype of this all-round musician and scholar, virtuoso and impresario, technologist, manager, composer of vocal and instrumental, sacred and secular repertoires. Dieterich Buxtehude would represent a somewhat less comprehensive counterpart who, in this respect, must nevertheless have made an impression on the younger generation around 1700, certainly on Mattheson, Handel, and Bach. For them, Buxtehude apparently signified a kind of father figure, one who anticipated in many ways the ideal of a later type: the autonomous composer.[16] The bourgeois, commercial, and liberal atmosphere of the Free Imperial City of Lübeck provided Buxtehude with considerable flexibility in developing and realizing his own various projects. He held, of course, the position of organist at St. Mary's, an office with specific duties. Nevertheless, his overall activities were characterized by a display of artistic initiative combined with unusual managerial independence. Courtly service would not have permitted such free conduct. Buxtehude was able to develop his career as a virtuoso, he traveled, and he surrounded himself with pupils. He seized opportunities for composing vocal works of both sacred and secular orientation, and as his own impresario, he organized and financed performances of large-scale "Abendmusiken." For this purpose he even created a new oratorio type far beyond the scope of the Carissimi model and regularly published the librettos for these works. Moreover, to broaden the compass of his activities he printed two chamber music collections, the sonatas opp. 1 and 2 of 1694 and 1696, respectively. In other words, Buxtehude conducted his office of organist very much in the style of a municipal "Capellmeister," thereby providing a clear role model, most notably for Telemann in Hamburg and Bach in Leipzig.

Buxtehude exemplified the ideal type of the universal musician in a further way. First, he balanced theory and practice. Since the generation of Praetorius or even earlier, scholarly theoretical erudition had been among the prerequisites for a pre-eminent musical office, and Buxtehude was no exception. His theoretical background reflected the Italian tradition of Zarlino, supplied most likely through Matthias Weckmann and Johann Adam Reinken. However, unlike the theoretically inclined Christoph Bernhard and Johann Theile, Buxtehude placed more emphasis on musical practice, with a strong theoretical foundation. Rather than writing treatises, he demonstrated his contrapuntal sophistication in diverse practical applications such as the *Klag-Lied* of 1675

16 Cf. Christoph Wolff, "Buxtehude, Bach, and seventeenth-century music in retrospect" in *Bach: essays on his life and music* (Cambridge, Mass., 1991), 41–55.

(BuxWV 76), or his canons (BuxWV 123–4). In this regard, Buxtehude provided an immediate example for the Bach of the *Well-Tempered Clavier* or the *Art of Fugue* – that is, for Bach the musical scholar.

Second, Buxtehude involved himself in organology and, generally, the technology of musical instruments. A widely recognized organ expert, he held close ties with Andreas Werckmeister, seventeenth-century Germany's premier musical scientist and speculative theorist. Buxtehude not only became the most prominent advocate of Werckmeister's new systems of temperament, but also explored in his works the immediate compositional implications of a more flexible and expressive harmonic language (through employment of keys with three and more sharps and flats, as well as through a notable preference for "functional" harmony, with frequent use of double dominants and the like). Again, and on a larger scale, Bach fits into that very tradition if we think of his practical experimentation with modes and keys, his exploration of unprecedented harmonic progressions; then of his close involvement not only with organ building, but well beyond that with the development of the fortepiano, the lautenclavier, the viola pomposa, and possibly the oboe da caccia and other instruments designed to broaden the spectrum of instrumental sonorities – ultimately in the interest of creating ever more individualized possibilities of sound.

Third, Buxtehude's compositional orientation included a broad spectrum of styles and genres, in the complementary use of retrospective as well as modern tendencies, the merging of Dutch and Hanseatic traditions (via Sweelinck, Scheidemann, and Reinken), English elements (in his viola da gamba writing), French manners (in the style brisé of his harpsichord works or in the choral movements emulating opera choruses of the Lullian manner). Italian influences (Frescobaldi, Legrenzi, Carissimi) are discernible too, but Buxtehude always aimed at synthesizing these elements. Practically all new genres of the seventeenth century occur in his music: concerto, motet, chorale, aria (strophic and free), and recitative in the vocal realm; toccata/prelude, fugue, ciacona/ passacaglia, canzona, suite, sonata, dance, and variation in the instrumental realm. This is not to suggest that Buxtehude's works serve as full-scale models for everything Bach did. Yet in terms of scope and breadth of stylistic orientation, formal design, and genre distribution Buxtehude's attitude and behavior are atypical of the prevailing tendencies in the eighteenth century. These are well represented by the standardization of instrumental and vocal genres and forms that occurs in the music of a Handel or Telemann, and sharply contrasts with Bach's emphasis on non-standardized works, even within a single genre of musical composition. A case in point is provided by the endless variety within the partitas of Bach's *Clavier-Übung* I (1731) as opposed to Handel's comparatively uniform *Suites de Pièces pour le Clavecin* I (1720), or even more impressively within the pieces of Bach's extremely varied chorale cantata cycle (1724–25) compared to those in Telemann's *Harmonischer Gottes-Dienst* (1725–26).

The image of the "universal musician," in whatever abstract or concrete form it existed, appears as a seventeenth-century phenomenon that did not conform to the changed ideals of the era of the enlightenment, and hence was certainly not an ideal that Bach's sons, for instance, wanted to adopt. The father must have recognized their drifting away from traditions he treasured, although he seems basically to have supported their course. At the time when the two oldest sons went about their own professional paths in the early and mid-1730s, Bach turned his attention more closely to the family background. If the pertinent documents do not mislead us, it is none other than Johann Sebastian himself who first systematically collected information on his family and especially on their seventeenth-century members. Around 1735 he put the family genealogy together.[17] Whether his efforts to collect the musical works of the earlier family members, the so-called *Alt-Bachisches Archiv*, stem from this same time is hard to tell. The extant sources documenting Bach's performances of pieces from the *Alt-Bachisches Archiv*, however, generally belong to the 1740s and thus suggest at least a general temporal connection.[18] It seems as though at this time of his life, the point when he observed the musical and professional emancipation of his own offspring, Bach develops an awareness of his position in the microcosm of the generations of his family and, in a more general sense, of his own historical position – including his relationship to seventeenth-century traditions.

In the Leipzig period, a time when Bach's artistic choices were rarely limited by external conditions, his links to those traditions manifest themselves obviously in a number of ways. For instance, he was apparently not ashamed to use chorale harmonizations from a seventeenth-century chorale book (1655) by Christoph Peter as a point of departure for his own more sophisticated elaborations;[19] he also integrated Johann Rosenmüller's famous six-part setting of "Welt ade, ich bin dein müde" (1649) in his 1726 cantata "Wer weiß, wie nahe mir mein Ende" BWV 27 – without changing a single note; he designed his *Christmas Oratorio* in 1734–5 according to the Buxtehudian fashion of a multi-sectional work spread over an extended period of time; he clearly had a

17 *Dok* I/184.
18 Cf. Daniel R. Melamed, "J. S. Bach and the German motet" (Ph.D. diss., Harvard University, 1989), 117–29.
19 BC IV, 1271.

special predilection for seventeenth-century chorale melodies and texts by Johann Crüger, Paul Gerhard and others; he paid attention to seventeenth-century theological tracts by Heinrich Müller and Abraham Calov, he turned to seventeenth-century librettists like Paul Thymich and Christian Weise. These instances are by no means negligible, but do they justify speaking of a seventeenth-century legacy as a truly important factor? Let us go a step beyond.

Seventeenth-century scientific and philosophical thought was concerned with the notion of perfection: from perfection of the world system to the search for perfect government. The most important and universally recognized key figure in seventeenth-century science and philosophy, someone who explored the concept of "perfectio"[20] in many different ways, was Isaac Newton. When in 1784–5 Christian Friedrich Daniel Schubart wrote "Was Newton als Weltweiser war, war Sebastian Bach als Tonkünstler"[21] [what Newton exemplified as philosopher, Bach represented as composer], he was not the first to compare Newton the scientist-philosopher and Bach the artist-musician. The first reference to Newton and Bach was made by Bach's student Johann Friedrich Agricola, and this already in 1750.[22] The broader meaning of this analogy is explored extensively in Johann Abraham Birnbaum's long-winded essay of 1738 defending Bach against the accusations of Johann Adolph Scheibe. There Birnbaum discusses the foundations of Bach's way of composing: aiming at perfection, he is composing to discover the secrets of the nature of music and so to gain "Einsicht in die Tiefen der Weltweisheit"[23] [insight into the depths of the wisdom of the world]. Here the philosophical foundations of Bach's scholarly approach to musical composition are spelled out, especially with respect to the genres of canon and fugue. But the same principles hold true also in a more general sense, demonstrated by his habit of constant elaboration as represented, for instance, in parody, revision, correction, and expansion of earlier versions.

This compositional behavior accurately represents Bach's philosophy of musical composition, his understanding of *musicalische Wissenschaft* as the knowledge of all possible implications of a musical idea, how and why they are possible. This may perhaps also be one of the reasons that Bach, in comparison with his contemporaries, appears so little audience-oriented; his sole focus is the musical subject matter at hand. His compositional art manifests itself as an empirical science.

---

20 Cf. Christoph Wolff, "'The extraordinary perfections of the Hon. court composer': an inquiry into the individuality of Bach's music" in *Essays*, 391–8.
21 *Dok* III/903.
22 *Dok* II/620.
23 Cf. Wolff, *Essays*, 389.

A genuine eighteenth-century composer, that is an artist clearly and unequivocally committed to musical progress, Bach did not aim to achieve his musical and aesthetic goals at the expense of breaking with and discarding traditional values. At the same time, he had no use for *stile antico* and *stile moderno* as mutually exclusive concepts. His virtuosity and technical command permitted him to combine, in a complementary manner, cutting-edge scholarly exploration of contrapuntal and harmonic frontiers on the one side, and pursuit of novel stylistic fashions on the other. Thus, Bach had no problem in his last large-scale work, the Symbolum Nicenum of the B Minor Mass, in putting the oldest and the newest movements side by side: the radically modern and freshly composed "Et incarnatus" and the re-modelled "Crucifixus," then forty years old.[24] It is not the remodeling process that makes the two divergent movements compatible but, rather, their common foundation. This permits the ultra-modern and emphatically homophonic "Et incarnatus" to close with densely knit, imitative canonic lines, whereas the old-fashioned and rigid "Crucifixus"-passacaglia ends in a gesture that basically dissolves the structural framework of the piece.

The composer here establishes principles that are both radically new and, at the same time, firmly grounded in the substance of the musical material itself. The musical legacy of the seventeenth century is not limited to the influence of the music of Schütz, Buxtehude, and the like; or to the treatises of Praetorius, Bernhard, Niedt, and others. First and foremost it consists in the establishment of a categorical benchmark, an absolute and measurable standard for the integration of practical composition and theoretical reflection. Recognizing this benchmark, Bach's idea of musical perfection reflects the fusion of theory and practice. Johann Sebastian Bach and Isaac Newton: Agricola's and Schubart's juxtaposition of the two names does not seem so far-fetched, for Bach's musical art established fundamental principles that changed the future of musical composition as much as Newton's discoveries affected the course of mathematics and physics. In that sense, Bach truly brought the legacy of the seventeenth century into the eighteenth.

---

24 Christoph Wolff, "'Et incarnatus' and 'Crucifixus': the earliest and the latest settings of Bach's B Minor Mass," in *Eighteenth-century music in theory and practice. Essays in honor of Alfred Mann*, ed. Mary Ann Parker (New York, 1994): 1–17.

Chapter twelve

Wilhelm Friedemann Bach's Halle performances of cantatas by his father

---

PETER WOLLNY

I

It is a commonly held view that in the second half of the eighteenth century the reception of Johann Sebastian Bach's music was focused mainly on his keyboard works, and among these particularly on the two parts of the *Well-Tempered Clavier* and the *Art of Fugue*; his vocal compositions, and primarily his church cantatas, are generally believed to have fallen into oblivion almost immediately after his death.

Indeed by around 1800 even the Bach specialist and first biographer Johann Nicolaus Forkel retained only a vague conception of Bach's compositions in the vocal genres.[1] Similarly, the Romantic writers on music E. T. A. Hoffmann, Wilhelm Heinrich Wackenroder, and Johann Karl Friedrich Triest appreciated Bach exclusively as a composer of instrumental music.[2] A decisive turn occurred only with the restoration of Protestant church music that began in the second quarter of the nineteenth century and culminated in the famous "centennial" performance of the St. Matthew Passion by Mendelssohn and the Berlin Sing-Akademie in 1829.[3]

The present study is based on research that appears in a more detailed and comprehensive version in my recently completed dissertation "Studies in the music of Wilhelm Friedemann Bach: sources and style" (Ph.D. diss., Harvard University, 1993). An earlier version was read at the Annual Meeting of the American Musicological Society, Pittsburgh, November, 1992.

1 Cf. particularly the list of J. S. Bach's vocal works in Forkel's *Ueber Johann Sebastian Bachs Leben, Kunst und Kunstwerke* (Leipzig, 1802), 61–2.

2 Cf. Carl Dahlhaus, "Zur Entstehung der romantischen Bach-Deutung," *BJ* 64 (1978): 192–210.

3 Under the direction of Carl Friedrich Zelter, regular performances of Bach cantatas by the Berlin Sing-Akademie appear to have started shortly after 1800, however. Cf. Georg Schünemann, "Die Bachpflege der Berliner Singakademie," *BJ* 25 (1928): 138–71.

Thus we are generally aware that around the turn of the century Bach's vocal works were largely neglected, yet we tend to overlook numerous clues that indicate an interest in his cantatas well into the 1780s. Examining the pertinent sources and documents without prejudice, we find that during the first three or even four decades after his death the awareness of Bach's vocal music was significantly greater than hitherto assumed.

To be sure, the reception of Bach's vocal music cannot be likened to that of his keyboard works. And it is also true that Bach's cantatas were never as widely disseminated as those of Georg Philipp Telemann. A number of documents suggest, however, that his merits as a vocal composer continued to be known outside his immediate circle. Johann Ernst Bach, for instance, in his preface to Jacob Adlung's *Anleitung zur musikalischen Gelahrtheit* (1758) names Bach and Telemann as the greatest masters of the sacred cantata,[4] and there are similar statements by Christoph Daniel Ebeling (1770) and Ernst Platner (1774).[5]

We are accustomed to the distorted view that Bach's death in 1750 represents a decisive turning point in the cantata genre, yet in fact there is no such caesura: not only did the generation of Bach's sons and students continue to use the same texts (or at least texts written in the same manner) as their teachers and predecessors, they also continued to compose in the same forms. To give an example: in the 1750s and 1760s, the Bach students Johann Gottlieb Goldberg and Gottfried August Homilius as well as Wilhelm Friedemann Bach continued to set texts from the *Geistliche Poesien* by Johann Jacob Rambach, originally published in 1720 and reissued in 1734 and 1735.[6] Only in the

---

4 Cf. *Dok* III/691.

5 Cf. *Dok* III/760 and 800. See also the anonymous recognition of Bach's merits as a church composer in the *Wöchentliche Nachrichten und Anmerkungen die Musik betreffend* (1768), quoted in *Dok* III/748.

6 M. Joh. Jacob Rambachs, / HALLENSIS, / Geistliche Poesien, / Davon / Der erste Theil / Zwey und siebenzig CANTATEN über / alle Sonn= und Fest=Tages=Evangelia; / Der andre Theil / Einige erbauliche Madrigale, / Sonnette und Geistliche / Lieder / in sich fasset. / Mit Königl. Preuß. Allergn. PRIVILEGIO, / HALLE, 1720. / In Verlegung der Neuen Buchhandlung . . . (copy: Halle, Universitätsbibliothek, Dd 3807); D. Joh. Jacob Rambachs, / Hoch=Fürstl. Hessen= Darmstädtischen Professoris / Theologiae Primarii, Ersten Superintendentens / und Consistorial-Accessoris zu Giessen, / Geistliche Poesien, / . . . / Zweyte Auflage. Leipzig, bey Christian David Schrötern, 1734 (copy: Hamburg, Staats- und Universitäts-bibliothek, A/112051). Johann Jacob Rambachs / Geistliche Poesien, / in zweyen Theilen. / Andere Auflage. / Gießen / Bey Johann Philipp Krieger, 1735 (copy: Brussels, Conservatoire Royale de Musique, 16718 FRW). The 1735 edition in many instances contains alternative chorale stanzas. Goldberg's setting of a text by Rambach, his cantata for the feast of St. John "Durch die herzliche Barmherzigkeit," dates from around 1743–46 and is generally believed to have been composed under the guidance of J. S. Bach; if so, the text might have been recommended to Goldberg by his teacher. Homilius's cantatas on Rambach texts, however, do not suggest J. S. Bach's influence; cf. Hans John, *Der Dresdner Kreuzkantor und Bach-Schüler Gottfried August Homilius: Ein Beitrag zur Musikgeschichte Dresdens im 18. Jahrhundert* (Tutzing, 1980), 166–7. W. F. Bach's Rambach settings comprise his Ascension cantata "Gott fähret auf mit Jauchzen" Fk 75, his Christmas cantata "Ach, daß du den Himmel zerrissest" Fk 93, and his aria "Zerbrecht, zerreißt, ihr schnöden Banden" Fk 94. It would be tempting to assume that J. S. Bach recommended Rambach's texts both to his son and to his student; yet as settings by Telemann

1780s did the madrigalian cantata gradually become obsolete, and by around 1790 it had vanished altogether. It was, in fact, with the end of the madrigalian cantata as a genre that Bach's sacred vocal music finally fell into oblivion.

After his death, J. S. Bach's cantatas continued to be performed in Leipzig and in towns like Chemnitz, Delitzsch, Grimma, Naumburg, Ölsnitz, and Merseburg, perhaps also in Leisnig;[7] traces are even found in the south-German city of Kaufbeuren.[8] In Berlin the former Bach students Agricola, Kirnberger, and Nichelmann gathered important collections of his vocal music.[9] We still know little about the performing activities of these musicians; it seems, however, that Agricola's complete or partial copies of twelve sacred cantatas and two "Sanctus" settings, for instance, were performed in his private musical society, which met every Saturday and in which, according to a remark published by Friedrich Wilhelm Marpurg, "not only instrumental but also vocal music was performed."[10] Similarly, the copies written by the unidentified Berlin scribe Anonymous 300 and by the musician S. Hering (who was closely

and Georg Benda demonstrate, the *Geistliche Poesien* continued to be popular for about forty years after their first publication. J. S. Bach himself twice used cantata libretti based on texts by Rambach; these were, however, significantly altered: "Es ist nichts Gesundes an meinem Leibe" BWV 25 is based on Rambach's text "Ich seufze Jesu, lieber Meister," and "Falsche Welt, dir trau ich nicht" BWV 52 makes use of Rambach's text for the seventeenth Sunday after Trinity, "Wehe mir, daß ich ein Fremdling bin unter Mesech."

7   For Chemnitz cf. *Dok* III/907; for Delitzsch see Winfried Hoffmann, "Leipzigs Wirkungen auf den Delitzscher Kantor Christoph Gottlieb Fröber," *Beiträge zur Bachforschung* 1 (1982): 54–73; for Grimma cf. NBA I/16 KB, 84 (Robert Moreen, George S. Bozarth and Paul Brainard). In Naumburg, Johann Christoph Altnickol probably performed his father-in-law's music on a regular basis. For Altnickol's copies of Bach's vocal music see Alfred Dürr, "Zur Chronologie der Handschrift Johann Christoph Altnickols und Johann Friedrich Agricolas," *BJ* 56 (1970): 44–65, esp. 45–7 (Dürr's list can be supplemented by Altnickol's copy of "Mit Fried und Freud ich fahr dahin" BWV 125 at Vienna, Gesellschaft der Musikfreunde, Ms. 15535); whether in addition to his own copies Altnickol inherited portions of J. S. Bach's original performing materials cannot be determined. Cf. Yoshitake Kobayashi, "Zur Teilung des Bachschen Erbes," in *Acht kleine Präludien und Studien über B A C H: Festgabe für Georg von Dadelsen zum 70. Geburtstag* (Göttingen, 1988), 66–76, esp. 69 and 72f. Ölsnitz and Merseburg are documented through performing parts for numerous cantatas by Johann Georg Nacke and Christian Friedrich Penzel; for details see Yoshitake Kobayashi, "Franz Hauser und seine Bach-Handschriftensammlung" (Ph.D. diss., Göttingen, 1973) and Hans-Joachim Schulze, *Studien zur Bach-Überlieferung im 18. Jahrhundert* (Leipzig, 1984), esp. 21f. On Leisnig see Werner Neumann, "Über die mutmaßlichen Beziehungen zwischen dem Leipziger Thomaskantor Bach und dem Leisniger Matthäikantor Stockmar," in *Bachiana et alia Musicologica. Festschrift für Alfred Dürr zum 65. Geburtstag*, ed. Wolfgang Rehm (Cassel, 1983), 201–8.

8   For evidence of performances of Bach cantatas in Kaufbeuren see Klaus Hofmann, "Ein süddeutsches Bach-Dokument aus dem Jahre 1751," *BJ* 72 (1986): 109–12.

9   On Agricola's collection see Dürr, "Zur Chronologie," 49–53; Kirnberger's collection is documented in Eva Renate Blechschmidt, *Die Amalienbibliothek. Historische Einordnung und Katalog mit Hinweisen auf die Schreiber der Handschriften* (Berlin, 1965); for Nichelmann's copies see Schulze, *Studien*, 130–45.

10 "Das Concert, welches alle Sonnabend bey dem Königl. Kammermusikus und Hofcomponisten Herrn Agricola gehalten, und worinnen nicht allein Instrumental- sondern auch Vocalmusik aufgeführt wird." *Historisch-Kritische Beyträge zur Aufnahme der Musik*, vol. 1 (Berlin, 1755), 387.

associated with Anon. 300) must have been intended for practical purposes, as is demonstrated by the large number of performing parts they prepared.[11] Because a number of these sources were owned at some point by the Berlin Singakademie, it is possible that they, like Agricola's copies and the performing materials written by Anon. 300 and S. Hering, were used at one of the Sing-Akademie's forerunner organizations, that is, in a private musical society.[12] How frequently Bach's vocal music was performed in these circles and who the audiences were remain unanswered questions.

Clearly the most persistent cultivation of J. S. Bach's vocal music in the eighteenth century took place in Halle and Hamburg, where the two eldest Bach sons held positions that required them to perform sacred vocal music on a regular basis. Bach scholarship has almost always taken a biased view of C. P. E.'s and, even more, of Friedemann's performances of their father's works;[13] in the pertinent literature one repeatedly encounters the more or less outspoken reproach of an unconsidered, even unscrupulous use of J. S. Bach's vocal compositions by his sons, although – or perhaps because – the exact circumstances of these performances have never been given much attention.

II

Friedemann Bach's practical use of his father's vocal works is limited to the eighteen years between May, 1746 and May, 1764, which mark the time of his tenure as organist and *Director musices* at the Halle Marienkirche.[14] Church music at Halle was organized quite differently from that in Leipzig, even though, as the title *Director musices* indicates, Friedemann held the same rank as his father. The three central churches of the city (St. Mary, St. Ulrich, and St. George) had to share their orchestra and singers, so that each church had

---

11 Cf. the sources identified by Paul Kast, *Die Bach-Handschriften der Berliner Staatsbibliothek* (Trossingen, 1958), esp. 135 and 139. Less well known are the numerous sources housed at the Berlin Hochschule der Künste (Ms. 6138) from the collection of Ernst Rudorff.

12 Thus the above-mentioned performances by Zelter would represent a more or less unbroken continuation of the Berlin Bach tradition.

13 Cf. particularly Georg Feder, "Bachs Werke in ihren Bearbeitungen 1750–1950. I. Die Vokalwerke" (Ph.D. diss., Christian-Albrechts-Universität Kiel, 1955). Friedemann's interest in his father's works has been colored by a famous anecdote concerning his "misuse" of one of J. S. Bach's passions. Cf. Friedrich Wilhelm Marpurg, *Legende einiger Musikheiligen. Ein Nachtrag zu den musikalischen Almanachen und Taschenbüchern jetziger Zeit* (Cologne, 1786), 60–2. A more moderate view than that of Feder is taken by Gerhard Herz, *Johann Sebastian Bach im Zeitalter des Rationalismus und der Frühromantik: Zur Geschichte der Bachbewegung von ihren Anfängen bis zur Wiederaufführung der Matthäuspassion im Jahre 1829* (Cassel, 1935).

14 For biographical details see Martin Falck, *Wilhelm Friedemann Bach: Sein Leben und sein Werk* (Leipzig, 1913), 22–43; and Walter Serauky, *Musikgeschichte der Stadt Halle*, vol. II/2, *Von Wilhelm Friedemann Bach bis Robert Franz* (Halle, 1942), 6–32.

concerted music only every third Sunday. This rule was modified, however, to the effect that the Marienkirche, as the main church in Halle, had the prerogative of concerted music on every high feast, both in the morning and in the afternoon. These feasts are listed in an appendix to the revised liturgy of 1660.[15] According to this *Kirchenordnung*, the Marienkirche had a cantata performed on the first day of each of the three high feasts of Christmas, Easter, and Pentecost. In addition, there were performances on the following feasts: First Sunday of Advent, Circumcision (January 1), Epiphany (January 6), Baptism of Christ (January 13), Purification of Mary (February 2), Annunciation of Mary (March 25), Palm Sunday, Ascension, Trinity, St. John the Baptist (June 24), Visitation of Mary (July 2), and St. Michael (September 29). Whenever any of the moveable feasts fell on a Sunday, the regular alternation between the three churches was interrupted and the music transferred to the Marienkirche. Thus altogether each year there were roughly forty-five to fifty cantata performances at the Marienkirche.

In Leipzig it had been the tradition since Johann Kuhnau's time that both on regular Sundays and on feast days the Thomascantor performed only compositions of his own,[16] a tradition that J. S. Bach respected at least through the 1720s; in Halle, in contrast, Friedemann's predecessor Gottfried Kirchhoff composed cantatas only for the fifteen high feasts and for special occasions, whereas for regular Sundays he relied on cantatas by Telemann, Fasch, and Förster.[17] Friedemann did not break with this local tradition and, like Kirchhoff, he composed cantatas almost exclusively for solemn occasions. Unfortunately we have only very scarce knowledge of this repertoire, because – except for Friedemann's copies of pieces by his father – neither musical sources nor contemporary inventories from the Halle Marienkirche are known. Judging from a number of printed cantata librettos documenting performances in the Marienkirche during Friedemann's tenure, Werner Braun suggested that Friedemann might have performed mainly cantatas by Telemann, especially from his so-called "Französischer Jahrgang" (1721/22), his "Sizilianischer Jahrgang" (1722/23), and his "Engel-Jahrgang" (1748/49).[18]

15 *Kirchenordnung der Stadt Hall in Sachsen, welche E. E. Hochweiser Rath daselbst A.1541 zuerst ablassen, A.1640 revidiren und A.1660 samt dero Anhang und Beylagen publiciren lassen* (Halle, 1660). The passages relating to the performance of music are quoted in Serauky, *Musikgeschichte*, II/1, 266f.

16 Cf. Arnold Schering, ed., *Sebastian Knüpfer. Johann Schelle. Johann Kuhnau: Ausgewählte Kirchenkantaten*, Denkmäler deutscher Tonkunst 58/59 (Leipzig, 1918), xli.

17 The inventory of Kirchhoff's music library is published in Serauky, *Musikgeschichte*, II/1, 497f.

18 "Materialien zu Wilhelm Friedemann Bachs Kantatenaufführungen in Halle," *Die Musikforschung* 18 (1965): 267–76, esp. 274. Because Friedemann took the text for his cantata "Ach Gott, vom Himmel sieh darein" Fk 96 from the "Engel-Jahrgang," we have proof that he indeed did know this cycle; contrary to Braun, however, Fk 96 demonstrates that not every text from this cycle automatically

From the once certainly rich collection of vocal works by Telemann at the Halle Marienkirche, today only a single piece can be traced: a copy of the *Missa alla Siciliana* in F major (TVWV 9:12), preserved at the Berlin Staatsbibliothek under the shelf number Mus. ms. 21744/75. As the owner's mark on the title page shows, the source was copied by Johann Christian Berger, cantor at the Marienkirche during the time of Friedemann's tenure as organist.[19] This secure sample of Berger's handwriting allows his identification as an occasional copyist for W. F. Bach (cf. BWV 12 and BWV 167 in Table 12.1).

One of the libretti discovered by Braun can now be identified as the text of a composition by Carl Heinrich Graun. The text print designated for Palm Sunday contains the complete Passion oratorio "Ein Lämmlein geht und trägt die Schuld" (1730).[20] As the libretto demonstrates, in Halle the work was presented in its original form, and not in the pasticcio version transmitted in a copy by J. S. Bach's student Johann Christoph Altnickol.[21] Moreover, for eight of his cantatas Friedemann used texts that were originally written in 1723 by Johann Friedrich Möhring for the *Schloßkapelle* in Zerbst and set to music in the same year by Johann Friedrich Fasch; this suggests that Friedemann might have known (and performed) Fasch's compositions as well.[22]

indicates a composition by Telemann. For a stylistic comparison of Telemann's and W. F. Bach's compositions of "Ach Gott, vom Himmel sieh darein" see my dissertation, 391–6.

19 For a description and facsimile of the source see Joachim Jaenecke, *Georg Philipp Telemann. Autographe und Abschriften*, Staatsbibliothek Preußischer Kulturbesitz. Kataloge der Musikabteilung, Series I, vol. 7 (Munich, 1993), 246 and 340. This source was first mentioned by Werner Menke, *Das Vokalwerk Georg Philipp Telemanns: Überlieferung und Zeitfolge* (Cassel, 1942), 12; Menke, however, gives no exact reference. Berger (1702–71) moved to Halle in 1749 and kept his post as cantor at the Marienkirche until his death. For details of his biography see Serauky, *Musikgeschichte*, II/2, 43–5. That the scribe and owner of the Telemann Mass is indeed identical with the Halle cantor can be verified through numerous samples of his handwriting preserved at the archive of the Marienkirche (particularly in the *Belege zur Kirchenrechnung*, 1749ff.).

20 *Texte / zur / Music, / welche / zu Halle / am / Sonntage Palmarum / Vor= und Nachmittags / in der / Haupt=Kirche / zu / U. L. Frauen / aufgeführet werden soll.* (copy: Halle, Universitätsbibliothek, Pon. QK, Y 3424k).

21 On this pasticcio, which has been suggested represents a compilation by J. S. Bach, see particularly John W. Grubbs, "Ein Passions-Pasticcio des 18. Jahrhunderts," *BJ* 51 (1965): 10–42; and Kirsten Beißwenger, *Johann Sebastian Bachs Notenbibliothek*, (Cassel, 1992), 89–100. Considering the differences between the pasticcio and the version performed in Halle, it seems unlikely that Friedemann received a copy of this – in any case widely distributed – work from Leipzig.

22 *GOtt geheiligtes / Beth= und Lob= / Opffer der Christen, / Bestehend / in Biblischen Sprüchen, geist= / lichen Cantaten und dahin gehö= / rigen Chorälen, / GOTT zu Ehren, / dem Evangelischen Zerbster Zion / und allen fromen Seelen zur Erbauung / Aus denen / Sonn= und Fest=täglichen Episteln / Auf gnädigste Anordnung / vor die Hoch=Fürstl. Schloß=Kirche / verfertiget, / Und vor GOtt in Wahrheit und Demuth / dargelegt / von / Johann Friedrich Möhringen. / ZERBST / Druckts Samuel Tietze, H. F. A. Hof= und Regierungs=Buchdrucker, 1723* (copy: Zerbst, Stadt- und Kreisbibliothek, wissenschaftliche Abteilung, call no. A 547). The text incipits for each movement are given in *Johann Friedrich Fasch (1688–1758): Kirchenkantaten in Jahrgängen*, 2 vols., ed. Gottfried Gille (Michaelstein, 1989); none of Fasch's compositions from Möhring's cycle seem to have survived. Friedemann used Möhring's texts – entirely or partially – for his cantatas Fk 73, 74, 80, 81, 85, 89, 91, and 92. In passing I would like to mention

Apart from his own compositions the most important component of Friedemann's Halle repertoire, however, was undoubtedly cantatas by his father. The first list of cantatas by J. S. Bach for which performances in Halle can be documented was compiled by Martin Falck. A corrected and expanded list was presented by Braun and later supplemented by Hans-Joachim Schulze. For the present list, given in Table 12.1, all the available original sets of performing parts of J. S. Bach's cantatas have been examined for traces of Friedemann's mature handwriting.[23] Because of the major gaps in the transmission of Friedemann's portion of his father's estate, there can be little doubt that this list represents only a fraction of the actual repertoire. One should also consider that whenever Friedemann inherited a complete set of parts (as he did, for example, for BWV 174), his performance might not have left any trace.

The precise dating of Friedemann's cantata performances constitutes an extremely difficult task. Only for two performances do we have a dated textbook (BWV 205a); for another piece (BWV 167), the date of performance can be deduced from circumstantial evidence.[24] To establish a reliable chronological frame, I have compared the paper types found in the additional parts prepared for Friedemann's performances with those found in approximately 150 autograph receipts preserved at the archive of the Halle Marienkirche.[25]

that an anonymous passion oratorio performed in 1745 and 1748 under the direction of the cantor of the Marienkirche, Johann Gottfried Mittag (cf. Serauky, *Musikgeschichte*, II/2, 43), is largely identical with a work performed by Gottfried Heinrich Stölzel in 1720 at Gotha (*Die leidende und am Creutz sterbende Liebe Jesu*, Gotha 1720; printed libretto at Gotha, Forschungsbibliothek, Cant. sac. n. 884,[2a]).

23 For this project I relied mainly on the photocopy collection at the Bach-Archiv Leipzig.

24 The watermark found in Friedemann's parts of BWV 167 is identical with that of the vocal parts of his cantata "Verhängnis, dein Wüten" Fk 87, which, as certain clues in the text indicate, was almost certainly intended to be performed at a mourning service for Sophia Dorothea, Queen of Prussia and mother of Frederick the Great, who died June 28, 1757. Her death was commemorated at Halle with mourning services in all three main churches on July 24, 1757 (7th Sunday after Trinity); cf. "Nachricht von der, bey Gelegenheit der Gedächtnis=Predigt Ihro Maj. der verwitweten höchstseligen Königin von Preussen, in der Ulrichskirche allhie beobachteten Feyerlichkeit," in *Wöchentliche Hallische Anzeigen*, no. XXXI (August 1, 1757), col. 538–9. This date is supported by another observation. In 1836, Franz Hauser made a copy of Friedemann's set of parts (which at the time was in the possession of Adolf Friedrich Rudorff). Hauser's copy (SBB P 1159/VIII adn. 7) transmits a title that can no longer be found on the parts; probably it was copied from a now-lost title wrapper. The title reads: "Dom III post Tr / in Festo Johannis / Auf Menschen rühmet Gottes Güte / di / Bach." Supposing that this title goes back to Friedemann, one can assume that the performance in Halle took place on the third Sunday after Trinity, and that in this particular year the Feast of St. John the Baptist was observed on the same day. The two occasions coincide only when the third Sunday after Trinity falls directly on June 24, or when it occurs in such close vicinity to that date that the Feast of St. John is moved to that particular Sunday. During the eighteen years of Friedemann's tenure at Halle, the third Sunday after Trinity never fell exactly on June 24, and only three times did it occur nearby: 1749 (June 22), 1757 (June 26), and 1760 (June 22).

25 In the fall of 1993, I was able to recover and catalogue the archival materials of the Halle Marienkirche relating to Friedemann Bach's tenure there. This material, which was hitherto inaccessible, supplements and occasionally modifies the chronology of the Halle works proposed in Part III of my dissertation. For kind support I am grateful to Hildegard Seidel, librarian at the Marienkirche.

Table 12.1. *Cantatas by J. S. Bach performed in Halle*

BWV 9 "Es ist das Heil uns kommen her"

Jahrgang II, 6th Sunday after Trinity
Source: several parts in W. F. Bach's hand: D–EIb (S), D–KÖ (A, T), B–Bc (B), A–Wgm
   (Va), US–CA (Bc/Org obl); added dynamic markings in movement 3 of original duplicate
   continuo part (US–NYp)
Changes of instrumentation: Fl and Ob d'amore replaced by Org obl in BWV 9/5
Date: probably fall, 1759. The watermark of the alto part (Hollandia, Pro Patria) is found
   among W. F. Bach's receipts only in one instance, dated September 28, 1759 (see also
   BWV 178).

BWV 12 "Weinen, Klagen, Sorgen, Zagen"

Jahrgang I, Jubilate
Source: SBB St 109; additional vocal part (soprano or tenor) for movement 5 in the hand of
   Johann Christian Berger, indicating separate performance of this movement
Date: after 1749

BWV 19 "Es erhub sich ein Streit"

Jahrgang III, St. Michael
Source: SBB P 45 (additional part for Org obl); revisions in SBB St 25, consisting of added
   trills at cadential points (S, mvt. 3, m. 37 and 62) and of an added title for movement 5 (V
   2, second copy, "Aria").
Changes of instrumentation: Ob d'amore 2 replaced by Org obl in BWV 19/2
Date: probably 1752 or before. The watermark of the additional organ part (INM in
   cartouche) is also found in a receipt of September 22, 1752.

BWV 30 "Freue dich, erlöste Schar"

Jahrgang –, St. John
Source: SBB St 31
Changes of instrumentation: addition of Tr 1, 2, Timp
Date: probably 1752 or before. The watermark of the additional trumpet and tympani parts
   (INM in cartouche) is also found in a receipt of September 22, 1752.

BWV 31 "Der Himmel lacht! Die Erde jubilieret"

Jahrgang I, Easter Sunday
Source: PL–Kj, St 14
Changes of instrumentation: strings in BWV 31/8 replaced by Org obl
Date: perhaps before 1750

Libraries other than SBB are identified in this table by their abbreviations established by
Répertoire International des Sources Musicales (RISM).

BWV 34 "O ewiges Feuer, o Ursprung der Liebe"

Jahrgang –, Pentecost
Source: SBB Am.B. 39
Date: possibly May 29, 1746, or May 21, 1747

BWV 43 "Gott fähret auf mit Jauchzen"

Jahrgang III, Ascension
Source: text print, D–HAu, Yb 3424i (only mvts. 1–5); SBB St 36 (revisions in S, A, T, B, Ob 1, Ob 2, V 1, V 2, Va); SBB P 44. The revisions include the addition of numerous trills and dynamics (e.g. Ob 1, mvt. 5, mm. 28, 29, 35, and V 1, first copy, mvt. 5, mm. 7, 9, 13, 15, 21, 26, 28, 29, 35), the counting of rests (particularly striking in the alto part for mvt. 9), the insertion of tacet indications (T, mvt. 10 "Rec. tacet", B, mvt. 10 "Recit: tacet", Va, mvt. 9–10 "Aria et Rec: tacet") and movement titles (Va, mvt. 5 "Aria" and mvt. 6 "Recit:"). In SBB P 44 Friedemann added the indication "Rec. segue" after the first movement.
Date: after 1750 (at least two different performances)

BWV 44 "Sie werden euch in den Bann tun"

Jahrgang I, Exaudi
Source: revisions in SBB St 86, including added trills in Ob 1 (mvt. 3, mm. 1, 21, 51, 67; mvt. 6, mm. 1, 4, 8, 10, 12, 15, 16).

BWV 45 "Es ist dir gesagt, Mensch, was gut ist"

Jahrgang III, 8th Sunday after Trinity
Source: revisions in SBB St 26 and P 80. The revisions in St 26 include added trills in T (mvt. 3, mm. 25, 82, 107, 141), Ob 1 (mvt. 1, mm. 36, 100, 122, 127), V 1 (mvt. 1, mm. 31, 36, 100, 106, 157, 222, 227), added dynamics in V 1 (mvt. 3, mm. 25, 61, 80), insertion of the left-out measure 194 in V 1; sometimes rests are counted. In P 80, on p. 11 (at the beginning of movement 3) J. S. Bach notated the continuo part in tablature, over which Friedemann pasted a strip of paper with the properly notated continuo part.

BWV 51 "Jauchzet Gott in allen Landen"

Jahrgang III?, Leipzig: 15th Sunday after Trinity; Halle: unspecified feast day
Source: revisions in SBB St 49, including added trills in V 1, first copy (mvt. 1, mm. 8, 17, 23, 38, 49), and Tr 1 (mvt. 1, mm. 5, 7, 8, 27, 35, 36, 37, 38, 49).
Changes of instrumentation: addition of Tr 2 and Timp
Date: perhaps before 1750

BWV 80/1+5 "Ein feste Burg ist unser Gott"

Jahrgang ?, Reformation Festival
Sources: SBB P 72; US–Wc, ML96.B.188

Changes of instrumentation: addition of Tr 1, 2, 3, Timp
Date: probably around 1761–3. The watermark (a) GCK in cartouche, (b) crescent moon between two stars (coat of arms of Halle) can be found in receipts from September 1761, June 1762, and June 1763.
The two movements are furnished with the Latin texts "Gaudete omnes populi" and "Manebit verbum Domini."

BWV 101/1 "Nimm von uns, Herr, du treuer Gott"

Jahrgang II, Leipzig: 10th Sunday after Trinity; Halle: possibly in connection with Catechism Prayers
Source: SBB P 830
Date: probably around 1761–3. For the dating of the watermark (a) GCK in cartouche, (b) crescent moon between two stars, see BWV 80.

BWV 128 "Auf Christi Himmelfahrt allein"

Jahrgang II, Ascension
Source: original score, private collection
Changes of instrumentation: Ob d'amore replaced by Org obl in BWV 128/4; Halle performance probably without woodwinds
Date: after 1750

BWV 147/1 "Herz und Mund und Tat und Leben" and BWV 170/1 "Vergnügte Ruh, beliebte Seelenlust"

Jahrgang I+III, Leipzig: Visitation of Mary/6th Sunday after Trinity; Halle: after Catechism Prayers
Source: D–LEb, Ms. R 7
Changes of instrumentation: Halle performance probably without oboes
Date: perhaps September 1752. The watermark of the score (INM in cartouche) is found in a receipt of September 22, 1752, which acknowledges payment for a cantata performance in connection with the Catechism Prayers.

BWV 149 "Man singet mit Freuden vom Sieg"

Jahrgang IV, St. Michael
Source: text print (copies: D–HAu, Pon. QK an Zb 6495, D–HAmk, H 1700 and one uncatalogued copy)
Date: October 3, 1756

BWV 167 "Ihr Menschen, rühmet Gottes Liebe"

Jahrgang I, Leipzig: St. John; Halle: St. John and 3rd Sunday after Trinity
Source: S–Ssmf, set of parts in the hand of W. F. Bach (S, A, T, B, Vne, Org), J. C. Berger (text underlay in movement 5 of S and A), and one anonymous scribe (2 V 1, 2 V 2, Va)

Changes of instrumentation: in BWV 167/3 Ob da caccia replaced by Va d'amore (?); Clar in BWV 167/5 omitted
Date: probably June 26, 1757

BWV 172 "Erschallet, ihr Lieder"

Jahrgang I, Pentecost
Source: revisions in SBB St 23, including added movement title for mvt. 1 and tacet indications for mvts. 4–6 in Tr 1 ("Coro", "Aria Ten: et Duetto tacet", "Choral tacet", "Coro repet"), added trills in Tr 1 (mvt. 3, mm. 4?, 15), counted rests in Tr 2 (mvt. 1, m. 43), Tr 3 (mvt. 1, m. 43, mvt. 3, mm. 13, 18).

BWV 178 "Wo Gott, der Herr, nicht bei uns hält"

Jahrgang II, 8th Sunday after Trinity
Source: SBB, St 596
Date: probably fall 1759. The watermark of the alto part (Hollandia, Pro Patria) is found among W. F. Bach's receipts only in one instance, dated September 28, 1759 (see also BWV 9).

BWV 194 "Höchsterwünschtes Freudenfest"

Jahrgang I, Leipzig: Trinity; Halle: unspecified
Source: SBB St 346 (added continuo part for mvts. 7 and 9) and St 48 (revisions in T and B). The revisions in St 48 include added trills in T (mvt. 8, m. 53) and B (mvt. 3, mm. 25, 34, 36).

BWV 205a "Blast Lärmen, ihr Feinde"

Jahrgang –, Leipzig: Coronation of August III; Halle: Inaugural Sermon of F. E. Rambach, and Thanksgiving Service for Victory at Lissa
Source: text prints, D–HAu, Pon. QK an Zb 6495
Date: November 21, 1756 and December 18, 1757

Of particular interest is the question whether any of J. S. Bach's cantatas were performed in Halle during his lifetime. Hitherto it was commonly assumed that Friedemann had access to his father's cantatas only after 1750; this assumption lacks substance, however. A number of documents attest that it was not uncommon for J. S. Bach to lend performing materials of vocal works to friends and former students. A letter written by Bach's nephew and private secretary Johann Elias Bach to the Ronneburg cantor Johann Wilhelm Koch in January of 1741, for example, illustrates how very frequently Bach was asked to make his compositions available. From this letter we learn that Koch had to wait patiently for the performing materials of a cantata he had requested until another borrower returned them, and that Bach had decided not to give out his scores any more, "because in that way he had already lost many things" ("weil er auf solche Art schon um viele Sachen gekommen ist").[26]

The Pentecost cantata "O ewiges Feuer, o Ursprung der Liebe" BWV 34 exists in an autograph score prepared by J. S. Bach around 1746/47 apparently specifically for a performance outside Leipzig, as detailed instructions concerning the sequence of movements indicate. Because Friedemann completed the instrumentation in the last movement of this cantata, and because the score was transmitted through him, it is likely that his father prepared the piece especially for him.[27] Possibly the work was heard during Friedemann's first official function in Halle on May 29, 1746, where it would have been performed together with his own cantata "Wer mich liebet" Fk 72. If so, BWV 34 would be a parallel case to the organ prelude BWV 541 with which J. S. Bach seems to have provided his eldest son for the job competition at Dresden in 1733.

J. S. Bach's support of his eldest son was apparently not one-sided, as the following example will show. The original set of performing parts for Friedemann's Advent cantata "Lasset uns ablegen" Fk 80, which shows traces of at least four performances in Halle during the late 1740s and the 1750s, contains an unfigured continuo part labeled "Violoncello e Bassono" (see Figure 12.1). These two instruments were not usually part of Friedemann's cantata ensemble, because in his performances the bass line was played by the organ, which was reinforced by a violone only in tutti movements. Such a part would, however, not be uncommon for J. S. Bach's continuo practice in Leipzig. And indeed a close look at the heading reveals that it was written by none other than J. S. Bach himself; the rest of the part is in Friedemann's hand. Friedemann noted on the title page "composuit anno 1749"; if this date is correct, then the heading represents the latest datable sample of J. S. Bach's handwriting.[28]

An examination of the paper-types reveals that Friedemann must have copied this "Violoncello e Bassono" part in Leipzig, whereas all the other parts were prepared in Halle. This suggests the following scenario: Friedemann composed the cantata and prepared the performing materials in Halle. He then brought them to Leipzig for a specific performance and apparently wrote out the extra bass part immediately prior to the performance. The fact that

---

26 *Dok* II/484. Cf. also *Dok* I/20, and *Dok* III/638.
27 Friedemann's completion of the original score is described in NBA I/13 KB, 116–7 (Dietrich Kilian). The possible connection with a Halle performance before 1750 was first pointed out in BC I, 334.
28 For a more detailed discussion see my dissertation, 303–14.

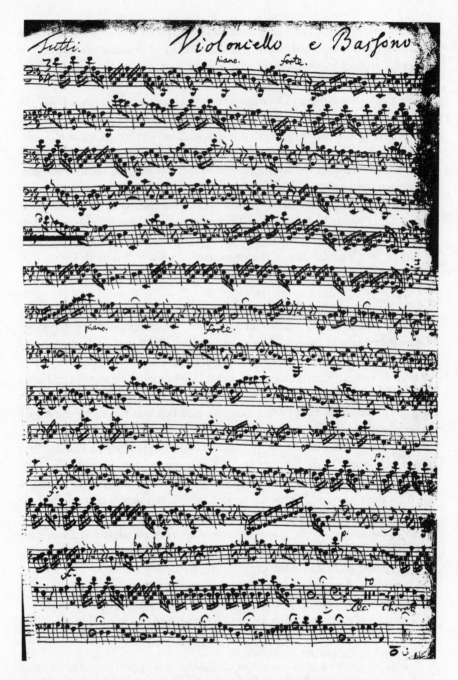

Figure 12.1 W. F. Bach, cantata "Lasset uns ablegen die Werke der Finsternis" Fk 80, first page of *Violoncello e Bassono* part, Mus. ms. Bach St 172, from the collection of the former Preußische Staatsbibliothek, preserved at the Jagiellonian Library, Cracow.

Friedemann alone is responsible for all the parts suggests that he – and not his father – was in charge of the Leipzig performance of this cantata.

This Leipzig performance of Fk 80 is difficult to interpret. Perhaps it was common practice for father and son to exchange their cantatas; but it is also possible that this specific undertaking was part of J. S. Bach's counter-offensive against the town council's tactless decision in June, 1749, to make arrangements (probably under the pressure of the Saxon Prime Minister Count Heinrich von Brühl) for a trial performance of Gottlob Harrer as the prospective successor, "in case the Capellmeister and Cantor Mr. Sebastian Bach should die."[29] We can only speculate about J. S. Bach's reaction to this, but his performances, in the summer of that year, of the Town Council Election cantata "Wir danken dir, Gott, wir danken dir" BWV 29 and the secular cantata "Geschwinde, geschwinde, ihr wirbelnden Winde" BWV 201 (with a number of changes in the text of the last recitative that could be read as allusions to Count Brühl) might have something to do with the incident. As Hans-Joachim Schulze has pointed out, after Harrer's trial performance Bach himself might well have become active and suggested a potential successor of his choice. This hypothesis is corroborated by the fact that C. P. E. Bach, too, performed his *Magnificat* at Leipzig shortly before his father's death.[30]

III

There is a puzzle of transmission here. Friedemann's revisions in J. S. Bach's original performing parts suggest Halle performances of a relatively large number of cantatas from *Jahrgänge* I and III, which are commonly assumed not to have been contained in his portion of his father's estate. His revisions, however, definitely display his mature handwriting and cannot possibly originate from the time he was still living at home (before 1733). Nevertheless, most of these sources later show up in C. P. E. Bach's estate catalogue of 1790. This situation allows for the following possibilities, which certainly are not mutually exclusive.

(1) Friedemann borrowed these materials from Leipzig during his father's lifetime and returned them soon after. After J. S. Bach's death the relevant sources came into the possession of other heirs.

29 Cf. *Dok* II/584. For a discussion of this event and J. S. Bach's possible reaction see particularly Christine Fröde, "Zu einer Kritik des Thomanerchores von 1749," *BJ* 70 (1984): 53–8, and Hans-Joachim Schulze, "'Wer der alte Bach geweßen weiß ich wohl': Anmerkungen zum Thema Kunstwerk und Biographie", in *Johann Sebastian Bachs Spätwerk und dessen Umfeld. Bericht über das wissenschaftliche Symposion anläßlich des 61. Bachfestes der Neuen Bach-Gesellschaft, Duisburg 28.–30. Mai 1986*, ed. Christoph Wolff (Cassel, 1988), 23–31, esp. 29.

30 Cf. *Dok* III/703.

(2) After 1750, Friedemann borrowed performance materials from his brother Carl Philipp Emanuel. According to statements by Johann Philipp Kirnberger and Friedrich Rochlitz the two brothers became alienated later in their lives, yet in the first years after their father's death contacts between them are documented by Friedemann's extended visit to Berlin in the fall of 1750 and through their joint appearance as commissioners of the first edition of the *Art of Fugue* (1751).[31] The case of BWV 172 indeed suggests that Friedemann borrowed parts inherited by his younger brother. For this piece, Friedemann owned an apparently incomplete set of parts (Musikbibliothek der Stadt Leipzig, ms. R 1). Traces of a revision from his hand, however, are found on the trumpet and timpani parts that belong to another, complete set of parts owned by Emanuel (SBB St 25). A plausible explanation for this would be that when he decided to perform the work, Friedemann asked his brother to supply the missing parts.

(3) Friedemann originally inherited portions of *Jahrgänge* I and III, but passed much of this material on to his brother at a later point. This possibility is supported by the fact that C. P. E. Bach's wrapper for the original parts of BWV 30 apparently stems from well after 1750, which could suggest that he did not inherit them but came by them only later.

A satisfactory explanation is still lacking for those cantata sources from the first and third cycles that certainly or most likely were transmitted through Friedemann (see Table 12.2). If we assume that they were indeed inherited by him, we have to modify the traditional conception of the division of J. S. Bach's cantatas among his heirs. According to Alfred Dürr, the cantata cycles were divided in the following way:[32]

> *Jahrgang* I: J. C. F. and C. P. E. Bach
> *Jahrgang* II: A. M. (parts) and W. F. Bach (scores)
> *Jahrgang* III: J. C. (parts) and C. P. E. Bach (scores)
> *Jahrgang* IV: W. F. Bach?

Although there is much evidence for such a distribution, this suggested allotment does not concur with Forkel's remark according to which Friedemann received most of the cantatas, because among the brothers he could best use them at Halle.[33] The large number of cantatas for feast days and special occa-

---

31 Cf. *Dok* III/639.

32 Cf. NBA I/15 KB, 205f. (Alfred Dürr, Robert Freeman, James Webster), and Kobayashi, "Zur Teilung des Bachschen Erbes."

33 "Die Jahrgänge wurden nach des Verfassers Tode unter dessen älteren Söhnen vertheilt, und zwar so, daß Wilh. Friedemann das meiste davon bekam, weil er in seiner damahligen Stelle zu Halle den meisten Gebrauch davon machen konnte." Forkel, *Ueber Johann Sebastian Bachs Leben, Kunst und Kunstwerke*, 61.

Table 12.2. *Original sources from J. S. Bach's first and third* Jahrgänge *transmitted through W. F. Bach*

Composition	Evidence for transmission through W. F. Bach
Jahrgang I	
BWV 12 (Jubilate)	Additional tenor part copied by J. C. Berger
BWV 172 (Pentecost)	Provenance of original parts (D–LEm, Ms. R 1)
BWV 194 (Trinity)	Provenance of some of the original parts (SBB St 48 and St 346) through W. F. Bach
BWV 167 (St. John)	Parts for Halle performance (S–Ssmf), probably copied from lost original score
BWV 147 (Visitation)	First movement used after 1750 in a pasticcio
?BWV 25 (14 p. Trin.)	Copied by Penzel (Aug. 25, 1770), presumably from original source in W. F. Bach's possession
Jahrgang III	
BWV 43 (Ascension)	Original parts transmitted through W. F. Bach
BWV 176 (Trinity)	Original parts transmitted through W. F. Bach
BWV 187 (7 p. Trin.)	Original parts transmitted through W. F. Bach
BWV 168 (9 p. Trin.)	Original parts transmitted through W. F. Bach
?BWV 79 (Reformation)	18th–century copy on paper manufactured in Halle

sions in what seems to have been Friedemann's share could suggest, however, that these pieces were distributed (and perhaps had been kept) separately when J. S. Bach's musical estate was divided among his heirs. As Table 2 demonstrates, from *Jahrgang* I W. F. Bach owned the cantatas designated for Pentecost, Trinity, the feast of St. John, and the Visitation of Mary, and from *Jahrgang* III the cantatas for Ascension, Trinity, and the Reformation Festival. Because Friedemann at Halle could make particularly good use of such works, it seems indeed possible that his special needs were given preferred consideration.[34]

IV

The question of what the existing sources are able to tell us about the specific circumstances of Friedemann's performances of cantatas by his father shall be addressed in two case studies. In every one of these performances Friedemann probably had to seek a compromise between the demands of a specific composition and what he could achieve under the working conditions at the Marienkirche. When on one occasion he decided to perform only the first

---

34 The habit of separating the pieces for solemn occasions from an annual cycle of cantatas can also be observed in the nonthematic Breitkopf catalogues, particularly those of 1761 and 1764.

Figure 12.2   J. S. Bach, Cantata "Höchsterwünschtes Freudenfest" BWV 194, W. F. Bach's additional leaf to the continuo part, SBB Mus. ms. Bach St 346/8b (front and back)

part of BWV 43, for example, he may have had to adapt the piece to the limited time available in a specific service;[35] when the text of BWV 167 was substantially changed, this may have been caused by the Marienkirche consistory exerting their right of censorship.[36] And changes in instrumentation do not necessarily reflect divergent musical tastes, but may simply have been necessitated by the absence of certain instruments in Friedemann's orchestra. These and similar possibilities have to be considered before we can try to assess Friedemann's attitude to his father's music.

35 Friedemann's revisions of the original parts of BWV 43 (SBB St 36) demonstrate that at least in one instance he performed the entire cantata and not only its first part. His mature handwriting can be identified without doubt in the following instances: St 36/4 (tacet indication for movement 10), St 36/14 (tacet indications for movements 6 and 10), St 36/15 (caption titles for movements 5 ["Aria"] and 6 ["Recit:"]). My identification of St 36 as the basis for Friedemann's performances also sheds new light on the transmission of the parts in the second half of the eighteenth century. Hitherto it was not possible to trace their provenance before the middle of the nineteenth century, but we can now be certain that Friedemann inherited them in 1750; they probably found their way to the Berlin Sing-Akademie by around 1800.
36 Cf. the passage in Friedemann's contract: "Vornehmlich aber hat er . . . nöthig die zur Musique erwehlten Textus und Cantiones dem Ober Pastori Unserer Kirche Tit. Consistorial Rath und Inspectori, Johann Georgi Francken zu dessen Approbation in Zeiten zu communiciren." Quoted after Falck, *Wilhelm Friedemann Bach*, 22.

(1)   "Höchsterwünschtes Freudenfest" BWV 194

Wilhelm Friedemann Bach's performance of "Höchsterwünschtes Freudenfest" BWV 194 is documented by an additional leaf inserted in one of J. S. Bach's original continuo parts and through revisions in the original tenor and bass parts (see Figure 12.2).[37] The additional part appears puzzling at first because it contains only the two recitatives BWV 194/7 and 9; on a closer look, however, it allows us to draw a number of interesting conclusions about the Halle performance of this cantata.

In the two movements contained in this part, the figured continuo line is supplemented by a superimposed cue staff containing the untexted vocal line. Although the leaf does not bear any designation for a specific instrument, it was certainly intended for the organ. At the end of the first recitative, Friedemann noted "Seque Aria ¢," and at the end of the second we find a similar instruction: "Seque Aria 3/4." These cues indicate that for these arias, the organist had to use a different part. The function of the additional sheet now becomes clear: it helped the organist in performing the recitatives, and it determined the sequence of movements, which in Friedemann's performance departed from all of J. S. Bach's versions.

Because Friedemann's part is inserted in the continuo part written by J. S. Bach's copyist Johann Christian Köpping, it seems logical to assume that it was used in conjunction with this particular part. Yet we find that there is a discrepancy in the notation of the two parts – Köpping's is notated a whole tone lower to fit an organ tuned in *Chorton*, whereas Friedemann's part is notated at pitch, for an organ tuned in *Cammerton*. This is easily explained, however: Like most mid-German organs of the time, the organ of the Halle Marienkirche was tuned in *Chorton* (that is, a whole tone above *Cammerton*), but in addition the instrument contained a small number of *Gedacktregister* tuned in *Cammerton*, the so-called *Musiziergedackt*. As the term indicates, these *Cammerton* stops were only used when the organ accompanied other instruments in concerted music. For obbligato parts, however, they were not strong enough, so that the organist had to rely on the *Chorton* stops.

As Table 12.3a demonstrates, the continuo part written by Köpping for J. S. Bach (St 348/8+8a) presents the cantata in an abridged version with a reduction of the original woodwind group, which is partially substituted by an obbligato organ. Friedemann apparently based his Halle performance on this abridged version,[38] but he changed the sequence of movements further. The

37 St 346/8b. For a detailed discussion of the sources see NBA I/31 KB, 104–12 (Frieder Rempp).
38 Accordingly he must have used the following original parts: St 48/1–4 (S, A, T, B), St 346/1 (Ob 1),

first instruction noted on his part probably refers to the Aria "Hilf, Gott, daß es uns gelinge" BWV 194/5, while the second definitely refers to the duet "O wie wohl ist uns geschehen" BWV 194/10, both of which had to be played from the original continuo part. In the performance, the organist played the arias from the original organ part and for the recitatives switched to the additional sheet. The congregation thus might have heard the piece in the form outlined in Table 12.3b.[39] The inserted leaf allows a rare glimpse at some details of performance practice at the Halle Marienkirche; at the same time it documents Friedemann's intention to make use of the original performing parts whenever possible.

(2)　*"Es ist das Heil uns kommen her" BWV 9*

The above findings can now be applied to another piece, whose puzzling appearance has been noted repeatedly: the cantata "Es ist das Heil uns kommen her" BWV 9. Friedemann's performance of this piece has often been mentioned in scholarly literature, but a satisfying interpretation of the complex problems surrounding the Halle performance has been lacking.[40]

After his father's death, Friedemann inherited the original score of the piece, the duplicate parts for violin 1 and 2, a duplicate flute part, and one of the two untransposed continuo parts. The remainder of the original performing materials was inherited by Anna Magdalena Bach, who soon after gave it to the Thomasschule. Friedemann's performance of this cantata took place definitely after 1750; paper-type and handwriting suggest a performance in the second half of the 1750s. To complete the performance materials, he provided additional parts for soprano, alto, tenor, bass, and viola as well as a continuo *particell* (Table 12.4a). Today, the set is not quite complete, because a part for oboe d'amore (containing at least movement 1) and most probably one for violone are lost. Perhaps Friedemann also prepared duplicate parts for the two violins.

The continuo *particell* appears puzzling because it contains only the three recitatives and the transposed obbligato parts for movement 5 (see Figure 12.3). From observations gained from other materials, however, we can easily

---

St 346/4+4a (V 1), St 346/5+5a (V 2), St 346/6+6a (Va), St 346/8+8a (Continuo and Organo obligato, used together with St 346/8b).

39　It cannot be securely determined which vocal parts Friedemann used for this performance. Traces of his revisions in the tenor and bass part of SBB St 48 indicate, however, that he must have used them at some point; because of a number of incongruencies with the instrumental parts preserved in St 346, however, one has to allow for the possibility that Friedemann performed BWV 194 at least a second time, but with a different sequence and selection of movements.

40　Cf. Falck, *Wilhelm Friedemann Bach*, 27, and particularly Gerhard Herz, *Bach-Sources in America* (Cassel, 1984), 229–33.

Table 12.3. J. S. Bach, "Höchsterwünschtes Freudenfest" BWV 194

(a) Sequence of movements in the two organ parts

SBB St 346/8+8a (Köpping)

BWV 194/12   Chorale "Sprich ja zu meinen Taten"
    2 Recit. "Unendlich großer Gott"
    3 Aria "Was des Höchsten Glanz erfüllt"
    4 Recit. "Wie könnte dir, du höchstes Angesicht"
    5 Aria "Hilf Gott, daß es uns gelinge"
    7 Recit. "Ihr Heiligen erfreuet euch"
   10 Aria "O wie wohl ist uns geschehen"
   12 Chorale "Mit Segen mich beschütte"

SBB St 346/8b (W. F. Bach)

BWV 194/7   Recit. "Ihr Heiligen erfreuet euch"
   [5] ("Seque Aria ¢ ") "Hilf Gott, daß es uns gelinge"
    9 Recit. "Kann wohl ein Mensch"
  [10] ("Seque Aria 3/4") "O wie wohl ist uns geschehen"

(b) Reconstructed sequence of movements and instrumentation in the Halle performance

?12	Chorale	"Sprich Ja zu meinen Taten"	S, A, T, B, Ob, V1, V2, Va, Bc
?2	Recit.	"Unendlich großer Gott"	B, Bc
?3	Aria	"Was des Höchsten Glanz erfüllt"	B, Org obl(=Ob1+Bc), V1, V2,Va
7	Recit.	"Ihr Heiligen, erfreuet euch"	T, Bc
5	Aria	"Hilf, Gott, daß es uns gelinge"	S, V1, V2, Va, Bc
9	Recit.	"Kann wohl ein Mensch zu Gott"	S, B, Bc
10	Aria	"O wie wohl ist uns geschehen"	S, B, Ob, Org obl (=Ob2+Bc)
?12	Chorale	"Mit Segen mich beschütte"	S, A, T, B, Ob, V1, V2, Va, Bc

explain its function in Friedemann's performance: again, the organist used it in conjunction with the untransposed original continuo part. From the continuo part, he accompanied movements 1, 3, and 7, but for the recitatives (mvts. 2, 4, and 6) he switched to the *particell* as it facilitated his playing by providing him with a cue staff. And again, for all these movements the organist made use of the *Cammerton* stops.

In movement 5, however, Friedemann decided to assign both obbligato parts to the organ. As I pointed out above, the *Cammerton* stops could be

Table 12.4. *J. S. Bach, "Es ist das Heil uns kommen her" BWV 9*

(a) Parts used for the Halle performance

Original duplicate parts, inherited by W. F. Bach in 1750
    Traverso (mvts. 1 and 7 only)   [US–NY, private coll.]
    Violino 1   [A–Wgm]
    Violino 2   [US–NYp]
    Continuo   [US–NYp]
Parts provided by W. F. Bach
    S, A, T, B   [D–EIb, D–KÖ, B–Bc]
    Viola   [A–Wgm]
    Organo   [US–CA]
    (to be used in conjunction with the original continuo part; contains only mvts. 2, 4–6)
Missing parts
    [Violone] (WFB?)
    [Oboe d'amore] (JSB?)

(b) Instrumentation in J. S. Bach's and W. F. Bach's performances

Movement		J. S. Bach	W. F. Bach
1 [Chorus]	"Es ist das Heil"	tutti	tutti
2 Recit.	"Gott gab uns ein Gesetz"	B, Bc: Vc, Vne, Org	B, Bc: Org
3 Aria	"Wir waren schon zu tief gesunken"	T, V 1 unisono, Bc: Vc, Vne, Org	T, V (solo?), Bc: Organo
4 Recit.	"Doch mußte das Gesetz erfüllet werden"	B, Bc: Vc, Vne, Org	B, Bc: Organo
5 Duetto	"Herr, du siehst statt guter Werke"	S, A, Fl, Ob, Bc: Vc, Vne, Org	S, A, Org obl, Bc: [Vne]
6 Recit.	"Wenn wir die Sünd aus dem Gesetz erkennen"	B, Bc: Vc, Vne, Org	B, Bc: Organo
7 Chorale	"Ob sichs anließ, als wollt er nicht"	tutti	tutti

used for continuo accompaniment, but they were not suited for solo passages. Therefore these parts had to be transposed for use with *Chorton* stops. Interestingly, Friedemann did not include the continuo line in his organ *particell*; thus, the organist did not play a trio in the style known from J. S. Bach's organ sonatas (BWV 525–30), but merely a duo consisting of the two upper instrumental lines. The bass line must have been played by the violone alone.

The number of parts used for BWV 9 is typical for Friedemann's Halle performances, as it corresponds to the number of instruments owned by the Marienkirche listed in an inventory of 1746: six violins, two violas, and one

Figure 12.3 J. S. Bach, "Es ist das Heil uns kommen her" BWV 9, continuo *particell* in the hand of W. F. Bach, Cambridge, Harvard University, Houghton Library, pfMS Mus 62, fol. 1r

violone.[41] Judging from all the extant sets of performing parts originating in the Halle period, the number of musicians Friedemann had at his disposal was indeed relatively small, particularly when compared to the resources J. S. Bach had at Leipzig. These restricted means are exemplified in a striking manner in Friedemann's staffing of the continuo group (as demonstrated in Table 12.4b). Whereas in his Leipzig years it was J. S. Bach's practice to reinforce the continuo line by one or two cellos, sometimes an additional violone, and frequently even to favor a double accompaniment of organ and harpsichord,[42] in W. F. Bach's performances the organ alone was responsible for most of the continuo line. There are no cello or bassoon parts, and the violone is used exclusively as a ripieno instrument. This practice echoes J. S. Bach's Mühlhausen and Weimar cantata performances and is also typical of seventeenth-century instrumentation.[43]

In several arias Friedemann replaced the woodwinds by an obbligato organ. As BWV 9 demonstrates, this sometimes reflects his deliberate choice (as flute and oboe are required in the opening chorus) rather than being caused by external circumstances.[44] In other instances, however, the replacement of an oboe by the organ made it possible to perform the entire work without woodwinds altogether.[45] BWV 9 is thus typical of Friedemann Bach's revisions, which are frequently characterized by an adjusting of the cantatas he performed to more intimate forces.

V

When we compare the number of surviving cantatas by J. S. Bach that Friedemann performed at the Marienkirche (at least twenty) with the number of his own (about twenty) he performed there, it appears that the two composers were represented at Halle almost equally. Interestingly, Friedemann tended to use the standard repertoire (Telemann, Fasch, C. H. Graun, perhaps Kirchhoff, and others) for regular Sundays, and to reserve both his father's and

41 Falck, *Wilhelm Friedemann Bach*, 27.
42 Cf. *Dok* I/22; and Laurence Dreyfus, *Bach's continuo group: players and practices in his vocal works* (Cambridge, Mass., 1987), *passim*.
43 Cf. Dreyfus, *Bach's continuo group*, 132–4.
44 As J. S. Bach's autograph score does not specify the instrumentation of the duet, and because this movement is not contained in the flute part Friedemann inherited, he might have been uncertain about how to cast the two instrumental parts.
45 See, for example, BWV 128. The assumption in NBA I/12 KB, 188 (Alfred Dürr) that J. S. Bach himself may have originally planned to assign BWV 128/4 to the organ is unfounded because the designation "Organo" is certainly in Friedemann's hand. Cf. the facsimile in NBA I/12, x. I am grateful to Joshua Rifkin, who suggested I take a closer look at this designation.

his own compositions for high feasts. There are no distinct criteria for Friedemann's selection of certain of his father's compositions over others, but it appears that he tended to choose from the more difficult, intricate, and ornate cantatas with extended choral movements.[46] As surviving textbooks suggest, on these festive occasions he favored the joint performance of a work by his father and one of his own. Thus on October 3, 1756, he performed his cantata "Der Höchste erhöret das Flehen der Armen" Fk 86 in the morning and his father's St. Michael's cantata "Man singet mit Freuden vom Sieg" BWV 149 in the afternoon;[47] on another occasion, as a textbook for an unspecified Ascension Day reveals, he performed the first half of his father's piece "Gott fähret auf mit Jauchzen" BWV 43 in the morning and his own cantata "Wo geht die Lebensreise hin?" Fk 91 in the afternoon.[48] As stated above, he might have performed BWV 34 and Fk 72 together as well.

Friedemann's adaptations of his father's music for his Halle performances show remarkable restraint and an obvious concern for the preservation of the original conception of a work. Whatever changes he made remained strictly within the limits of what J. S. Bach himself would have altered when adjusting his own works for a renewed performance. The replacement of woodwinds by an obbligato organ, for example, as practiced by Friedemann in BWV 9, 19, 31, and 128, can be found in J. S. Bach's revisions of his cantatas BWV 63 and 73. The more serious alterations in the sequence of movements that Friedemann made in his performance of cantata BWV 194 interestingly concern a piece that previously had undergone several fundamental revisions by the composer himself.[49] Even his parody of the secular cantata BWV 205a as a sacred work shows no features that would have been unusual in Johann Sebastian's own parody practice. It might not be accidental that from Friedemann's hand we find no arrangements of the kind that his brother Carl Philipp Emanuel favored, for example with the cantata "Herr, deine Augen sehen nach dem Glauben" BWV 102, where – among other changes – vocal lines are substantially rewritten, a recitative is furnished with an additional string accompaniment, an

46 This is most obvious in Friedemann's well-known arrangement of the two choruses from BWV 80. Interestingly, at least three of the cantatas performed by Friedemann were later revived by his brother Carl Philipp Emanuel in Hamburg (BWV 19, 30, and 44). Whether this is simply a matter of coincidence or an indication of common aesthetic predilections is difficult to assess.

47 According to the textbook *Music, welche bey der feyerlichen Abschiedspredigt des . . . Herrn George Ludewig Herrnschmids, bisherigen . . . Oberpfarrers zur L. Frauen-Kirche . . . am 16ten Sonntage nach Trinitatis, den 3ten Octobr. 1756 . . . aufgeführet wird* (copy: Halle, Universitätsbibliothek, Pon. QK an Zb 6495). Cf. Hans-Joachim Schulze, "Ein 'Drama per Musica' als Kirchenmusik. Zu Wilhelm Friedemann Bachs Aufführungen der Huldigungskantate BWV 205a," *BJ* 61 (1975): 133–40, esp. 134.

48 Cf. Braun, "Materialien," 273.

49 Cf. NBA I/15 KB, 23–5; NBA I/31 KB, 122–7; NBA I/35 KB, 143–51 (Alfred Dürr).

Figure 12.4 J. S. Bach, "Es ist dir gesagt, Mensch, was gut ist" BWV 45, original Violino I part in the hand of Johann Heinrich Bach with revisions in the hand of W. F. Bach (addition of omitted measure 194, all trills, several accidentals), SBB Mus. ms. Bach St 26

entire aria is canceled, and a second chorale stanza is added in the middle of the piece.[50] Friedemann's meticulous revisions of the original parts suggest great care when preparing a work for a performance; consider, for example, BWV 45, where the entire set of performing parts was proofread and corrected against the autograph score (see Figure 12.4). There is nothing to indicate indolence, indifference or unscrupulousness toward his father's works.[51]

This general restraint in the handling of his father's cantatas appears also to have been in accord with Friedemann's reluctance to follow the popular practice of creating pasticcios by mixing works of his own, his father, and other composers. His insertion of a short simple recitative between two choruses by J. S. Bach (BWV 147/1 and 170/1) in a cantata he produced for the conclusion of the so-called catechism prayers does not really constitute an exception here, since simple recitatives are of quasi-impersonal style. It appears that the aesthetic principle behind Friedemann's rejection of pasticcios was probably a strong sense of stylistic homogeneity and auctorial identity. This attitude, by the way, contrasts with the Hamburg cantata performances by C. P. E. Bach, who when performing one of his father's cantatas often replaced the arias with works of his own.[52]

In light of the privileged role his father's cantatas played in Friedemann's repertoire at Halle, it is clear that his own cantata style cannot be understood without taking into account that influence. But how he adopted certain stylistic features and how he managed to define his own identity against his father's overwhelming genius – are topics for another paper. Further study of the impact of J. S. Bach's music on the artistic development of his sons and of his students is essential if we wish to deepen our understanding of how the tradition of his vocal music was carried on in the decades after his death.

---

50 Cf. NBA I/19 KB, 229–30 (Robert L. Marshall).
51 Feder, "Bachs Werke in ihren Bearbeitungen," 11–15.
52 Cf., for example, C. P. E. Bach's arrangement of BWV 19, which is documented in NBA I/30 KB, 72 and 82–4 (Marianne Helms). On C. P. E. Bach's use of his father's passions see Hans-Joachim Schulze, "Carl Philipp Emanuel Bachs Hamburger Passionsmusiken und ihr gattungsgeschichtlicher Kontext," in *Carl Philipp Emanuel Bach und die europäische Musikkultur des mittleren 18. Jahrhunderts. Bericht über das internationale Symposium der Joachim Jungius-Gesellschaft der Wissenschaften Hamburg 29. September – 2. Oktober 1988*, ed. Hans Joachim Marx (Göttingen, 1990), 333–43.

Index of J. S. Bach's works

Page numbers in italic refer to music examples.

229

Secular cantatas

Other concerted vocal works

Motets

Orchestral suite

Contrapuntal works

General index

This index does not include J. S. Bach. Page numbers in italic refer to music examples.